SAGE was founded in 1965 by Sara Miller McCune to support the dissemination of usable knowledge by publishing innovative and high-quality research and teaching content. Today, we publish over 900 journals, including those of more than 400 learned societies, more than 800 new books per year, and a growing range of library products including archives, data, case studies, reports, and video. SAGE remains majority-owned by our founder, and after Sara's lifetime will become owned by a charitable trust that secures our continued independence.

Los Angeles | London | New Delhi | Singapore | Washington DC | Melbourne

Legitimising Standard Languages

LEGITIMISING STANDARD LANGUAGES

Perspectives from a School in Banaras

NIRMALI GOSWAMI

Sociology and Social Anthropology of
Education in South Asia

Series Editor
Meenakshi Thapan

Los Angeles | London | New Delhi
Singapore | Washington DC | Melbourne

First published in 2017 by

SAGE Publications India Pvt Ltd
B1/I-1 Mohan Cooperative Industrial Area
Mathura Road, New Delhi 110 044, India
www.sagepub.in

SAGE Publications Inc
2455 Teller Road
Thousand Oaks, California 91320, USA

SAGE Publications Ltd
1 Oliver's Yard, 55 City Road
London EC1Y 1SP, United Kingdom

SAGE Publications Asia-Pacific Pte Ltd
3 Church Street
#10-04 Samsung Hub
Singapore 049483

Published by Vivek Mehra for SAGE Publications India Pvt Ltd, typeset in 11/13 pt Minion Pro by Fidus Design Pvt. Ltd., Chandigarh and printed at Chaman Enterprises, New Delhi.

Library of Congress Cataloging-in-Publication Data
Name: Goswami, Nirmali.
Title: Legitimising the standard languages: perspectives from a school in
     Banaras/Nirmali Goswami.
Description: New Delhi, India; Thousand Oaks, California: SAGE
     Publications, 2017. | Series: Sociology and social anthropology of
     education in South Asia | Includes bibliographical references and index.
Identifiers: LCCN 2017020477| ISBN 9789386446527 (print hardbound: alk.
     paper) | ISBN 9789386446534 (e pub 2.0) | ISBN 9789386446541 (e book)
Subjects: LCSH: Native language and education—India—Vārānasi (Uttar
     Pradesh)—Case studies. | Language and education—India—Vārānasi (Uttar
     Pradesh) | Language policy—India—Vārānasi (Uttar Pradesh) |
     Education—Social aspects—India—Vārānasi (Uttar Pradesh) | Education,
     Secondary—India—Vārānasi (Uttar Pradesh) |
Classification: LCC LC201.7.I4 G67 2017 | DDC 306.44/60954—dc23
LC record available at https://lccn.loc.gov/2017020477

ISBN: 978-93-864-4652-7 (HB)

SAGE Team: Supriya Das, Guneet Kaur Gulati and Rajinder Kaur

Contents

Thank you for choosing a SAGE product!
If you have any comment, observation or feedback,
I would like to personally hear from you.
Please write to me at **contactceo@sagepub.in**

Vivek Mehra, Managing Director and CEO, SAGE India.

Bulk Sales

SAGE India offers special discounts
for purchase of books in bulk.
We also make available special imprints
and excerpts from our books on demand.

For orders and enquiries, write to us at

Marketing Department
SAGE Publications India Pvt Ltd
B1/I-1, Mohan Cooperative Industrial Area
Mathura Road, Post Bag 7
New Delhi 110044, India

E-mail us at **marketing@sagepub.in**

Get to know more about SAGE

Be invited to SAGE events, get on our mailing list.
Write today to **marketing@sagepub.in**

This book is also available as an e-book.

List of Abbreviations

AMU	Aligarh Muslim University
BHU	Banaras Hindu University
CAD	Constituent Assembly Debates
CHGS	Central Hindu Girls School
HKHSS	Hind Kishor Higher Secondary School
NCF	National Curricular Framework
NEP	National Education Policy
NKCR	National Knowledge Commission Report
NWPO	North-Western Provinces and Oudh
OBC	Other Backward Class
TLF	Three-Language Formula

Series Editor's Note[*]

This series is an initiative in the field of sociology and social anthropology, as research in education has been a neglected dimension of the broader disciplinary framework in India and the rest of South Asia. The aim of the series is to build and develop a focus on the sociology and social anthropology of education, taking different aspects of education into consideration for analysis. The idea is to develop perspectives that do not rely on educational misgivings, institutional features, financial outlays and state failures alone. These are only some social aspects of educational practices. There are other dimensions that envelop students, teachers, the community and society in complex ways that we need to uncover in order to provide an understanding of how education and society connect in diverse ways.

At one level, this series seeks to problematise our understanding of education, as a process, in the context of the making of citizens in a 'modern', changing India. Education has been examined in its institutional avatar ad nauseam. Such efforts view schools, for example, as organisations that transmit and evaluate educational knowledge and provide certification based on academic achievement. The causes of inequality located in gender, caste, class and religion have perhaps been examined in this context as these shape individuals' lives in multiple and complex ways.

---

[*] This book is second in the series after Anuradha Sharma's *School Worlds: An Ethnographic Study* published in 2016.

At the same time, schools and institutions for tertiary education are spaces, processes, through which participants bring meaning and create worlds that hugely impact their personal and intellectual development. These remain largely unexplored. The experience of inequality, for example, as it is manifest within educational institutions, needs to be understood as much as the structural features of such inequality and how they impact student and familial aspirations for inclusion, educational attainment and employment.

Conflict, crises and events in everyday life are significant aspects of these processes. The ways in which youth may be both shaped by and engaged with the unfolding of crises, events and everyday life remain opaque in our understanding of how education plays an important role in the making of citizens. It is this understanding of human agency in institutional contexts that has somehow eluded scholars who seek to establish the significance of the structural and ideological frameworks within which educational processes are embedded. Once we understand that students are keen and active participants in the processes into which they are inserted, our views about education and its possible outcomes may perhaps change. It is indeed possible to examine and understand the vastly differing and multiple practices that students engage in as agents within, and outside, an institutional framework. Do they, in fact, seek to push the possibilities for making their voices heard or do they succumb to the authoritarian practices prevalent in our educational institutions? How do students seek to rise above not just the normative expectations associated with their 'roles' as students but also with asserting themselves in deeply meaningful and contextually significant ways? This means that we must pay attention to critical consciousness as it reveals itself in pedagogic encounters of different kinds and also in peer cultures and student-led organisations and movements in different parts of South Asia.

We may also see teachers as agents of both change and reproduction in education. It becomes important to identify and examine some of the processes that enable them to be pioneers and facilitators for transformative practices, rather than only being viewed as toothless agents of the state or private bodies, as they usually are, without any possibilities for bringing about change in their limited worlds. Both teachers and students are engaged participants in processes pertaining to education and the series needs to unpack the possibilities and potential for movement underlying the constrained and encapsulated worlds they inhabit.

This series, therefore, seeks to understand aspects of educating contemporary South Asia in different educational contexts and settings. It is important to reiterate that we need to focus on social inequalities in the context of educational processes, whether these are based on caste, class, gender and/or ethnic issues, keeping in mind an analysis of students' networks, their lives and regional variations. The homogeneity with which we seek to build an understanding of the writing of textbooks based on religious fundamentalism alone is not the point. It is equally essential to draw out other significant aspects of not only the writing of textbooks but also the aspects of their transaction and impact on children's learning. This transaction depends on teachers and students and their interaction inside classrooms. It is imperative to understand these processes by focusing on children's views and their perspectives on textbooks, and their significance in their lives. At the same time, we need to also recognise the use of language, curriculum and evaluation in educational processes that tend to define educational practice in particular ways. What are the political tools that are used to do this and how do these play out in the everyday life of institutions and of the people in them? It is imperative to understand both aspects of the organisation of knowledge in particular ways: the state and its agents as well as the actors (students, teachers and administrators) at the receiving end. Evaluation and certification are other tools in the hands of those who seek to govern educational practice and become instruments through which pedagogic encounters take place within institutions.

Educational spaces are also about place and location in multiple ways, whether these are at the intersection of caste, gender and class or are about location as both territorial and imagined spaces. The sociology of education must unpack these complexities and bring out their implications in a variety of contexts. The significance of gender, caste, religion or language as defining characteristics of educational processes are germane to our understanding and need to be examined in different contexts in the region that make each experience unique and similar at the same time.

The series also seeks to foreground scholarship that uses a range of methodological tools and theoretical constructs to understand the phenomena under study. Thus, studying forms of inequality must be based on fieldwork in different contexts and not rely on statistical information alone; an analysis of textbooks must also take into account other social and cultural dimensions of schooling and students' perspectives rather than the content of the texts or political dilemmas alone. It is not necessary that the series will be concerned with only the institutional aspects of education; studies of childhood and youth are also an essential component of the proposed series. The educational outcomes for youth and their families have remained almost untouched in contemporary work on the theme in India and the region. One of the lenses through which this series aims to develop the sociology of education is through a focus on youth and aspects of their experience, both within and outside institutional spaces.

Meenakshi Thapan

Preface

While your child is learning your maid's language, someone else's child is learning a foreign language with us. This was the tagline of an advertisement for a kindergarten school in an Indian city. It was targeting an upper-middle-class urban family in which women go out for work leaving their kids in the care of another woman from a different class background. The other woman usually comes from a different status group even if from a similar linguistic background and is presumed to be using the non-standard and the low prestige form of a language. The message is unabashedly loud and clear—save your children from the working-class cultures even if your lifestyle demands dependence on their labour. The advertisement taps on the deep-seated fears of the middle-class parents and proposes a kind of schooling as a counter to that. While many of us may feel dismayed at the tone and tenor of the message, most schools in India, including those which cater to the lower income groups, are always expected to train children in refined versions of languages used by formal people at formal places rather than in those varieties which are used at native place, marketplace, *mohalla* or street corners of cities and villages by domestic help, relatives, neighbours, grandparents and parents. In other words, schools are meant to teach standard rather than popular form of languages.

Standards are often meant to bring in uniformity and to control variations which might lower the value of a product. In other words, they suggest an agreement on the minimum level of acceptability of a product for use. These terms of acceptability are usually based on the tastes and preferences of high status groups. Similarly, standard languages convey uniformity and, sometimes, also claim purity of one form of a language over others. Such languages are important resources in the modern world, as they bring materialistic and symbolic rewards to their users and help them connect with the wider social world. Even as the age of popular and social media has worked towards proliferation of and at times, celebration of non-standard hybrid languages, one cannot overlook the continued significance of standard forms. If we probe deeper, we find that there is a difference between what is considered 'hep' and 'lame' usage of such hybrid forms. The difference, ironically enough, is contingent on the facility with the standard form. What is considered cool or high class usually calls for a creative engagement with the standard forms, and is considered the prerogative of the higher status group.

Historically, the battle over forms of languages have triggered conflicts and violence and, at times, led to new definitions of national communities and recognition of one form of a language as the standard language. Clearly, the claims of any one particular form of a language as the standard form necessarily involves power struggle. The form of language which is accepted at official level represents the dominant group of the state and is prescribed and propagated though agencies of the state. In everyday context, such power is exercised in a more subtle way. In such contexts, standard language forms have the potential to inflict a kind of symbolic violence which is so routine and mundane in nature that it hardly gets noticed. They express relations of power and have the ability to make or mar a person's chances of success in social and economic fields, which explains how their usage has become a quintessential part of middle-class identity. It is not surprising that in the educational domain these standard forms have a particularly hallowed existence. Most schools, in spite of the variations in funding pattern, affiliations and resources, are united in their insistence on the correct form of the languages taught. Even the most dysfunctional schools tend to engage in a puritanical approach to language-learning.

At this point, my personal and professional engagements with school education merge with each other to uncover the symbolic violence of Language-used in different contexts. Some of these issues were very clear to me even as a child growing up in a Hindi heartland where everyone used Hindi but it varied immensely between different classes of people. Between a variety of usage of Hindi, the skilful use of standard which is considered *shudh* (pure) brought social distinction. My own learning of shudh Hindi helped me to exploit the same in various platforms in and outside school. My growing up in two different cultural worlds also helped me to notice that one can be simultaneously complemented and ridiculed for using a pure form of language, if the language is acquired exclusively in school. My colloquial Assamese, learnt in family circles and puritanical Hindi, learnt at school, enabled me to be at ease in certain circles while kept me out from others. Once a form is identified as standard, it tends to be rigid and ceases to be dynamic and flexible. On the other hand, non-standard, popular languages enjoy a kind of liveliness and exuberance that is remarkable in striking camaraderie, gaining trust and inducing laughter.

For these very reasons, a study of the practice and social consequences of standard language-learning becomes very important. This book is located in the interdisciplinary tradition of sociology and anthropology of education which follows Pierre Bourdieu's argument that language and power relations should not be studied from a narrow technical perspective without taking into account their wider social context.

This work seeks to examine the social context in which power struggles over forms of language are wrought and how the same context mediates the teaching and learning processes at school. The city of Banaras is selected for fieldwork because of its historic association with the Hindi Nationalist Movement which was instrumental in defining the standard form of Hindi. The field material is drawn primarily from a private school and its community located in Banaras. In Banaras, English and standard Hindi are used by high status groups cutting across class, community and ethnicity backgrounds. Owing to its cosmopolitan character, some other languages are also used for schooling. Prominent among them are Sanskrit, Bengali and Urdu. In this work, I have examined standard

Hindi as one such form of language produced by complex historical and social processes in India. It deals with the question of how
ideas about languages are expressed in and with regard to school
as a space of learning by differently located actors. These ideas are
then examined with a view to understand the dynamics of class,
caste, gender and religion. It is assumed that a close analysis of how
the markers of languages are employed by actors, in and outside
school, is necessary to understand the process of boundary making
across groups; and how these processes influence language-learning
practices at school.

Acknowledgements

Writing an academic text can not be accomplished at an individual level. In my case, the idea of this book has evolved and acquired its current shape because of the joint intellectual efforts and creative engagements of many other actors. It draws on my doctoral work which was extensively revised and new materials were added to give it the present form. The basic idea evolved in the many conversations and discussions that I had with my advisor Professor Amman Madan. His intent listening and kind assurances gave me the strength to articulate my argument and give shape to this work. I remain indebted to him for his constant support and encouragement, professionally and otherwise. I am grateful to Professors Ashok Kaul and A. K. Sharma, for trusting my abilities at a very early stage of my student life and who provided support in this project at various stages from its inception. For this work, I have immensely benefitted from the learning experience gained in the Department of Humanities and Social Sciences of IIT Kanpur. In particular, my interactions with Achla Raina, Suchitra Mathur, Rahul Verman, Manali Chakravarti led to enriching discussions which afforded me many valuable insights into this work. I am also thankful to Professor Ranu Jain for her detailed comments on an earlier version of this work. Professor Mullick, Professor Bhat, Professor Pandey and Late Dr Bhanu Mehta, from Banaras Hindu University very kindly responded to my queries and helped me gain clarity of thought on various issues.

I am deeply indebted to Professor Thapan who saw merit in this project and helped me revise the work extensively. It was only

because of her careful reading of the manuscript and constant
reminders that the manuscript reached a logical conclusion. I must
also thank the anonymous reviewers at SAGE who gave critical
inputs to enrich and improve the work. Special thanks are due to
the SAGE team who helped me in getting the manuscript ready
for publication.

My heartfelt thanks are due to my friends from Banaras all
of whom I cannot name here, who have contributed in the most
direct and intimate way to this project by trusting me and by
sharing their world and invaluable friendship with me. Mehdiji
and his family provided me not just free access to the school but
also shared with me their warm hospitality and sumptuous meals.
I cannot thank enough the teaching staff of Hind Kishor Higher
Secondary School (HKHSS), Sumedha and her family, for their
friendship and sharing their life at school with me from close
quarters. Thanks are also due to the students at HKHSS and their
family members for the sheer love and exuberance with which they
welcomed me. I shall remain forever grateful to them. Academic
engagement with a subject like this dilutes the boundaries of one's
personal and professional worlds and one tends to live with the
ideas all the time. I must thank my family members Ma, Dada,
Sanchita, Mummy and Papa for understanding this and for their
unconditional love, patience and support throughout the project.
At this moment I fondly remember my late father who initiated me
into the pursuit of critical inquiry long before my life as an academic
began. I must mention the warm and loving company of my friends
at IIT Kanpur and in Tezpur, for keeping me in good humour
during the busiest and the most stressful days of my work. Finally,
words fail to describe the kind of support I received from Vivek in
this project. He not only helped me with formulating many of these
ideas but it is through his writings and actions that now I see the
possibility of a form of communication, that can be engaging with
people with humility and love. In this journey together we have
been joined by our daughter Amal who lit up our lives with hope.
Thanks are due to her as well.

1

Introduction

Nij bhasha unnati ahai, sab unnati ko mool.
'All forms of progress sprout from one's own language.'

—Bharatendu Harishchandra (1877)

Boli ka prasar ghar se hota hai ... shuddhta ka prachar skool se hota hai.
'Speech spreads from home, correctness is propagated in schools.'

—Shankarlal, Hindi teacher (2008)

Bharatendu Harishchandra, known as the pioneer of Hindi prose writing in nineteenth-century Banaras, was one of the literati who sought to create a discourse of modernity rooted in *nij bhasha* or one's own language, referring to a community of fellow speakers. It is not clear, however, who all comprised the members of the community to which he seemed to belong, and who are the ones whom the imagined community of the language excluded. Because of his well-documented role in establishing the standard version of modern Hindi and the historico-political context of the nationalistic movement of the nineteenth-century India, it could very well be interpreted that he is referring to the community of Hindi speakers as a whole. However, at the time of speech, he was still engaged in the process of creating a space and community for Khariboli Hindi (Dalmia 1997). So it could not have been referred to as nij bhasha by many at that point in time. It must have been a nij-bhasha-community in the making rather than an already existing reality, and yet it was claimed to be the preferred route for all kinds of progress.

The hopes and aspirations of modernity, of progress and of the construction of a distinct national identity through language are typical of colonial societies. However, their dilemmas are revealed when one finds that there seems to be no real consensus over the legitimate language in these societies for all spheres/domains of use. The plurality of speech within a seemingly homogenous 'Hindi-speaking community' is a well-known fact. Census data, a diversity of literary traditions and academics, have time and again suggested the heterogeneity of speech practice that comprise the Hindi-speaking population.[1] This is best exemplified in the practice of Bharatendu Harishchandra himself, when he used a different variety of Hindi for writing poetry, as manifested in the couplet quoted earlier, and a different variety for his prose (Dalmia 1997; Rai 2002).

The second epigraph, by Mr Shankarlal, an old Hindi teacher in a school in the same city, articulates the positions of language forms in two differing contexts. He contrasts *boli* or speech with correctness of form associated with *Bhasha* and relates them with home and school respectively. This separation of home and school as two distinct spheres presents a dilemma regarding the language of education in post-colonial societies. On the one hand, schools are constructed as a learning space for valued knowledge, building the grounds of an aspiring modern society, one that Bharatendu sought to create. On the other hand, it also indicates a separation of the school from home in terms of different forms of speech in both spheres.

The present work emerges out of a similar dilemma about the experience of modernity through standard languages in a culturally contested world of post-colonial societies. I am interested in uncovering the conflicts and negotiations that take place in educational arena over identities of nation, state, region, class, community and gender. Through these processes one can unravel the power dynamics around languages in which some varieties are preferred over others and others are silenced in certain domains. My interest in examining the processes of legitimisation is focused on the institutional context of school located in a north-Indian city, Banaras, which has been a centre of the movement for recognition of Hindi as the official language in the nineteenth and early twentieth centuries.[2]

Legitimacy of Languages

In this work, language is viewed as a marker of group identity in the framework of the nation-state project. In this project, a uniformity of culture is sought to be created, among other things, of language/s for economic, political and cultural integration (Anderson 1983; Gellner 1983). As such, the national/official languages become the markers of an apparently common culture. One of the major features of these national/official languages is that these are in standardised forms, as Anderson calls them, 'frozen in time' (1991). By standardisation processes, the variability of a language is controlled through various institutions and agencies.[3] These standard languages serve the purpose of making communication possible at a wider national level and across communities in plural societies at the economic, political and social levels. Therefore, the emergence of standard languages is also seen as a sign of modernity and progress. Standard language, then, is intimately bound with the state and can be seen as the one which imposes itself upon a territory as the legitimate way of communicating in the formal sphere.

These languages derive their legitimacy from the state on the claims of their commonality and cultural neutrality. The ideal of commonality may be seen as the quality of belonging to everyone. It is one of the crucial components of modern liberal state as it assures participation of all. However, the claim of commonality of standard languages does not hold much ground, as the literature on history of nation-states and empirical studies in anthropology and sociolinguistics suggest that these languages are usually closer to a dominant group.[4] From a critical perspective, these languages derive authority from their proximity to the dominant group and through various mechanisms contribute to the creation of a culturally homogeneous community.

Another ideal is that of cultural neutrality of these languages. A liberal conception of state sticks to the ideal of a culturally neutral procedural equality (Dworkin 1978, as cited in Taylor 1994, 56–57). The notion of cultural neutrality, which is presented as a touchstone of a liberal state and all its institutions, has come under the scanner from various theoretical perspectives (Appiah 2005; Fraser 2000; Taylor 1994). The multiculturalist and a feminist probing of this framework suggest that the state and its institutions may actually be favourable to the dominant groups and legitimise their languages over others. When a particular cultural form is superimposed as representative of a wider community, or as belonging to everyone, there emerges a problem of misrecognition of minority cultures. Misrecognition in this sense stems from a failure to give 'due recognition' to those cultural forms which are different from the majority (Taylor 1994, 25–26). It leads to an invisibilisation of minority cultures and silencing of minority tongues in public life.

If we extend the argument to schools as public institutions, the question of what should be the language of school curriculum in a pluralistic society is essentially a cultural and political question. A clear formulation can be seen in the work of Pierre Bourdieu who conceptualised official languages as normalised product ([1976] 1991). He visualised the interconnectedness of the economic, political and symbolic fields in defining the social estimation of official languages. A structural disparity exists between a very unequal knowledge of the legitimate language and the much more uniform recognition of this language. In its wide acceptance, by both speakers and non-users, government policies and state directives play only a partial role. It becomes a norm only when the unification of the labour market aligns with that of the educational and symbolic markets. The effective silencing of popular language varieties and hypercorrection by ordinary speakers in formal contexts is made possible when linguistic unification is complete. Educational institutions, grammarians and teachers play important roles as agents of legitimisation of these languages over other forms. This understanding has influenced a variety of scholarly traditions, examining language-use in its political context in anthropology, sociolinguistics and sociology of education (Collins 2009; Reay 1999; Woolard 1985). Some of these works offered significant leads to understand how macro-level changes in relations between labour markets and educational fields affect the status claim of a language (Haeri 1997; Woolard 1985). Similarly, the political context of colonial societies influenced the fluid multilingual reality of such societies and created discrete and distinct linguistic communities which were in hierarchical relation to each other (Chakrabarty 2002; Kaviraj 1997). These societies have witnessed a trend towards polarisation of the elite and popular languages in the realm of education (Bhokta 1998; Brass 2004; Kumar 2005d). Some of these relations between state and its role in establishing the legitimacy of standard language in colonial contexts will be examined in detail in the next chapter. Here, I focus on the institutional sphere of the school and its relation with family to understand the process of transmission and negotiation of legitimate cultural forms.

Misrecognition of Cultures in Schools

The school as a public institution manifests many of the cultural conflicts in its curricular and other aspects of life. Ethnographic studies have revealed that the rituals and everyday practices of schools, whether funded by state or not, are culturally coded and implicated in power relations (Giroux 1983; Mehan 1987). The problem of misrecognition cited previously has also been a major area of academic investigation in the sociological study of schools and their role in the larger process of social and cultural reproduction of power relations. According to Bourdieu, misrecognition refers to the process and mechanisms through which the social conditions in which a cultural artefact becomes valued are rendered invisible. With reference to standard languages, it refers to the conditions where listeners accept the authority of a dominant language, but fail to recognise the historical developments and the material power difference between social groups that underlie such authority (Woolard 2004). The concept of misrecognition tells us that the standard isn't really everybody's language and that it really does belong to specific 'someone's' more than to others.

Drawing from Bourdieu's analytical framework of misrecognition and of differential access to cultural capital among different class fractions, a number of studies started analysing the mismatch of home and school environment for some groups. The relationship of social class and language-use was also analysed by Basil Bernstein through his theory of codes, seen as central to his conception of social class, which is linked in complex ways with classroom processes. He argued that the experience of work process reinforces kinds of family role relations, themselves realised as discursive identities that are carried by 'elaborated' and 'restricted' codes (Bernstein 1971). However, it faced criticism for supporting a deficit-model of socialisation for a working-class family. The other studies focused on the differences in families' relation with schools in terms of parenting style, child-rearing practices along class and racial divide (Lareau 1985; Reay 1998). These differences, in some contexts, had implications for the academic preparedness of children coming from different class and racial backgrounds. The focus was often on the class differentiated power relations that parents, especially mothers, shared with school personnel. For example, Diane Reay in her study of mothers' involvement in children's schooling found that a mother's class and educational background influences her interaction with school staff and shapes the power dynamic between the two (Reay 1999).

Meanwhile, linguistic anthropology contributed towards a nuanced understanding of language socialisation process in varying class and racial contexts and its implications in terms of wider power relations. S. B. Heath's work (1983) focused on three neighbourhoods from varied class and ethnic backgrounds to describe their differential communication patterns. He could relate some of these communication styles with teacher expectations and curricular demands from students in schools. Collins found similar patterns in his examination of the schools and their language pedagogy where he highlighted the role of difference between the language patterns of the home and community and those of the school in producing the low educational achievement of many working-class and minority students (1988).[5] As discussed above these findings were supported by the studies of home and school relationship which pointed towards the inability of working-class non-white mothers to use their linguistic capital to their advantage while negotiating with school expectations (Reay 1998).[6] This body of work has contributed towards a fine grained analysis of the reproduction of class, race and gender differences through schooling in which language plays a key role.

However, education is no longer viewed as merely a site of reproduction of dominant relations. The deterministic/structuralistic view of schooling has faced criticism for presenting a rigid hierarchy of class, ethnicity and gender, and for presenting social actors particularly from minority groups as passive actors. New approaches have been employed to make sense of how people construct social identities in school contexts, without necessarily missing on the structural constraints (Collins 2009; Fine and Weis 2003). A close examination of school processes is deemed necessary to understand the school actors in their complex relations and how they negotiate with the official agenda of the school. Paul Willis (1977) in his classic work brought a cultural dimension to the structural analysis of schooling and focused on counter-cultures sustained by peer-group contexts in school. One of the various strategies that the 'lads' in his study used was to mock the teacher authority and the practice of 'successful' boys. It included having a 'laff' at the use of standard language by the other boys. This approach led to a focus on cultural forms employed by students in schools as signs of resistance against structural constraints. Foley's ethnographic study of classroom performance of students from different class and ethnic backgrounds presents a rich account of both resistance and reproduction in classroom, where he makes a class-differentiated analysis of the communicative speech acts of the students. He was able to show that middle-class cultural capital helps students, from varied racial backgrounds, to mock teacher authority in more subtle and nuanced ways while remaining successful at school (Foley 1991). In these studies there is a shift towards visualising schools as a space which resonates with conflicts and contradictions of various types, with an emphasis on durable yet negotiable aspect of constraints in school life (Collins 2009; Reay 2010).

Relatively fewer studies have focused explicitly on difference between home and school cultures in post-colonial settings. In the Indian context, inequality of caste, gender and class have been the major focus of studies addressing students' experience of school cultures. Even fewer have attempted an understanding of the role of dominant language cultures in these processes.[7] In this regard, historical studies of colonial model of education have been particularly insightful in highlighting its cultural dominance and continued influence over school relations in contemporary India (K. Kumar 2005a, 2005b; N. Kumar 2000). Particularly, Krishna Kumar's investigation of the political agenda of education examines the role of an identity-based movement in establishing a particular form of school language (2005). His analysis of school textbooks in contemporary India also point towards a growing schism between the cultures propagated by school and the children's social contexts (Kumar 1988).

Some recent studies have focused on how school education of a particular kind becomes a means of articulation of class and citizenship identity in India. These studies have examined ideologies of language, focusing on English education from middle-class standpoints in a globalising India (LaDousa 2014; Proctor 2010; Ramanathan 2005). In other words, the schools are viewed through the caveat of 'medium of instruction' dividing them into English-medium and Vernacular-medium types. These schools represent two different worldviews about schooling and aspirations of social mobility. In this framework, associating with any one of these depends on one's class identity and assures a mobility of a particular kind (LaDousa 2014). Ramanathan's work (2005) details the processes through which vernacular-medium students are excluded from participation in college education of a certain type. However, the middle-class category is too complex to be neatly packed in terms of their aspirations in relation to the English language alone. The analysis of the discourses of schooling and mobility shows that such hopes are not necessarily fulfilled through education in English. For Bhattacharya (2013), English language discourse in the era of globalisation has constructed an ideology that places English language education as the surest way of attaining social mobility while undermining the social inequalities associated with it. She argues that the notions of 'homogeneity' and 'uniformity' are constructed around English education in India. She points out that the English-medium schooling market is varied and, in any case, not enough for reproduction of class-based mobility. Proctor (2010) also points out the contradictory and conflicting nature of such mobility discourses. However, in their exclusive focus on English language schooling, and fieldwork in locations which in economic terms seems to be more integrated with a national and global labour market, these studies do not account for the legitimacy processes that construct language ideologies within a vernacular language market. Sociolinguists in India have pointed out that in places where literacy is not yet universal, and not yet integrated with work life, people tend to identify with the prestige variety of language leading to underestimation of other language varieties in census reports (Dasgupta 2001; Khubchandani 1977). These prestige varieties are the dominant standard languages operating within a region and may reveal similar power dynamics when examined closely in their own context. Many of these languages are juxtaposed to not just the minority language of the region but also to innumerable other varieties which are unrecognised by any official machinery. Some of these issues have been addressed in sociolinguistic studies of multilingualism in India and its relation with school education.

Echoing the work of Woolard (1985), Annamalai (2001) has used the notion of the domain use of language where different varieties of languages serve different purposes for public and private life. Languages operating in the public domain like schools serve to acquire power and wealth, while languages used in private domains such as family and community help to develop solidarity and identity[8] (Annamalai 2001, 68–71). While highlighting both the neighbourhood and literate forms of multilingualism in India, many of these scholars are critical of the role of schools in maintaining multilingualism in India. Agnihotri (2007), in particular, has not only questioned the disjuncture between monolingual assumptions of school processes and the multilingual home environments of students, but also identifies it as a limitation of the dominant discourse of language-learning in India. This approach extends the sphere of power dynamics to the sphere of 'vernacular education' itself as long as the language-learning practices in schools are trapped in standard language ideologies. This work attempts a critique of the discourse of standard languages in education for creating schisms which are intrinsic to the very techniques and tools of modernisation, leading to the classification of good over bad and legitimisation of good over bad kind of language. It is with this assumption that an enquiry is being made into such processes of schools located in a plural and multilingual society of Banaras.

Field of Study

Banaras is a north-Indian city in the state of Uttar Pradesh. It is a large urban settlement with a population of more than 13 lakh,[9] concentrated mainly on the northern bank of the river Ganga. Banaras has a sacred-city image among Hindus and is a major pilgrimage centre for them which has always attracted immigration from across India. This immigration has shaped the spatial arrangement of the old city. *Ghats*[10] were constructed on the river bank which lead to the city through lanes lined with settlements of people from specific communities (Kumar 2000). The residence pattern of the city, except in the recent expansions, follows a mohalla pattern of living, that is, in close neighbourhood settlements formed by narrow lanes lined by commercial as well as residential buildings. Because of the settlements from various corners of India, there are many ethnic conclaves inhabited by one community and closely followed by another. In the older city, or the *Pakka Mahal*, there are different settlements which can be described as 'pockets of ethnicity' (Sinha and Saraswati 1978).[11] Singh (1996) has identified and mapped settlement patterns of Muslim, Christian, Buddhist, Jain, Sikh, Bengali, Marathi, Gujarati, Sindhi, Tamil, Telugu, Kannada, Marwari and Nepali communities in the city (refer Tables 1.1 and 1.2). During my interaction with several residents of the city, the regionally diverse character

Table 1.1
Distribution of the Population of Banaras/Varanasi by Mother Tongue

Language	Population	%
Hindi	28,91,755	92.13
Urdu	2,21,016	7.04
Punjabi	1,929	0.06
Bengali	11,485	0.37
Others	12,492	0.40
Total		100.00

Source: Census (2011).

Table 1.2
Distribution of the Population of Banaras/Varanasi Among Various Religious Communities

	Population	%
Hindu	31,07,681	84.5
Muslim	5,46,987	14.88
Christian	7,696	0.21
Sikh	3,309	0.09
Buddhist	1,146	0.03
Jain	1898	0.05
Others	298	0.01
Unspecified	7826	0.22
Total	36,76,841	100

Source: Census (2011).

of the city life strongly emerged. Frequent references were made to Bengali *paras* (neighbourhoods) and Kannadiga *mathas* (settlements around religious centres) and to the Punjabi, Sindhi, Khatri, Gujarati and Marathi communities, in general. It continues to be a major city for national and international tourism. The economy of the city largely depends on the informal sector, consisting mainly of trade and small-scale and cottage industries in the manufacturing sector. While the city has witnessed conflicts between the Hindu and Muslim communities, they are linked through trade relations in the major industry of the Banarasi saree.

Despite the diversity of the cultural profile of the city, in census results, Hindi remains the language of the overwhelming majority of the population where over 90 per cent of the population speaks Hindi (refer Table 1.1). It is evident that the non-Hindi speaking communities must be smaller in size and are bilingual. The numerical strength of Hindi is also consolidated because it is often used as an umbrella term for most of the varieties spoken widely in the city and in the region, subsuming several popular varieties having a large community of speakers (Census 1991 as cited in Paul Brass 2004). The state of Uttar Pradesh is a good example of the normalisation of standard language Hindi, where almost everyone (99.98 per cent of the total population) claims to be a speaker of the scheduled languages.[12] Hindi has the distinction of subsuming the maximum number of mother tongues under it, as identified in Census 2001, almost 49. Some of the mother tongues within Hindi have a vast number of speakers such as Bhojpuri (33,099,497), Rajasthani (18,355,613), Chhattisgarhi (13,260,186), Magadhi (13,978,565) and others.[13] Hindi thus emerges as a heterogeneous category with several varieties of regional importance clubbed within it. Bhojpuri and Banarasi are the two popular varieties which are widely spoken in the city. While Bhojpuri is considered to be an important language variety of eastern Uttar Pradesh, Banarasi is seen as a distinct variety of Western Bhojpuri specific to the city of Banaras (Grierson 1967). According to Simon (1998, 252), a diglossic situation exists in Banaras where switching between Hindi and Banarasi is common. It suggests that the popular Language-used in the city is a more informal variety than the standard Hindi and people are using both of them. Urdu is the second major language after Hindi, yet the Urdu-speaking population of the city is less than 7 per cent (refer Table 1.1). However, census results have not proved to be a reliable record of speakers of the Urdu language because of the inconsistencies in defining and identifying the language (Simon 1998). It is often argued that the institutions that once supported Urdu are themselves declining, and that Urdu is now surviving only in madrasas because the Muslim elite have abandoned it. The city is also famous for having been a major centre of education. The city boasts of some Sanskrit schools even in contemporary times. However, a major transformation was brought through colonisation of education which introduced a more common and bureaucratic structure of education. The nationalist response to the colonial rule was also reflected in the struggle over educational institutions and the kind of knowledge that should be imparted in them. The two major educational institutions, Banaras Hindu University and Mahatama Gandhi Kashi Vidyapeeth, present themselves as key symbols of such struggle.[14] It is also important to note that because of its reputation as a centre of Hindu learning, several reformers also engaged with the schooling system in the city. One such effort at modern schooling with Hindu system of learning was initiated by Annie Besant through the Theosophical Society of India. Even in contemporary times, the city presents a bewildering variety of schooling ranging from government funded to private, both for-profit and not-for profit schools, including those following specific educational philosophy. Krishna Murthy Trust, based on educational ideals of Krishnamurthy, has also opened its school on the banks of the river Ganges. It is because of its central location in the educational discourse of the nation that I chose the city of Banaras to explore the issue of the legitimacy of certain languages in schools. Here, it is important to note that Banaras has had a history of a diversity of educational institutions, some of which exist from pre-colonial period in the form of Sanskrit school and Mahajani Pathshala (Kumar 2000). However, to unravel the ideas of legitimate language-use in contemporary times, it is important to select a school which follows the state curriculum of school education and also caters to a diversity of population at least in terms of caste, community and gender. For this reason, a 'modern' school has to be explored by examining its structure and practices with a view to understanding how it handles group identities of class, community, caste and gender, while conforming to the expected ideal of cultural neutrality.

In this study, I aim to explore the relationships of official/ standard languages among themselves and with popular languages in the school setting, and their implications for the school community in and outside school. I also seek to examine how the dominant languages are transmitted, transacted and negotiated in modern institutions. I am focusing on the construction of official and standard languages in the school context. Through this exercise, I also hope to understand the cultural consequences of the process of standardisation and legitimisation of languages in institutions in societies where variability and diversity have been the norm, otherwise.

Organisation of the Book

This book has seven chapters. Chapter 1 poses the issue of the legitimacy of languages in the school by problematising the notions of cultural commonality of modern nation-states and neutrality of the procedures in their various institutions. The legitimation of some cultural forms over others and resistance of others is examined at some length in the domain of education. Here I have focused on the separation of the domains of home and school in terms of language-use and how it is shaped by the dynamics of class, status, gender and community identities within a nation-state. It appears that we need to closely examine the world of 'vernacular-medium education' to understand the power dynamics which operate at local level and how they connect with national discourses of modernity and progress through education. It also briefly introduces the field of Banaras in North India and the main objectives of the study.

Chapter 2 discusses the standard language ideology and the role of state in perpetuating it by taking the case of standard Hindi in India. The assumption of cultural homogeneity and commonality implicit in the idea of standard language in the Western European states has been criticised from the multiculturalist and post-colonial perspectives. Anthropological studies of language markets within a nation-state point towards complexity of issues surrounding maintenance of and resistance to the standard language ideologies. Literature on the social reproductive role of school through its official curriculum of languages helps us in problematising the role that the school plays in the transmission of legitimate knowledge and languages. Further, I take the case of Hindi nationalism in India to exemplify the aforementioned debates. I have also examined select policy documents related to the education policies in India to explore the official curriculum of language in India. In the end, I argue that Hindi in spite of gaining the official status has not been particularly successful in establishing its claims at national level, and to project itself as a vehicle of social mobility and one that belongs to everyone, both of which are essential to bestow authority to language in public life.

Chapter 3 describes the school system in Banaras in the context of political, economic history of colonial rule and the identity politics which shaped modern schooling in the city. This chapter delves deeper into the question to make sense of schooling in present-day Banaras against its history of identity politics over the issue of language and vis-à-vis their link with the labour market situation. These issues are informed by an understanding of the conflict between the colonial and indigenous forms of knowledge in schools located in a city like Banaras. It also gives a brief discussion of the various kinds of schools visited in the city as per their students' composition, the nature of their affiliations with the state on one hand and with other organisations, religious or otherwise on the other.

Chapter 4 presents the authority structure and practices of the school selected for detailed examination of the aforementioned themes. I take this school, Hind Kishor Higher Secondary School (HKHSS), as an example of a modern school embedded in a culturally contested social universe of school market in Banaras. In this chapter, I explore the organisation of school life in terms of conflicting norms of commercial school-market, state prescribed curricula and community norms of schooling. After locating the school and its major social actors, I have closely examined the organisation of school life and dominant ethos of school culture as perceived by teachers and school administrators. This chapter brings out the inherently conflicted nature of a modern school, reflected in its attempt to maintain its position within the school market of the city. In this effort the school is seen adjusting the state prescribed curricula as per the the class and community specific expectations of its students community.

In Chapter 5, the concept of middle class and its linkages with formal schooling has been explored through an examination of families associated with the HKHSS. A major problem with the usage of the category of middle class to understand educational experiences is its inapplicability in an urban context like Banaras, which, unlike other industrial cities, is largely reliant on informal sectors of economy based on cottage style industries, a condition which prevents full integration of labour market and symbolic market. Majority of the existing literature on the subject have exclusively focused on upper-middle-class families from professional backgrounds and settled in metropolitan centres, and how they use their better access to cultural resources like English language to maintain their class position through school-choice. In a very different context of lower-middle-class families associated with a particular kind of school, one can argue that learning cultures and language-use patterns are influenced by their current occupational associations and have an effect on the kind of educational strategies adopted for upward mobility.

Chapter 6 examines the processes of labelling and classification employed by school teachers which have implications for construction of learner-identity of students. This is part of the larger process of legitimisation of standard language identities through transaction of the official curriculum of standard languages in school. It shows how the norm of Hindi is constructed against the local influences of Banarasi/Bhojpuri. The fact that Urdu has a special significance for the school population and yet occupies a marginal space in discourse of the modern school is also looked at. English, on the other hand, is widely perceived to be a language of progress and modernity. In all these processes, students and teachers are also engaged in a process of negotiating the formality of school culture by creating their own domains of informal language-use which is governed more by norms of solidarity, intimacy, trust and fun. In conclusion, I summarise the major insights gained from this exercise. My major arguments pertaining to the legitimacy of certain knowledge with reference to standard languages are presented in terms of its consequences for an understanding of class- and status-based hierarchies and classification with reference to schooling and their implications for language curricula in practice at school. Some insights gained from the exercise have been shared with reference to educational planning and policymaking.

Notes

1. Hindi has the distinction of subsuming the maximum number of mother tongues under it, as identified in Census 2001, namely 49. Some of the mother tongues within Hindi have a vast number of speakers such as Bhojpuri (33,099,497), Rajasthani (18,355,613), Chhattisgarhi (13,260,186), Magadhi (13,978,565) and others.

2. For further details on Hindi National Movement, refer to Alok Rai (2002), King (1989) an Kumar (2005d). Also refer to Chapter 2 in this volume.

3. The phrase 'frozen in time', though of metaphorical value, is not meant to suggest that all such institutions and agencies actually succeed in standardising a particular form of language. However, this seems to be the dominant trend in most modern institutions.

4. Such historical works include Hobsbawm (1983), Anderson (1983) and Paul Brass (1974) for an analysis of elite interests in nationality formation in Indian context. In sociolinguistic studies and anthropological studies of language, refer to Woolard (1985), and Woolard and Schieffelin (1994).

5. Collins has differentiated between deficit and difference approach in this regard.

6. For exceptions to the approach of cultural difference between home and school environment of racial groups, look at the work of J. G. Ogbu (1981) who argues for using a relational framework through which differential achievement of students from varied ethnic groups can be explained.

7. For some of the notable exception in this regard which have suggested the difference in tribal contexts of learning and school education, see Nambissan (1994) and Sarangapani (2003).

8. This dichotomy has been questioned by LaDousa (2014) in his recent work, where he has been able to show how some people associate Hindi-medium schools with notions of mother tongue.

9. The total population of the district is 31.30 lakh (10 lakh = 1 million) as per Census 2001.

10. Construction of steps, concrete or kaccha, which lead to the river bank for bathing purpose. In Banaras, there are numerous ghats for differential functions such as ghats for washermen, for funeral service, and there are some ghats which serve as common space for the community for multiple uses of worships, ceremonies of birth and death, bathing, exercise and other forms of recreation.

11. Pakka Mahal refers to the residential settlements in the heart of the city near the bank of the river Ganga. It claimed a higher status in popular perception, literally meaning

a neighbourhood which is based on pukka construction, and also because it formed the hub of commercial activity and symbolised urban life of the city.

12. From the table on the distribution of the population by scheduled and other languages, States and Union Territories (Government of India 2001). The figure varies in other states from more than 90 per cent in most Hindi-speaking states to a much lower proportion in the states of Northeast India. Northeastern states (Nagaland, 9.83%; Mizoram, 12.51%; Meghalaya, 16.57% and Arunachal Pradesh, 33.7%) have the least population of scheduled-language speakers.

13. From the table of Abstract of speakers' strength of language and mother tongues (Government of India 2001).

14. Refer to Krishna Kumar's Quest of Self-identity (2005d) which examines how the battles of national identity focused on educational institutions and sought to forge an exclusively Hindi and Hindu identity through education. It also discusses the significance of educational institutions such as Banaras Hindu University and Kashi Vidyapeeth in this regard.

2

Nation-State and Language Markets: Hindi as a School Language in India

Hindi ko kursi ka paap laga hai. [1]

Bhanu Mehta, 78, Senior Theatre artist, Varanasi

The provocative statement which could be roughly translated as 'Hindi suffers due to sins of power', was made during my fieldwork in Banaras by Dr Bhanu Mehta, a doctor by profession and a well-known literary figure. In a city like Banaras, this statement comes as a surprise, because here Hindi's association with power, symbolised by *kursi*, appears to be almost unchallenged. He believed that Hindi as a language is better off without its proximity to state authority. Being a Gujarati by birth and a Hindi columnist by choice, he was well aware of the regional sentiments which oppose Hindi in its avatar as a national language. He further explained that whenever he writes in English for a magazine he is paid four times the remuneration that he gets for writing in Hindi, indicating the dynamics of publishing industry, where the apparently unchallenged power and authority of Hindi is checked by a much stronger contender, English.

In Indian context, making sense of power relations embedded in the language-use and its ideology is a complex exercise. The multiethnic and multilingual fabric of Indian society requires that the appraisal of any language that is considered 'standard' has to be done with a bifocal gaze. One has to keep focus on the development of its particular form and its position vis-à-vis other language varieties simultaneously. For example, if one is interested in understanding Bengali and its uses in various domains, one has to inquire which among the various varieties of Bangla comes to be recognised as the *sadhu bhasha* associated with *bhadralok*[2] and how is the same language perceived by the speakers of Oriya and Assamese.

This chapter examines the political history of Hindi in order to explore the interrelation between state and educational institutions through the concepts of standard language ideology and culture. Here, standard language ideology refers to a belief in uniformity of language and standard language culture refers to the development of a consciousness of the correct form of a language (Milroy 2001). The focus is on two major questions here. One concerns the varying modes of imagining languages and communities in the modern state. To this end we examine the critiques of linguistic model of nation-state and the ideology of language that emerges within this framework. Second, we examine the mechanisms through which such visions are maintained and negotiated in the realm of education. I would be drawing on Pierre Bourdieu's work on linguistic market and symbolic power and Kathryn Woolard's notion of linguistic authority for this purpose (Bourdieu 1976a; Bourdieu and Wacquant 1992; Woolard 1985, 2004).

An analysis of language and identity issues in India, helps us open up the question of standard language cultures for further scrutiny. The last two sections of this chapter examine the social implications of adopting standard Hindi as the official language of the state and as a language of education. A close scrutiny of official discourse and scholarly literature around Hindi in post-independence period indicates that its legitimacy is gradually being eroded through concerns similar to the ones expressed previously by Dr Mehta in Banaras and also from pedagogic concerns about a school-going child and her local context.

Standard Language Cultures and Linguistic Nationalism

The salience of language issues in public life has a relatively recent history. It is only with the advent of the modern state that policy decisions regarding languages began affecting people's lives via their access to educational and employment opportunities. With the development of the modern state and mass societies, the grounds of legitimacy changed from divine will to that of popular will. It is in such societies that the people's languages began mattering in polity (Brass 2004; Hobsbawm 1996). But not all languages belonging to people had equal significance. In this period, some varieties of languages came to represent the modern nation-state.

Scholars of nationalism have highlighted the historic processes through which certain language varieties emerge as an important cultural marker of a nation. Ernest Gellner (1983, 1987) discussed at length the structural changes induced by the processes of industrialisation which helped in the formation of nation-state. Large-scale factory-based production displaced community-specific village economies and, accordingly, a centralised and uniform system of education came into being replacing a community-centred education. Populations culturally divided into small inward-oriented communities, governed by thin political and administrative strata, gradually opened up to form a larger society where political and cultural boundaries coincided. Gellner termed this new political–cultural entity as the nation-state (1983). A significant component of this process was the development of standardised and impersonal languages with which these nation-states came to identify themselves.

Anderson (1991) emphasised the common cultural marker of language even more in the emergence of the nation-state. In his account, linguistic nation-states emerged in Europe because of the convergence of capitalism as a mode of production and the development of print technology on the linguistic scenario. The logic of capitalism and the emergence of modern ideas of science and rationality created conditions which made it possible to imagine a community based on a common language, 'national print languages' (Anderson 1991, 67). In colonised societies, such conditions were created through a colonial model of governance and public education system which fuelled the emergence of a nationalist consciousness among native elites.

The notion of a common language within the territory of a nation-state has also been challenged in sociolinguistic and anthropological studies of minority language communities through empirical findings of prevalence of code-switching, parallel-bilingualism and of alternative language markets.[3] In many studies, the concept of standard language ideology is employed to discuss how myths of a uniform official language are created and sustained even when multiple language markets exist (LaDousa 2005; Woolard 1985; Woolard and Schieffelin 1994). These studies are informed by Pierre Bourdieu's analysis of symbolic power of official languages in a modern state. In his view, a language becomes 'normalised' when labour market is completely integrated with education market. That is when a dominant group language acquires 'impersonal' character of anonymity by successfully concealing its association with the dominant group. Following this, Kathryn Woolard put forward two ideological complexes within which languages claim authority in modern societies (2004). The ideological complexes of 'anonymity' (referring to a kind of 'universalism') and 'authenticity' (a form of romanticism and particularism) help us to understand two kinds of authority claims, each sustaining a certain kind of myth about people and their relationship with language.

In the discourse of authenticity, a particular way of speaking gains credence because of its rootedness in a particular location. Authenticity is achieved through marked language-use, in which accents are celebrated rather than muted. Though the claims of authenticity can be traced back to the linguistic nationalist projects of the eighteenth and nineteenth century Europe, now it is mainly used with particular reference to the articulation of minority languages seeking recognition in political sphere (Woolard 2004). In the Indian context, scholars have written about regional and sub-national discourses of language which seek to establish the claim of authenticity of the variety which echoes the native spirit of the land.[4]

The ideological complex of anonymity can be traced to the concept of public sphere of Habermas which is based on the conception of a realm of social life in which access is guaranteed to all the citizens (Habermas 1989; Woolard 2004). Just as a citizen is supposed to be speaking for everyone and no one in particular, similarly public language is a language which belongs to no one in particular, thereby, claims to belong to everyone. It is in this discourse that official languages are seen from the prism of 'disinterestedness'. It is also implied that such a language form can be used, if one is willing and smart enough to learn it, for communication at public spaces for personal benefits (Silverstein 1996 cited in Woolard 2004, 4).

The discourse of anonymity helped in establishing a culturally neutral claim for the official languages in western nation-states. Fishman (1966) for example, asserted that English in US is constructed as a language of mobility and assumes a de-ethnicised character in the process. According to Woolard, this assumption makes dominant public languages hegemonic in nature, because it is based on 'misrecognition' of the real social conditions which make these language varieties appear standard and neutral (2004). This acquired sense of anonymity and neutrality is essential for an official language to maintain its legitimacy in the field of administration and education.

However, once the authority is established, it is maintained through not just official but mostly through forces which appear to be naturally at work in most informal contexts. Bourdieu in his classic work on linguistic economy has asserted that the official languages are not just practiced in public institutions, but also become the norm against which all other linguistic practices are measured (Bourdieu 1976a). In everyday contexts, language-users make use of models that link types of linguistic forms with the types of people who stereotypically use them; Silverstein (1979) describes these models of typical language-use as 'linguistic ideologies'. These ideologies hold in both formal as well as informal situations.

Bourdieu used the concept of price formation to explain language behaviour in formal spaces and how they tend to overpower non-formal language-use. He characterises the standard language with formalism and adherence of norms while vernacular language markets with relaxed norms and an absence of such constraints, something that appears in more intimate contexts with close friends (Bourdieu 1976a). While referring to popular language and the value of the illegitimate linguistic products, Bourdieu also conceded that unification of market is never so complete that one can't find space, especially among friends, for its use and when one is not forced to watch oneself (1991). Nevertheless, he strongly presents the hierarchic relation between the formal and the popular because all the popular languages and their users are subdued when they come in contact with formal market.

> [T]he reality of linguistic legitimacy consists precisely in the fact that dominated individuals are always under the potential jurisdiction of formal law even when they spend all their lives ... beyond its reach, so that when they are placed in a formal situation they are doomed to silence ... (Bourdieu 1976b, 71)

However, the stereotypical use of formal language does not always hold and people make use of language forms for a variety of purpose. For example, during most of my school visits in Banaras almost all school administrators said they hold strict norms of formality regarding language-used in school space, but many others also admitted to the use of local language within and outside school contexts.[5] These aspects of formality of informal language-use has been examined in great detail in recent times and have also presented how careful deployment of language-use in various domains leads to construction of alternative identities (Hall 2015; Buscholtz 2001 as cited in Wortham 2011). These works suggest how actors are not simply cowed down by structural constraints of formalism and social prestige attached to the formal spaces, but also find creative ways of subverting them through mixing the different language styles.

In more recent studies it is found that such domain arrangements are frequently crossed by the social actors to negotiate identity (Rampton 2005 in Wortham 2011). However, during my interactions with varied actors in school contexts, this ability to cross the domains was unequally employed by social actors. There was a particular ease with which a senior school teacher could speak in Hindi and English and also make a switch to the non-standard variant Banarasi while interacting with the daily wage workers or some of the parents. However, similar ease was not visible on the other side. Those who predominantly used non-formal varieties at workplace and at home felt awkward when confronted with school staff. For example during parent–teachers meeting, the teachers would do the maximum talking while the parents would speak minimum and remain mostly silent.

The Field of Education and Languages

For certain language varieties to acquire formal or public role over others, the institutional arrangements of grammarians, schools and teachers is crucial (Bourdieu 1991). In this section we will focus on the role of educational institutions, particularly school education. This is because schools are often seen as modern public institutions which provide the necessary linkages between the employment market and the individual household through mechanisms of socialisation and selection. From this perspective, schools may also be viewed as providing opportunities to learning the standard languages in a nation-state for better participation in economy and polity.

However, a more critical tradition views schools as institutions which, amidst various contradictions, maintain the dominant ideology. From this perspective, schools ensure that children learn not just the skills, but also values and attitudes in conformity with their class positions, contributing to the reproduction of relations in society. In this process standard language acquisition in school plays an important role. In other words, standard language ideologies like all other ruling ideologies are nurtured and promoted in schools, even amidst contradictions.

> ... educational processes establish associations between 'educated' and 'uneducated', 'sophisticated' and 'unsophisticated', 'official' and 'vernacular' language-use and, accordingly, types of students. An understanding of language ideologies thus helps explain how educational processes move young people toward diverse social locations, and linguistic anthropological work on these processes helps to show how social individuals and group members are produced.
>
> (Wortham 2011, 144)

For Bourdieu, schools embody the culture of the dominant groups in society. He is credited with elaborating the reproductive role of the school by examining the linkages of the educational field with the political, economic and symbolic fields. He brings in the notion of the different forms of capital such as cultural, social and economic, and their convertibility across fields to explain the economic as well as cultural advantages for specific groups and actors in their respective fields (Bourdieu 1986). He applies these concepts in the domain of languages to explain how the official languages defined by the state acquire a normalised form through school processes (Bourdieu 1976b). Bourdieu critiques Saussure and Chomsky for their inadequate attention to the social and economic conditions of acquiring legitimate competency in languages, and to the properties of the field/market where this competency is established and imposed (Bourdieu 1976b, 1985). He seeks to resolve the problem of structure and agency by conceiving the speech act as not merely generated by linguistic competence, but also as the product of an encounter between linguistic habitus and properties of the linguistic field (Bourdieu 1976b). He further cautions against the tendency to treat the standard languages taught in schools as natural and common. Standard language, for him, is a normalised product. It is required in a state and in a bureaucratic set-up which calls for an impersonal and abstract nature of communication.

In the Indian context, Dasgupta and Gumperz have examined the process of emergence of standard languages as a consequence of modernisation of society which calls for democratisation of communication pattern and depends more on standardised form of communication through standard languages (Dasgupta and

Gumperz 1971).[6] Bourdieu, on the other hand, stresses on the political aspect of the process through which standard languages acquire dominant positions. For him, language politics is a struggle over symbolic capital and over the formation and reformation of mental structures. He is, therefore, concerned with the operation of symbolic dominance in the linguistic market through the processes of normalisation of standard language. For official languages to become normalised, it is important to have a complete integration of labour and linguistic markets.

Such a perfect integration of the labour and linguistic market does not exist in 'developing' third world societies and even in many of the industrialised western societies. Nonetheless, Bourdieu's work inspired a great deal of work among linguistic anthropologists who extended and qualified his ideas by applying them in different social political contexts.

Kathryn Woolard's work in Spain led to questioning of some of the assumptions of uniform linguistic field (1985). Her fieldwork revealed that in a specific political context, people held a non-standard language, Catalan, in higher esteem over the official language, Spanish. She came up with a formulation of alternative markets, which flourished in Catalan corresponding to the nature of the labour market in Barcelona. It suggests the role of specific historic conditions in which adherence to official standard language is sometimes normalised and at times some other languages enjoy greater authority.

Even in Bourdieu's work, a similar consideration is made in his discussion of conflicting norms of working-class masculinity which construe following the standard speech as effeminate (Bourdieu 1976). It would also not be fair to Bourdieu to evaluate his work on language by overlooking his later contributions to understanding cultural reproduction (1984, 1992). His later work reflects a more nuanced appreciation of the autonomous conception of several fields which may have differentiated evaluation of symbolic capitals attached to them. Therefore, we cannot speak of language without discussing the power play it assumes and the social context of its use. Any standard language, then, is intimately bound with the state and can be seen as the one which imposes itself upon a territory as the legitimate way of communication in the formal sphere. However, the language policy of the state alone is not a sufficient explanation of how the normalisation of language takes place in a society. It cannot, on its own, induce the willing acceptance of the dominant language-variety by all. Schools assume an important role in creating the willing acceptance of official languages. The education system plays a decisive role in Bourdieu's understanding of the reproduction of dominant culture, in general.

Even as Bourdieu's framework remains useful for establishing the macro-linkages between the nature of the labour market, the emergence of a common linguistic field and a common education system, it is important to take note of the nature of relation between the labour market and the school system and how it may vary in different contexts. If industrialisation is particularly weak in a region, then the school becomes the primary institution to access jobs in the bureaucratic apparatus set up by the government, but not otherwise. The colonial rule was successful in establishing stronger relations between school education and employment prospects in the bureaucratic apparatus of government in India. However, my understanding of labour market in the specific context of Banaras, which always relied more on small-scale industries, presents a different scenario altogether. An understanding of employment market dynamics in varied settings reveal that only certain occupational groups rely solely on schooling to access government jobs, while other groups rely more on their social networks for gaining an entry into labour market.[7] Woolard's work in the Catalan region of Spain (1985) questioned some of the assumptions of Bourdieu's emphasis on the efficacy of the school as an institution in establishing cultural hegemony. We may do well to focus not just on formal schools but also on other sites which sustain alternative linguistic markets. In case of the Catalan region, the alternative markets were sustained by the specific history of labour market. Similarly, transformations in the nature of labour market in the globalised world, marked by the rise of English as the dominant language, have also influenced the language of education policies of Asian countries (Tsui and Tollefson 2007).

Ethnographic and historicised accounts of varied political economic contexts suggest that complete unification of linguistic market is not realised in many societies, particularly so in the colonised societies.[8] In such societies, the official languages are rarely the language of the masses and not necessarily the most authoritative and prestigious language in various domains, including in education. For example, in Egypt, a conflict is seen in valuation of official language and foreign languages in terms of job-market where proficiency in a foreign language rather than the official language earns the highest reward (Haeri 1997). Similar patterns of alternative valuation of languages are also seen in south Asian societies, indicating the presence of competing rather than unified linguistic markets (Brass 1974, 2004; LaDousa 2005, 2014).

Anderson (1991) also revised his analysis of the nation building project in the context of the colonised societies of Southeast Asia and highlighted the role of modern governance techniques and tools such as census, mapping and museums. Bernard Cohn (1996), in his work on India, has probed deeper into the colonial governance techniques and their consequent effects on the linguistic landscape. He argued that the state-formation process in colonised societies was influenced to a great degree by the colonial projects of enumeration, classification and standardisation of languages which have shaped 'the languages of command' in colonial India. In the next section, we examine the rise of Hindi as an official language and the political context of its standardisation.

Colonial Governance and Standardisation of Hindi

Control over native languages remains the most potent source of power for the imperial centre, because it is through language that knowledge is produced about native societies (Ashcroft, Griffiths, and Tiffin 1995). Control over knowledge production is vital to the colonial project of imposing its own systems of values over native population. For example, the colonial conceptions of history and geography set the norms for power struggle over territories in native societies. This power over knowledge production through control of languages is systemically employed in the educational field. In the Indian context, we examine the role of colonial governance through an exploration of its educational policies and languages policies, and also the nativist response to the same which led to the formation of standard language ideologies in modern India.

Bernard Cohn in his seminal work (1985, 1996) contends that colonial rule over India works through the processes of 'objectification' and 'hierarchisation' of knowledge. It began the process of classifying and standardising languages for better control over new territories. Knowledge of the Indian vernacular languages was necessary and useful for administrative purpose, particularly in the law courts and schools and colleges. Second, and at a more pragmatic level, the process of standardising language connected the realm of education with employment through its bureaucratic apparatus and significantly raised people's stakes in such languages. What language is used by the bureaucracy and judiciary, and what languages are taught and learnt at school became a hugely contested issue.

Colonial Governance and Identifying 'Vernaculars'

Cohn (1996) has suggested that the conquest of a colony is also the invasion of a new epistemological space. The educated colonial masters tried to make sense of this new space through their familiar frames of reference, through translations of the indigenous texts and the creation of new ones. For this purpose, they set up institutions like Fort William College and employed scientific comparative methodologies of studying languages. Through these institutions and methods, an 'original' and 'pure' form of the language could be traced back through a process of historic reconstruction. In their urgency to make sense of the language scenario in India, the British administrators used the ideas of nationality and national languages prevalent in Europe, and simply identified the Hindus and Muslims as two separate national cultures with two different languages—Hindui and Urdu or Hindustani (Cohn 1985; Dalmia 1997).

The post-colonial perspective helps us to examine how the language boundaries were transformed and acquired more strong forms compared to the pre-colonial times when these had more fluid boundaries (Chakrabarty 2002). The process started with institution of language departments with strong classification of languages. It is also substantiated by scarce references to a uniform language like Hindi prior to the colonial rule. For example, John Gilchrist, who founded the Oriental Seminary in Calcutta in 1799, observed that there existed at least three levels or styles of Hindustani: the High Court or Persian style, which was pedantic and influenced by Arabic and Persian; the middle or genuine Hindustani style, in which foreign and indigenous words were in equal proportion; and the vulgar style or the rustic Hindui (Dalmia 1997). It was only after the establishment of Fort William College and his appointment as teacher of Hindustani, that separate arrangements were made for the teaching of Bhasha, or Hindui as, separate from that of Hindustani.[9] The institutionalisation and separation of these language varieties took place simultaneously. A similar role towards separation of language on community lines was played by the missionaries, in their development of vernacular primers for school education and through textbook societies (Kumar 2001, 2005d). Both contributed to the process of separation through classification on religious lines, by printing separate textbooks for Hindus and Muslims in different scripts. These developments illuminate the role of colonial institutions and other agents in selecting and, thereby, giving a print form to vernacular languages from their understanding of the linguistic situation in native society. This exercise changed the social reality of the colonised society by giving new forms and definitions to languages and by assigning them new meanings through their administrative apparatus.

Cohn (1985) views these processes of the colonial project as resulting in objectification of Indian languages like never before. More recently, Dipesh Chakrabarty has described the processes through which fluid identities and boundaries of languages were converted into discrete 'enumerated' entities, each with a well-defined population of its own (2002). Second, it was also an attempt to gain legitimacy in the eyes of the Indian people by giving patronage to the traditional sources of knowledge creation.[10] Third, it led to the creation of oriental knowledge in a way which positioned the orient and the occident in a hierarchical relationship of inferiority and superiority. Educational history of the subcontinent reveals the initial investments made by the colonisers in promoting oriental forms of knowledge, by establishing Madrasas in Delhi and Calcutta, and Sanskrit College in Banaras (Dodson 2002; Mir 2006). However, the educational policies soon took a turn towards an anglicised model of education, which privileged western knowledge over indigenous knowledge (Kumar 2005b).

In this process, vernacular languages of Indian origin were discovered and developed through colonial institutions. It is important to note that these vernaculars were defined by the classification systems enforced by the colonial government. The colonial mode of historical investigations was one of the tools through which Indian languages were identified as following two distinct traditions belonging to Hindus and Muslims. Ironically, the same methods of classification based on segregating one tradition from the other was later used by the 'native elites' to contest the colonial rule and present their own national alternative. In north India, the Hindi-elites led the movement for identification and political recognition of the Sanskritised version of Hindi by connecting it to a glorious Hindu past.

The 'Vernacular Turn' in School Education

In the education policy in colonial India, we can trace a shift from orientalism to an Anglicist approach and, finally, towards a vernacular turn. Macaulay's Minute of 1835 remains a document of seminal importance in the history of education in India through which foundations of a colonial system of education was laid and legitimised. The minute is a telling tale of devaluation of all forms of indigenous knowledge in favour of an anglicised form of education. In this form, school education was aimed at imparting European knowledge in English for a miniscule elite section of Indian society.

This section was expected to then impart knowledge to the masses in vernacular language.

However, there was a further shift towards use of vernaculars in education in 1830s and after the Wood's Despatch. Through an administrative Act of 1837, Persian was replaced by the vernacular languages as the language of administration at the provincial level. This move was believed to be rooted in a liberal political philosophy which accorded great importance to the administration in the vernacular languages. However, the said shift towards vernaculars did not necessarily reflect greater democratisation. The vernacular language, recognised by the colonial administration was not necessarily a popular language used by the majority of the population; rather, it continued to reflect the language of the cultural elites from the province. Urdu rather than Punjabi was introduced in Punjab, a pedantic form of Hindustani replaced Persian in the North-Western Provinces and Oudh (NWPO), and Bengali rather than Assamese was introduced in Assam (Borpujari 1998; Mir 2006). However, as King (1994) would claim, the Act had little effect in practice in NWPO because it only changed the grammar of the language from Persian to Urdu/Hindustani while all the technical terms used in judiciary and other domains of administration remained the same. Later, Wood's Despatch in 1854 marked a significant departure in its recognition of the important role of the vernacular languages in the dissemination of western education in India. It was justified on grounds of being a principle of directness as against the indirect filtration hypothesis of the earlier Anglicists (Evans 2002).

By these moves towards vernacularisation of administration and education, however limited they might be, colonial government brought together the realm of education and employment through its bureaucratic apparatus and raised people's stakes in official languages.

For example, in 1877, when the provincial government prescribed success in the middle-class vernacular or middle-class Anglo-vernacular examinations as qualification for the government services, it fuelled the demand for recognition of Hindi in Nagri script in the United Province (King 1989). In other words, what language is taught and learnt at school became a contested issue in this period. We are examining the details of political mobilisation around Hindi as separate from Urdu in the next section.

Before discussing the specifics of the movement in detail, one can summarise the effect of the same at three levels. The Hindi movement that ensued, had three lasting influences on the form of Hindi. One, it drew its legacy from Sanskrit, making it the basis of national-identity construction and linking it with Hindu heritage. Two, it was purged from Urdu influence, thereby distancing it from the composite tradition of Hindus and Muslims which together constituted Urdu. Three, it subsumed many popular varieties of languages as dialects of Hindi, in effect creating a wide gulf between the users of Sanskritised Hindi and popular variants of Hindi. Clearly, these developments had implications for not just the 'form' of Hindi but also for the hierarchical organisation of social relations in the province and later in the country on new grounds.

Hindi Movement

The issue of an appropriate language for education can also be seen through the discourse of national identity construction in a colonised society. The quest for a distinct identity of a nation and the search for a national language among the native elite form another narrative which explains the rise of Hindi nationalism in north India in the nineteenth century. The quest for identity was felt more in the domain of education, because education was the main site where cultural battles for representation and authority over what constituted appropriate knowledge were fought.

The major arguments against the Act of 1837, which established Hindustani in the Persian script as the language of the courts, came from the Hindu merchant class and other leaders of the Hindi movement. They argued that the majority of the population consisted of Hindus, and Hindi written in Devanagari,[11] being the language of the Hindus, should replace Urdu as the language of the courts (Dalmia 1997; King 1989). Meanwhile, the groups which occupied higher positions in the judicial and executive services were the Muslim elite and the Kayasthas, who were literate in Urdu. On the other hand, the high-caste Hindus, comprising Brahmans, Rajputs and Khatris constituted the second rung in the administrative hierarchy of the education department.

According to King (1994), from amongst these officials came most of the influential members of the Nagri Pracharini Sabha, the organisation which led the movement vigorously. Sabha members used their social, financial and cultural resources in the promotion of Hindi through mobilising support for the resolution of 1900, which finally granted Hindi status equivalent to Urdu. The sabha also contributed to the production of a corpus of standard Hindi literature through literary magazines and scientific publications. Among other activities, they instituted awards and prizes for Hindi-writing and lobbied in various government bodies for the cause of Devanagari Hindi (Dalmia 1997; King 1989).

The form of Hindi used for literary purposes was also greatly affected during the late nineteenth and early twentieth century by the Sabha members. Several literary magazines took up the responsibility of defining and promoting the correct usage of Hindi during this period. *Saraswati*, edited by Mahavir Prasad Dwivedi, was the most important amongst them. This magazine became an important platform for presenting a particular form of standard Hindi free from Urdu and regional dialects, and also in strongly criticising those who did not adhere to the norm. Later, Ram Chandra Shukla took upon himself the task of reinforcing Hindi in that tradition by writing the first extensive history of Hindi in his *Hindi Sahitya ka Itihas* in 1929, which excluded those literary works which had been strong in Urdu influence (Kumar 2005).The language of poetry also came to be questioned, as there were many people, including the pioneer of the Hindi movement Bharatendu Harishchandra, who used Brajbhasha for writing poetry. The move towards the standardisation of the language of poetry met with some initial resistance, but eventually, it was established. Ayodhya Prasad Hariaudh and, later, Maithili

Sharan Gupta firmly established Khariboli poetry in modern Hindi which drew from Hindu religious traditions for themes (King 1989).

The active construction of a national identity around a particular form of Hindi, witnessed a high level of engagement on the part of the local elite in the literary, organisational and political arenas, which made it exclusive of all 'foreign' influences and, simultaneously, marginalised the use of indigenous forms of language. All of this was a curious process of the construction of a tradition which redefined and re-allocated languages. This process of construction of a new, culturally homogeneous community while drawing from a classical tradition of Sanskrit transcended the duality of modernity and tradition (Dalmia 1997). As a result, Hindi could establish itself as the authentic 'native/national' variety only by marginalising the regional dialects, the rich oral traditions and the speech of the majority of the population.

Many post-colonial writers and scholars have presented a cultural critique of the colonial model of education, which places western culture and values vis-à-vis indigenous culture in a hierarchical relation and reproduces old social hierarchy of elite and masses (Kumar 2000; Viswanathan 1989). The response to the colonial discourse of education have largely acquired two forms, one is that of resisting the colonial language and adopting the native form through a radical decolonisation.[12] However, many others feet that this appeal to some essential native culture is also doomed to failure and creates new set of problems. For example, in Indian context if one closely examines the implications of colonial rule in terms of languages, one can argue that the new political discourse, institutions and movements have replaced an older hierarchy with a new one: the standard vernaculars used by the new cultural elite were placed against the popular languages of the masses. Similarly, colonial education policy created a class of educational and linguistic elites, and the gap between them and the masses continued to widen (Bhokta 1998). These gaps continued to persist in independent India and in its education policy.

Hindi in Language and Education Policies in Post-independence India

Independent India in its quest for a national identity through a language could not come to an easy consensus over the status of Hindi because of competing pressures from various quarters in the making of a federal republic. Two contradictory interests informed much of the debate over language policy of India and led to the development of a competitive language market. One was pertaining to promotion of a national link-language and the second was to provide political space to linguistic units within a federal structure. The political consciousness of linguistic units of the new nation had its roots in pre-independence struggles.[13] The standard Hindi written in Devanagri as the official language of the union gets constructed within such contested realms of nationalist ideology. A close examination of Constituent Assembly Debates (CAD) on language brings out the 'half-hearted compromise' over Hindi and its standard form (Austin 2009). Considerable attention has also been drawn to the political circumstances in the wake of partition and communal politics in which the standard form of Hindi, based on Sanskrit and distant from Urdu, came to be agreed upon (Agnihotri 2015). In CAD, questions were raised regarding the extent to which Hindi could claim legitimacy in a federal structure and the minimum time frame needed for its adoption by non-Hindi-speaking federal units (Austin 2009). Final agreement could be reached only by making provision for the continuation of English for official purposes of the Union, for interstate communication, and for administrative and judicial purposes in non-Hindi provinces. Though it is largely read as a compromise formula, many provisions were kept to enable Hindi acquire its legitimate status in due course of time. For example, the Article 351 directs the Union to promote the spread of the Hindi language and to develop it so that it may serve as a medium of expression for all the elements of 'composite culture'.

> It shall be the duty of the Union to promote the spread of the Hindi language, to develop it so that it may serve as a medium of expression

for all the elements of the composite culture of India and to secure its
enrichment by assimilating without interfering with its genius, the
forms, style and expressions used in Hindustani and in the other
languages of India specified in the Eighth Schedule, and by drawing,
wherever necessary or desirable, for its vocabulary, *primarily* on
Sanskrit and secondarily on other languages.

—Constitution of India, Article 351

The language of the Act itself contained contrary viewpoints
over the form of Hindi by making reference to Hindustani and
other languages in the Eighth schedule of the Constitution on
one hand, and by making Sanskrit the primary basis of lexical
development of Hindi on the other. In spite of the contradictions,
these provisions furthered the cause of standardisation of Hindi
by establishing Sanskrit as the primary source, and in earmarking
funds for preparation of Hindi terminology for scientific, social and
technical subjects. Some of the contradictions regarding official
language policy finally culminated in language-based conflicts in
the southern states until the passage of the Official Languages Act
of 1963 (as amended in 1967), through which the use of English
as the official language was extended from the previously decided
period of fifteen years.

Another strand of debate with implications for establishment of a competitive linguistic market within Hindi provinces
was based on the discourse of rights of the cultural minority.
Constitutional provisions identify the right to conserve one's language as the fundamental right to liberty. Article 29(a) grants the
fundamental right of any citizen or any section of citizens to conserve its own language, script and culture. Special provisions have
also been made for the protection of minority languages within
a state through educational institutions. Article 30 ensures the
rights of minorities to establish and administer educational institutions. Other provisions prescribe for 'mother tongue education' in
elementary-level schools. All these measures were taken with a view
to accommodate the demands of various groups in a democratic
polity (Bhargava 2010; Mahajan 2002) and laid the foundation for
a competitive linguistic market in India.

Position of Hindi in Education Policy

Post-independence, education policies bore imprints of the conflicting discourses of language. In other words, like many other postcolonial societies, the issue of official language in India is predicated on many conflicts which have implications for the status of Hindi in the educational realm. I begin with the central question of the conditions in which particular languages gain authority claims and then examine the case of Hindi as school language to explore the extent of these claims. Drawing on the work of Bourdieu (1976b) and Kathryn Woolard (2004), I am appraising the legitimacy claims of Hindi in public domain in terms of its recognition as official language of Indian state and as a language suitable for school education. The distinction between ideological complex of anonymity and authenticity, spelled out by Woolard,[14] helps one to argue that the claim of 'authenticity' is crucial for a language to get public recognition, and in case of Hindi, helped it to achieve the status of official language of the Union and be implemented in schools immediately after independence. However, simply achieving the official status is not enough. It is the claim of 'anonymity' which is essential for an official language to *maintain* its legitimacy in a multilingual context. In case of Hindi, it can be argued that despite its official status, it has not been particularly successful in concealing its linkages with a particular social group, a feat which can bestow the language an authority in public life. The authority of Hindi is also questioned because of its failure in creating strong linkages with the employment market. This is argued on the basis of an analysis of select education policy documents in post-independence India. These documents include the two major policy documents at national level and two reports aimed at curricular reforms, National Curriculum Framework, 2005 and National Knowledge Commission Report (NKCR), 2008. The analysis reveals that the question of school language is articulated through conflicting discourses of education. Particularly, two separate though interrelated articulations of education have been identified both of which present a different vision of nation-state.

1. Education for integration in a diverse society and,
2. Education for economic mobility in an unequal society.

While these articulations differ in their vision of education, they foreground the idea of a nation-state while legitimising the use of a particular form of language for schooling. It is interesting to note, however, that in both these formulations and the strategies adopted, Hindi seems to be on a weak position vis-à-vis English. A third and an alternative formulation is also identified which makes reference to the local context in a multilingual society, without necessarily relying on the essentialising notion of the authentic identity of a nation-state or a region.

Education for Integration Through the Incorporation of Diversity

The major education policy documents, immediately after independence, reflect a concern for a common language through its association with a 'national' education. Kothari Commission and National Education Policy (NEP) of 1968 were among the first to spell out the ideas of national education, setting some basic parameters with decisive influence on the position of Hindi in official school curriculum. These documents stated the need for a common schooling in the country for better national integration. However, the idea of integration was not based on simple uniformity of culture, because the same document (MHRD 1968) also talks about various other aims such as the promotion of regional languages for the release of 'creative energy', the raising of the standards of education and disseminating the same to the wider population, and the bridging of the gap between the masses and the intelligentsia. One innovative method to resolve the conflicting aims of maintaining national integration as well as protection of regional identity was the adoption of a three-language formula (TLF), which was incorporated in NEP 1968. The formula made the provision that secondary schools were required to teach the regional language of the state, in addition to Hindi and English. In the Hindi-using states of north India, a modern Indian language scheduled in the Constitution besides Hindi and English, preferably from southern India, was to be taught. This formula, while making space for regional languages, in effect, makes it mandatory for schools across India to teach Hindi and English as compulsory languages at the secondary level.[15]

The next major policy statement in MHRD (1986) also reiterates the need for 'common schooling' and the TLF. The political atmosphere had changed by then because of the anti-Hindi agitation in the South and the emergence of regional parties in the late 1960s and 1970s (Advani 2009). For the first time, the need for a national curricular framework (NCF) was expressed in this policy statement. It discusses a national system of education based on the NCF containing the idea of a cultural core, reflecting components such as the history of the freedom movement, constitutional ideals, etc. It is apparently a very clear statement favouring a more integrated society through its advocacy of a common cultural content through a centrally framed curriculum. However, it also sought to foster an understanding of the diversity of the cultural and social systems among students. It further recommends the conservation of the languages of minority communities and identifies the need for developing material for scheduled tribes in their own languages.

Braj Kachru (1986) has commented on this magical aspect of English language vis-à-vis other Indian languages whereby the latter are perceived as having factional associations.

> The native codes are functionally marked in terms of caste, religion and region, and so forth, English has no such markers, at least in the non-native context. In India the most widely used language is Hindi (46%) and its different varieties have traditionally been associated with various factions: Hindi with the Hindus; Urdu with the Muslims; and Hindustani with the maneuvering political pandits who could not create a constituency for it.
>
> (Kachru 1986 cited in Ashcroft, Griffiths, and Tiffin 1995, 272–75)

In this way, the idea of integration through the use of a common language across schools in India was tempered by concerns for regional languages and minority languages. The failure of TLF in many states in establishing Hindi and the continuation of English as an indispensable part of school education across India presents the dilemma of Hindi in school education scenario. English, on the other hand enjoyed greater success because of its supposed neutrality to other groups in a multilingual polity. In other words, English, rather than Hindi, came to acquire a kind of 'anonymous' and 'impersonal' character, which is considered to be the hallmark of authority of standard languages. This is a common phenomenon in all societies with colonial experience, where the attempt to provide a native alternative to the language of the colonisers have always been contested at various fronts. The alternatives have oscillated between providing a native alternative to the colonial language, to the approach which seeks to appropriate the colonisers' language by nativising it to those advocating hybrid form of languages in post-colonial societies (Ashcroft, Griffiths, and Tiffin 1995; Braithwaite 1984).[16]

Education for Social and Economic Mobility

The discourse of education for the sake of economic mobility, envisions the Indian state in terms of a unified labour market and languages as skills necessary to compete in this arena. Hindi being the official language held stronger claims in comparison to other vernacular and non-standard languages and weaker claims vis-à-vis English in national and global markets. In his recent work, Brass (2004) has discussed a three-tier hierarchic structure, delineating the inter-relations of education, language choices and life-chance in the Indian context. He has argued that the English-speaking elite and English-literate bilinguals from Hindi-speaking regions compete for top positions in the national market of India, while speakers of Hindi or the regional languages occupy only the intermediate-level positions. The illiterate and the speakers of only the mother tongues remain at the lowest rung of society, heightening the gap between the elite and the mass even further. Given the nature of competitive politics in India, even in the field of government administrative jobs at the union level where knowledge of Hindi had some additional value over other regional languages, authority claims of Hindi came under questioning in recent debates.[17]

In recent years, government policy documents started showing a preference for a stronger role of English in school education. This change is accelerated due to the change in the nature of language markets in the wake of globalisation, where Hindi is not seen as a vehicle of social mobility. This change is linked with post-1991 economic reforms and the expansion of service sector attributed to a boom in IT sector. These changes have unfolded a new dynamic of labour market and school education because of the growing reliance on learning of English for jobs in the specific sector which is free from bureaucratic control of government. The weakened share of bureaucratic jobs in government sectors which relied on use of official languages were further weakened in this period and English emerges much more strongly as a language of aspiration because of the new kinds of employment based on English competency. These developments brought a major shift in education policy discourse where English is no longer seen as a language of colonial masters alone (Advani 2009). This is also evidenced by the spurt of private English-medium school-market in India which has generated enormous interest among commentators.

In this official discourse, English education is identified as one of the strategy to counter the inequality of access to quality education in India. The policy document that most strongly presents the case of English from this position is the NKCR (National Knowledge Commission 2008). It set for itself the ideal of a 'knowledge society' and deems English as important for the realisation of the same to promote inclusive growth (letter to the Prime Minister of India, Pitroda 2006). The rationale for the promotion of English at school level is provided by the significance of English in higher education and in promising professional or white-collar jobs. The commission recommends the introduction of English along with the first language of the child from Class 1 in all schools. It is curious to note that, unlike previous documents the NKCR does not make any reference to mother tongue education.[18] This discourse has generated a lot of scholarly work in the field of education and language in India, both highlighting the growing schism between English and vernacular education (Ramanathan 2005) and highlighting the complexity of associating English with social mobility in a hierarchical society (Bhattacharjee 2013; LaDousa 2014; Proctor 2010).

It is in this discourse that Hindi's claim to legitimacy seems to be on a particularly weak grounding. In the wake of globalisation, it is argued that linkages of education and employment markets are continually eroded for Hindi and other regional languages in comparison to English. But it has to be mentioned that, the interrelation of education in English and social mobility in a hierarchical society is much more complex in nature and, more often than not, fails in its stated goals in the educational domain.

Education for a Contextually Sensitive Learning

An alternative conception of language and education, occupying relatively marginal space in public debates has emerged around the notion of the 'local context of child'. Unlike the previous discourses, it does not use the nation-state as its frame of reference. It is also different from the emphasis on the use of an essentialist notion of 'mother tongue' for education, which conflates the notion of regional languages with mother languages.[19]

Here, school education is premised on the idea of facilitating learning through being sensitive to the local context of a child. Critiquing the standard language ideologies which draw legitimacy from the state, it contests the use of a standard language like Hindi for classroom teaching for being too restrictive for a child to be able to express oneself with ease.

Particularly, in a caste- and class-stratified society, an insistence on standard norms of Hindi based on highly Sanskritised lexical items, may further add to the devaluation of the child's social identity and home context in classroom settings. For example, Dalit narratives of school education have questioned the foreignness of both English language as well as the language of the Brahmins (Rege 2010). The problems of a curriculum which is insensitive to a child's social identity of caste and class has been brought out in the work by many educationists in India (Bhog and Ghose 2014; Kumar 1985, 1988).

NCF of 2005 makes explicit recommendations related to the languages to be used in education from this perspective. Its executive summary foregrounds the issue of the failure of schools in relating with languages of students' homes and of neighbourhoods. The Position Paper of the Focus Group on Teaching of Indian Languages (2006) deals with language issues in their social and cultural contexts, and links them with the broader policy goals of social justice and equality. It views the goal of education as cultivating responsible citizenship based on communicative competence in a Habermasian sense in which citizenship ideals are based on an inclusive social world. The emphasis is on the need to move beyond a fixed rule- and curriculum-bound knowledge of language to a more creative, aesthetic engagement with language. It also affirms the belief in the ability of the child to be proficient in multiple languages simultaneously. One of the important shifts from the earlier approach was an attempt to treat the local context as a source of knowledge or a learning resource rather than as an obstacle to learning an official language.

The NCF also recommends allowing a multilingual atmosphere in the classroom which will solve the problem of providing mother tongue education in India. It foregrounds the issue of school failure for a child and relates it with a lack of connect of schools with languages of her homes and of neighbourhoods. Rather than dwelling on the question of selection of a suitable language for learning, it recommends allowing coexistence of several language varieties in the classroom. The learning of English will also benefit from an easy multilingual atmosphere in the classroom.

These provisions militate against a standardised understanding of languages in school setting. This is a major shift in NCF 2005 from the older paradigm which has several implications for language pedagogy in Indian classrooms. Khubchandani (1977) discusses the uncritical conflation of 'mother tongue education' with the regionally dominant language, while ignoring the linguistic diversity and complexity of India. He draws attention to the fact that the difference between the language spoken at home and the regional varieties taught in the school has been largely ignored by educationists. In studies of education and social inequality, the difference between the school variety and the variety at home is usually ignored. In sociolinguistic studies, it is reported that in India where formal education is not yet universal, people tend to identify with a prestigious, major language group, which happens to be the language taught at the school (Dasgupta 2001).

Conclusion

Historical contingencies created a peculiar condition regarding language of education in India which promoted multilinguality at official levels, without necessarily bridging the divide between elite and popular cultures. A reading of the education policies suggests that conflicting ideologies persist in official policies. The policies are concerned with goals of national integration and diversity on one hand and employability and mobility on the other. An alternative conception of language of education can also be seen which calls for a contextually sensitive language pedagogy premised on ideal of multilinguality. It is important to note that depending on the frameworks we adopt for the analysis of language of education at school level, there will be implications for pedagogic strategies adopted at school level. While some kind of curricular reforms are aimed at bridging the gap between different groups by a focus on universalisation of these norms of standard language, others look for a pluralisation of the norm itself.

Similar complexities in which school language is mired in post-colonial societies, make it imperative that the language issue has to be understood not just at the level of the official curriculum of language in education, but in the micro-politics of specific languages at the school level.

Notes

1. 'Hindi is cursed because of its proximity to positions of power'.
2. *Bhadralok* is used as an honorific term to refer to a gentleman in Bengali. It also connoted an educated man of letters in West Bengal as per Ruud (2003).
3. Refer to Gal (1988) and Monica Heller (1999). For a review of anthropological studies of languages refer to Wortham (2011) and Duranti (2004) and Bucholtz and Hall (2010).

4. For example, refer to Baruah (1999) for the articulation of the notion of sub-nationalism in case of assertion of Assamese ethnic identity in contrast to Bengali.

5. Refer to Chapter 3 and Chapter 6 in this volume for details about such patterns of language-use and its regulation.

6. Others have critiqued this notion of modernisation through language. Notable mention may be made of Gandhi's critique of colonial education in standard languages in his Hind Swaraj. Historians of education like Krishna Kumar, Poromesh Acharya and NP Bhokta have similarly criticised the idea of standard or elite languages.

7. Refer to David Drury's (1993) work in Kanpur city for a mapping of the relation between schooling choice and class and occupational categories. Also look at Chapter 5 of this volume.

8. In colonial societies, very different situations existed from the European industrialised nation-state. See Cohn (1985), Niloofar Haeri (1997) and Errington (2001).

9. According to Dalmia (1997), this separate department of Bhasha, or Hindui, under the leadership of Lallulalji and Sadal Misra took up the task of identifying Hindu literature and rendering it in Hindui (Bhasha), deliberately excluding the Persian–Arabic words from it.

10. The political implications of the knowledge-creation exercise regarding the orient (the 'other') has been elaborated by Edward Said (1979).

11. The Kaithi script used for account-keeping by the Kayasthas was rejected in favour of Devanagari, the script used in most of the Sanskrit texts (King 1989).

12. For example one can refer to the works of Ngugi Wa Thong' O and his refusal to write in English and instead adopting a Gikuyu identity in Ashcroft, Griffiths and Tiffin (1995).

13. The Motilal Nehru Committee (1928) and the later States Reorganisation Commission Report (1953) suggested that to ensure better participation of citizens in public affairs and for the educational advancement of the region, linguistic homogeneity should be made the criterion of state formation (Annamalai 2001; Thirumalai 2005).

14. Refer to Woolard (2004) and to Chapter 1 (pp. 22–23) in this volume for elaboration of these concepts.

15. There are differing views on the formula among scholars. Schiffman (1996) considers it a good reflection of the Indian multilingual tradition and a balancing act to control the dominance of Hindi. But, in practice it continues to be violated in both Hindi- and non-Hindi-speaking regions of India.

16. Apart from Braithwaite's (1984) work on 'nativisation' of English language to serve native interests, there are other approaches which emphasise on using 'hybridity' of language forms. Hybridity, as a norm, has the potential to be used against the essentialising tendencies of both the colonial language as well as that of the native's construction of its alternative.

17. Check G. Austin for debates in early years of independence and the debates over recruitment in Indian Public Service Commission & Railways.

18. Rao (2008) has criticised the recommendations of NKCR for regressing back to Macaulay's time and completely ignoring the needs of linguistic minorities whose languages are not yet recognised.

19. Refer to Brass (2004) and Passions of Tongue by Sumathy Ramaswamy (1997).

3

Languages and Schools in Banaras: State and Community Linkages

… in my opinion schools teach only subjects. Tehzib, and the way we speak, our culture and such things, we learn from our families.

Abdul, Urdu Teacher, 35

In Gujrat *kelvani* or a learning culture is stressed at, a way of speaking which you don't acquire from bookish knowledge.

Bhanu Mehta, Literary Critique, 67

These epigraphs come from persons very differently placed in the social and economic scale. Mr AlHindi, an Urdu writer and a private school teacher, comes from a religious family and his brother holds an important leadership position among Muslims in the city. On the other hand, Mr Mehta is a Gujarati, a trained medical doctor by profession and a noted theatre artist and literary figure in the city's cultural life. In spite of coming from so varied class and community backgrounds, they express a common concern about contemporary schooling. They believe that schools are deficient in a fundamental way that cannot be overcome within current discourses of education. That deficiency comes from the fact that schools, as institutions, *cannot* impart learning in the form of *tehzib* or *kelvani*—Urdu and Gujarati equivalents of learning—at the community level. Both of them implicitly know that contemporary schools are meant to make a separation between the life and the learning that takes place at community and school level.

In the history of education, particularly of the post-colonial societies, the genesis of this separation is usually traced to the colonial rule which introduced the norm of public schooling over private forms of community-specific learning. In the post-colonial literature, education is viewed as one of the most 'cryptic' and 'insidious' of colonial survivals where even after political independence unequal relations between colonial (educational) producers and peripheral consumers continue (Ashcroft, Griffiths, and Tiffin 1995). This is because most of these societies have maintained colonial pattern of school administration not just in terms of hierarchic and bureaucratic management of education, but more importantly, in terms of defining what constitutes worthwhile knowledge to be taught in schools and how it is to be taught.

As an example of the same phenomenon, we have seen how standard languages associated with cultural elites continue to persist in school education in post-independence India. However, it would be naïve to suggest that in the encounter between the colonial and the native forms of education, the native cultures have been completely replaced by the colonial cultures. Such an understanding undermines the capacity of native institutions to negotiate the colonial forms of knowledge. Rather new kinds of institutions emerge from such encounters which cannot be captured in the dichotomous categories of the modern and the traditional. Even as schools in independent India represent the dominance of the official narrative of the nation-state, their past remain entangled in cultural battles over what is worthwhile knowledge for schooling and for whom. The widely available historical scholarship on efforts by community leaders to define women's education is a testimony of this fact (Chanana 2001; Kumar 2000; Mahanta 2008). The history of educational institutions in Banaras also presents schools as sites of conflicts and negotiations between the colonial and the indigenous ideals of education (Kumar 1998).

An awareness of these issues problematises the classification of contemporary schools in simple and dichotomous categories like modern versus unmodern or the government controlled versus private funded schools. One of the ways to capture the plurality and the hybridity of cultural forms in contemporary schools in India, therefore, is to closely examine them as sites of conflicting narratives of community, nation building and modernity.

In contemporary times, schools also present opportunities to examine different visions of state and nation (LaDousa 2014). Particularly with reference to the transformations in labour market brought in the period of globalisation, many studies have examined schools either in terms of government funded or private funded, or through categories of medium of instruction, such as English vis-à-vis Vernacular languages (LaDousa 2014; Ramanathan 2005). An understanding of school-markets through this divide, while helpful in understanding the larger power structure in a globalising economy, misses out on the tussles and dynamism within and across these categories. Bhattacharya (2013) has problematised the category of English-medium private schools and simple associations of English-medium school with social mobility. Similarly, Hindi-medium schools cover an enormous variety of schools in north India, differing in their funding patterns and relationships with the government. Further, if we account for the myriad ways in which communities have historically engaged with schools in a city like Banaras, we arrive at a complex relationship between state and schools, mediated by their links with communities at different levels. Part of this tangle in independent India was resolved through provisions for minority languages and minority religious educational institutions in policies of education. This chapter delves deeper into the question of relation of schools with communities in the modern nation-state. It attempts to make sense of schools in present-day Banaras against its history of identity politics over the issue of language and vis-à-vis their link with labour market situation. These issues are informed by an understanding of the conflict between the colonial and indigenous forms of knowledge in schools located in a city like Banaras.

Educational Institutions and the
Tussle of State and Community

A historical assessment of educational institutions and changes in their form provides a vantage point to assess contemporary schools. Colonial rule becomes an important referential period because it had important bearings on the cultural struggle over knowledge, in general, and languages in education, in particular (Cohn 1985; Kumar 2005b). It did succeed in transforming the indigenous modes of education in many ways. It changed the system of education by bringing it under the ambit of the bureaucratic apparatus of state leading to new ways of using physical space, textbooks, languages, teaching methods, and the routines and rituals associated with learning. The relationship of the school teacher with the local community also changed when her/his services were bureaucratised and became part of educational hierarchy (Kumar 2005c). The relation of hierarchy between teachers and students continued in post-independence period as well and incorporated new forms of subordination to adult authority of a teacher, one tinged with bureaucratic impersonality (Kumar 2000, 2008).

Even curricular aspects of education underwent significant change in this period. Kumar (2005b) argues that the colonial administrators' view of school education was heavily influenced by the reformation ideas of knowledge which was specific to Europe. This led them to view indigenous school curriculum and pedagogic practice, particularly of language, literacy and logic, with contempt, resulting in official promotion of only colonial forms of knowledge in schools and discouragement and rejection of indigenous schooling (K. Kumar 2005b; N. Kumar 2000). Kumar also argues that such rejection of indigenous schooling created a conflict between education and culture (2005b, 72).

However, this rejection does not go uncontested from community leaders in India who actively supported and promoted 'new' forms of educational institutions in this period. N. Kumar (2000) in her work on the educational history of Banaras has examined the encounter of colonial schooling with indigenous modes of learning, by looking at the transformations in the various forms of educational institutions in Banaras. In her account of pre-colonial Banaras, there were Sanskrit schools, for the Brahmans; *Mahajani pathshalas*, for the merchant Hindus; Koran schools or *maktabs*, for the lower-class Muslim weavers; and Persian schools, for high-caste Hindus and the upper-class Muslims. Such a diversity of schooling system can be attributed to the community-specific nature of the educational system that existed in pre-colonial Banaras. Each of these learning systems helped to maintain and reproduce the existing class, caste and gender-based hierarchical social order, and transmitted the cultural values necessary for such reproduction. For example, Persian schools were more 'career oriented' and emphasised literary knowledge of Persian language necessary for official work among the better-off population of Hindus and Muslims, while Maktabs meant for Muslim weavers, emphasised on basic memorisation of Koran and being a good Muslim weaver (2000, 121–23).[1]

Colonial governance redefined the nature of interrelation between communities and schools by introducing a common education for all. The community-specific system of learning that existed under the earlier arrangement faced a crisis. The crisis was in terms of a change in the values of the educational system which had been fulfilling the social, reproductive needs of the communities in a particular political, economic and social order.[2] Gradually, the pre-colonial forms of community-specific schools weakened and ceased to exist in older forms. Although such forms of schooling could not survive in the long run, historical evidence about new versions of schools, relatively independent of colonial norms of education, are found in Banaras. These schools were either funded directly by local community of merchants or by the organisations created for setting up indigenous form of education as against the colonial ones.[3] The leaders of such organisations and communities negotiated the colonial model of education, by making the mandated curriculum suitable for community's educational requirements. This was most starkly visible in the arena of girls' schooling, where community-defined notions of suitable education for girls were incorporated in school curricula by introducing components of household skills or domestic education. Examples of these innovations can be found in some indigenous schools set up by community leaders or ideologues, to retain 'indigenous cultural values' within the colonial framework of 'secular' 'modern' schooling, such as the Annie Besant school, based on the principles of Theosophy, and Agrasen Kanya Mahavidyalaya and Arya Mahila Degree College, which sought to combine the ideal of the 'Indian woman' with the Western ideal of secular universal education. In Kumar's account (Kumar 2000), such schools are viewed as sites of 'creative responses' from community leaders, which transcend the dichotomy of the colonial and the indigenous. These responses were interlinked with the movement for a 'national' form of education, proposed by the Congress party at all-India level and, at the same time, were different in their local articulations, reflecting the power structures at the city level.[4]

In post-independence period, Indian state has emerged as the most important institution in terms of control over school knowledge. It grants recognition to schools, frames the curricula and sets the evaluation mechanisms of all kinds of schools. Even in minority schools, except religious instruction, most other aspects of education are largely controlled by the state.[5] In a way, the nation-state has overtaken communities in defining the content of school knowledge. But this monopoly over school knowledge is also contested at various levels, sometimes in the guise of identity-based movements for recognition of a certain language within education, and sometimes, in more tacit ways within school contexts. This aspect of conflict between communities and the state over school knowledge has not received enough attention in sociological research.

Nita Kumar, in her commentary on the contemporary schools in Banaras, argues that even though colonial model of schooling (both government and private funded) seems to have won the cultural battle over the indigenous forms, the present-day schools in the city continue to present a tussle between the requirements of the state and the local needs for modern schooling, and adjustments are made accordingly (Kumar 1998, 2000). For example, the state regulations prescribe all recognised schools to have sufficient space and provide basic facilities such as playground, library and yet the city is brimming with fully functional, privately funded schools of various types which do not fulfil such norms. Another requirement of the state is to teach three languages in the school at secondary level, one of which should preferably be out of the Hindi-speaking region. This expectation from schools is seldom seen to be fulfilled in the majority of schools and we will discuss that in greater detail later.

In recent times, there have been a number of studies on school education in context of globalising economy and the concomitant changes in the labour market and state, and how these changes have implications for school organisation, funding and curricula. Here, globalised employment market is believed to have presented significant challenge to state monopoly over school curricula, particularly with reference to the language of education. The recent spur in the research on privately funded English-medium schools vis-à-vis vernacular-medium schools have often alluded to this framework. However, the history of cultural resistance to the colonial model provides important insights to make sense of the nature of present-day schools in Banaras. The classification of school type based on school's relationship with state and market has to take into account the role of communities with an active stake in defining school knowledge. We have seen that, the rise of a Sanskritised form of Hindi as school language in Banaras presents an important case of how certain groups stake claim over school knowledge within a nationalist project. In Banaras, these questions of community and school knowledge are inevitably linked with the political and economic aspects of the city life.

The Political and Economic Context of Hindi in Banaras

The city of Banaras does not have a strong industrial base and is to a large extent dependent on informal and small-scale industries. The economic profile of the city is influenced by its status of a pilgrimage city and as an important centre of education. The major industries in the city are small-scale and handicraft based such as those of brocade, toys, hardware, etc. There is a huge dependence on the informal sector for the industrial development of the city for the employment opportunities in the city. Amongst manufacturing industries, the spinning and weaving industry is the largest in terms of number of employees, amounting to 50 per cent of the total employment in industry (Refer Tables 3.1 and 3.2).

These industries are not like the ones that are presumed to develop in an industrialised society, and are not fully integrated with a centralised education system and standard languages. The dominant industry of the Banarasi saree proves to be an important case study to examine how class and community relations intersect and set the political economic life in the city. It also has important implications towards understanding the social reproductive function of the education system embedded in a completely different system of production. The estimated labour force involved in the silk industry of Banaras is around 1–3 lakh weavers, 1,500 traders (a majority among them being Hindus) and around 2,000 *girastas* or master weavers, mostly Muslims (Varman and Chakrabarti 2007, 125–26). Trade relations between the Hindu mahajans and

Table 3.1
Employment Share in the City by Various Categories

Category	No. of Employees	Percentage Share
Manufacturing	1,28,930	8.44
Trade and commerce	82,035	5.37
Other services	60,466	3.96
Transport and communication	24,235	1.59
Agriculture	12,239	0.80
Construction	7,028	0.46
Marginal workers	5,938	0.39
Total employed	3,20,871	21.01
Not employed	8,85,425	57.98
Total	15,27,167	100.00

Source: JNNURM (2006).

Table 3.2
Employment Share of Different Industries Within Manufacturing

Category	No. of Employees	Percentage to Total
Spinning and weaving	65,368	50.70
Metal and metal manufacturing	19,223	14.91
Food and food processing	4,938	3.83
Timber and wood workers	4,487	3.48
Printing and publishing	7,981	6.19
Manufacturing machinery	4,435	3.44
Textile	1,354	1.05
Zarda and tobacco	1,147	0.89
Chemical production	2,669	2.07
Transport equipments	1,405	1.09
Electric machinery	6,472	5.02
Miscellaneous	9,451	7.33
Total	1,28,930	100.00

Source: JNNURM (2006).

the Muslim weavers have been important in the recent communal history of the city as well (Casolari 2002). The Ansari community is the dominant one among the weavers who work for others and earn wages for their work (Showeb 1994). One can see a gradual, upward socio-economic mobility among the community of Muslim weavers, as many among them have become master weavers and some have even become traders and exporters, although their proportion is still less than 30 per cent (Varman and Chakrabarti 2007). They are also seen as an educationally backward community, sometimes referred to as *jahil* (illiterate or uneducated), and as resistant to modern schooling, as compared to other communities and castes (Kumar 1998, 2000). They are also usually associated with a particular form of speech that is *Julehti* (of Julahas, the caste group associated with weaving).[6] The residents jokingly refer to it as *Aiyo jaiyo ki bhasha* (the language in which the words 'come' and 'go' are referred as *aiyo* and *jaiyo* in the place of more standard *aaiye* and *jaaiye* in Hindi). Some scholars classify it as a form of Banarasi prevalent among city residents (Simon 1998). The language variety resonates the world of saree production. The characters of Abdul Bismillah's award winning Hindi novel *Jhini Jhini Bini Chadariya* speak this variety within their world of domestic and work life. However, non-Muslim Banarasi speakers would not identify with it as their own, even if they could freely communicate with each other.

Historically, the upper-caste Hindus—comprising the merchant castes, the Pandits or Brahmans and the Bhumihars—occupied strategic positions in the political economy of Banaras (Bayly 1983; Freitag 1989). In the late nineteenth and early twentieth century, some of these groups constituted the 'vernacular elite' whose role was instrumental in getting Hindi in Devanagari recognised as an official language of the United Provinces (Bayly 1983; Dalmia 1997; King 1989). Their active participation in Hindi movement made the city of Banaras the centre of linguistic nationalism in the last two decades. Historically, the local elite of Banaras had played an important role in the ascendance of Sanskritised Hindi to a national symbol through institutionalised efforts. The movement for a particular form of Hindi had two distinct effects on the linguistic scenario of India, in general, and north India, in particular. Sanskritised Hindi, in the Devanagari script, was separated from Urdu, and even Hindustani. Second, it also absorbed Brajbhasha, Bhojpuri, Awadhi and other regional varieties within its fold and these varieties came to be called the 'dialects' of Hindi. All these developments led to the polarisation between the elite and popular languages (Bhokta 1998; King 1989; Rai 2002). Scholars have studied the role of institutions like Nagari Pracharini Sabha and literary and cultural icons like Bharatendu Harishchandra from the city, who pioneered the attempt in developing a form of Hindi for the national role (Dalmia 1997; Kumar 2005d).[7] In twentieth century India, some of the important contributions to the development of curricular material for school education and for teachers training were carried out in BHU by Ram Chandra Shukla and his associates (Kumar 2005d).

In a changed political scenario, post-independence Banaras witnessed another language movement in defence of Hindi and against the continuation of 'imperial' English as an additional official language of the union in the 1960s. While states like Tamil Nadu were engulfed in protests against the proposed move to make Hindi the sole official language of the union, there was a counter-movement of Angrezi Hatao, or Banish English, inspired by Ram Manohar Lohia in the north-Indian states such as Uttar Pradesh and Bihar.

Piyush Misra, a Hindi teacher in BHU and a former participant of the movement, recollected how many of the shopkeepers in Banaras had to change their signboards overnight from English to Hindi so as to avoid their shops being burnt.[8] The current scenario where Hindi has become the dominant language of the city can be seen in the backdrop of these conflicts over language identities. This predominance is unmistakable, even as the city inhabits diverse people from different parts of India.

It is against this backdrop of a history of cultural struggle over education on one hand and social demographics and language politics on the other, we can begin to make sense of schools, especially the Hindi-medium schools in the city and how these vary from one another.

Schools in Banaras: Beyond the Dichotomies

History of educational institutions in the city reveal them to be not just contributing to the reproduction of social and cultural dominance relationships, but also as innovative sites of cultural conflicts between the colonial and native ways of learning and defining knowledge. These conflicts have bearings on understanding the current status of Banaras as an important centre of education, catering to the diverse needs of not just city dwellers but also of the rural hinterland of eastern Uttar Pradesh and Bihar.

One of the ways of making sense of the diverse schools, is through their relation with the state in which schools are usually identified through their source of funding, management and the extent of state regulation. Government schools are managed and completely funded by the state at central, state or district level. Government schools also vary in terms of their affiliation with central, state or municipal boards. Others are privately managed but are either partially dependent on government for funding or completely independent in their funding sources. The latter are termed as private schools. The category of private schools is too broad to constitute a homogenous group of schools. They vary in terms of pattern of ownership and organisational affiliations and also in terms of diverse category of students' population they cater to. One major variation is in terms of class and status of parents because schools demand different forms of capital from the families of the students, in terms of school fee and other associated expenses and engagements expected from the students' home.

In matters of framing the curricula, state has more or less control over all kinds of schools which seek recognition, including the private ones. Only those schools which are managed as minority institutions have some freedom regarding their curriculum, which has space for religious instruction as well. Some of the non-minority, but government aided schools also have affiliations with some cultural–religious organisations like Saraswati Shishu Mandir which has implications for their curriculum. These forms of community affiliations mark the private and aided schools in the city and mediate their relation with the state and the market. More nuanced relationship of non-minority schools with religious communities, can only be explored by examining the informal and everyday aspects of curricula which will be dealt in later parts of the book.

Another way of examining the schools in the city would be on the basis of their medium of instruction. According to NCERT Report on language of education in India (2006), the largest number of schools offer education in Hindi medium at all levels of schooling in Uttar Pradesh. The second largest group is of English-medium schools, which is one-fifth of the Hindi-medium schools, followed by Sanskrit (refer Table 3.3).

The number of Hindi-medium schools top that of any other language-medium schooling as per NCERT all India surveys. For the year 2005, the proportion of Hindi-medium schools

Table 3.3
Secondary Schools by Medium of Instruction for the State of Uttar Pradesh

Medium of Instruction	All	%	Rural	%	Urban	%
English	1,614	11.95	654	8.44	960	16.67
Hindi	10,965	81.16	6,557	84.70	4,408	76.56
Sanskrit	735	5.44	448	5.78	287	4.98
Others	184	1.36	82	1.05	102	1.77
Total	13,498	100.00	7,741	100.00	5,757	100.00

Source: NCERT (2006).

at secondary level of school education was 32 per cent, while English-medium schools at this level were 20 per cent (NCERT 2006). In the state of Uttar Pradesh, the proportionate share of Hindi-medium-school was much higher at more than 80 per cent for all the categories except for urban areas where it was around 76 per cent of all the schools (Table 3.3).

Hindi, English and Sanskrit are the three languages taught in the majority of the schools of the city. In some schools, Urdu and Bengali are taught as subjects depending upon the students' social profiles and the availability of teachers. Hindi and English are the two most widely used medium of instruction in all these schools. The statistics related to combinations of languages taught in secondary schools also present Hindi as a common language in all the major combinations listed there.

Many of the educational studies in India have foregrounded the issue of language of education, which assumes significance in view of the changing ideas of nation-state in a globalising world (LaDousa 2005; Ramanathan 2005). The divide between the Hindi- and English-medium schools in Banaras is considered significant for examining the hierarchical relations between the national and/or metropolitan and the regional citizens (LaDousa 2005). LaDousa (2014) argues that multiple language markets operate in Banaras, one of which places Hindi- and English-medium schools in dichotomous categories. In that account, Hindi medium is identified with low-cost government schooling and English medium with fee-charging private schooling. In other words, most of the English-medium schools are believed to be expensive and privately managed while majority of Hindi-medium schools are deemed to be Government funded. However, the field data does not testify the same. During my fieldwork, I came across a wide variety of schools in the city within each of these categories on grounds of perceptions of quality, students' composition and affiliation with cultural organisations (Table 3.4).

These schools are also believed to be unequally placed in people's perception, in terms of what future they guarantee to students in the local and global labour markets. Hierarchical ordering of schools, on the basis of different markets located at the national and local levels highlight the conflicts between the national elite and the regional elite. Without denying the implications of such polarisations, in this research, we focus more on the multi-layered nature of the conflicts played out at the school, where the conflicting markets of English and Hindi present only one of the several strands. In other words, the language markets of Banaras are even more varied if we focus on lower-middle-class families and their perceptions of schooling within the local context of the city and its inner world. And the dynamics of this world can be revealed through the tension within what is termed as the 'local'. The universe of the language dynamics within 'local market' of Banaras includes Hindi, in relation with other varieties such as Bhojpuri, Banarasi and Urdu.[9]

Table 3.4
Number of Schools in Urban Uttar Pradesh Teaching Different Combinations of Three languages Taught as the First, Second and Third Languages

Combinations	Number of Schools	
	Upper-primary	Secondary
English Hindi Sanskrit	5,891	2,191
Hindi English Sanskrit	26,737	7,164
Hindi English Urdu	2,500	–
Hindi Sanskrit English	2,280	831

Source: NCERT (2006).

Various scholars have documented the relations of conflict between Hindi and Urdu in colonial India, and many others have commented on the declining status of Urdu as a language of education in post-independence India.[10] The number of schools with Urdu as medium of instruction is very limited as per the all India survey (NCERT 2006). While studies of madrasa education in India are available, very little attention has been paid to the Urdu-medium schools outside the ambit of religious instruction. I came across many Urdu-medium schools catering to the pockets of Muslim settlements, particularly for girls' education.

The variability of cultural affiliation of school, is often seen in terms of the distinction between secular and minority schools. The minority schools have been given the right to conduct religious instruction to protect and promote their cultures. For all other schools, the curriculum is common and defined by the state through its various bodies and the only legitimate community affiliation that they officially espouse is that of the nation. However, each school has its own unique ties to the local community it seeks to serve. During my visits to various forms of the school, I sought to explore the cultural affiliations of the school by examining the social profile of the students, as well as the affiliation with other organisations in terms of sources of funding and their effects on the school ideology and practices in brief. The schools presented below represent a wide variety of schools within the seemingly homogenous category of Hindi- and English-medium schools in the city. By presenting an account of these schools, the objective is to examine the heterogeneity of school types within a category of schools based on language of instruction or the degree of government support to run the school. The schools described below do not claim to represent all kinds of schools in Varanasi, but point towards some specific bases of variation in terms of organisational affiliation and composition of school population. Hindi-medium schools include one municipality school, one school funded by the Central University and one private school affiliated to a Hindu organisation. English-medium schools include three schools, each of these catering to different class and community of children. One is a high-end school catering to upper-middle-class families, another is affiliated to a Gurdwara trust, and another school cater-ing to girl students from lower-middle-class Muslim families. A government funded madrasa has also been examined with a view to widen the scope of enquiry. This account is based on a single day visit to each school. I visited these schools with a common set of questions and interacted mainly with teachers and school staff. This exercise helped me in not just mapping out the social profile of Hindi- and English-medium schools, but also identify key parameters for detailed enquiry later.

Municipality School

Government schools in the urban areas are a dying institution.

– Headmaster, Municipality School

The Municipality School of Piyari Kala is situated in a prime city location. The school premises house three separate schools, two primary schools, one for boys and one for girls and, a school for disabled children. In this school, most of the students come from very low economic backgrounds. Often, they are abandoned or orphaned children. Their parents work as daily wage earners by sweeping, selling peanuts, making envelopes, etc. They are either illiterate or have a very limited exposure to schooling. One-third of the students are from the Muslim community, because of the location of the school. The majority of the students as per their teachers come from the 'backward classes' or, are 'category students'. Students keep dropping out of the school and only 50 per cent of the remainder continue till Class 8 or 10. Hence, a very few number of the students join other schools to continue their studies. Most of the teachers are old, because recruitment in the government schools has been stopped for a long time. That is why the school principal asserted that these government schools in the urban areas are dying. He claimed that the schools in the rural areas are getting their due attention, but government schools are not needed any more in the urban areas. There is no appointment of regular teachers or even of *shiksha mitras*, the teachers appointed on a contract basis. There were only 9 permanent/regular teachers for all the sections of this school. He further claimed that in Banaras city alone, there are some 116 municipality-run schools for primary education and 22 junior-high schools, but there are just 240 teachers in all. Even the status of the teachers in government schools is very low, as they are required to do all kinds of duties from election duty to taking part in polio drives. Another senior teacher lamented about the overall condition of the government school now in comparison to an earlier time, when all the government officials were schooled in state-run schools. Their disappointment and despair is indicative of the shared belief that all government schools in India are facing a major crisis. It is in this context that the government school, located at the heart of the city, functioning with insufficient and inadequate teaching staff, and catering to students who either dropout from the school or are there because they do not have any other choice, is to be understood.

Central Hindu Girls School (CHGS)

This is a government funded school, but is under the adminis-tration of the central University in the city. It has an impressive infrastructure as compared to all other schools with a sprawling campus, separate auditorium, labs and library apart from big play-grounds for junior and senior sections of the school.

Most of the teaching positions are regularised and funded by government. It is a girls' school, branching out of the historic Central Hindu School, set up by Annie Besant in 1898. The origi-nal school was set up as a creative intervention into the educational set-up and with a view to combining principles of Western educa-tion and literature, but grounded in the principles of Theosophy. It is affiliated to BHU, which has been another major symbol of Hindu modernity, and a university which was funded by the local elite to create space for institutionalised knowledge with a Hindu-nationalist cultural agenda (Kumar 2005d).

But now, in the public image, CHGS exists as a government school offering quality higher education to girls. The school has a special place in the girls' education market of Banaras because it assures an easy entry into the University through reservation of seats.

The school is affiliated with the Central board of secondary education. Even as it is a Hindi-medium school, it has the provision of bilingual education for students, in which they have the choice to write their examinations in either Hindi or English which is unique among the city schools. The school offers Hindi and English as compulsory languages, and Sanskrit and Urdu as optional languages to its students. At senior secondary level, it offers the choice of science, arts and commerce streams to the students. The school caters to a heterogenous set of students from diverse caste and community backgrounds. All the government norms regarding the reservation are followed strictly. The students are selected through entrance tests conducted at specific levels of entry.

Even as it has a special space in the history of school education in the city, there were no visible markers of the memory of its association with the Theosophical Society of India. Most emblems of the school at the school entrance and in the principal's room reflected its association with the University. None of the teachers I interacted with mentioned anything about Annie Besant or her educational work. They mainly emphasised on the school's academic and extra-curricular activities.

Bhartiya Shishu Mandir

This is a non-government high school level Hindi-medium school. The school is located in a narrow residential lane of the city with an overbearing three storied building. Inside the school campus, I was led to the principal's room which was decorated with framed photographs of Gandhi, Bhagat Singh and Vivekananda among others. He spelt out that the objective of the school was to impart modern education with Indian values. The school comes under the organisation of Saraswati Shishu Mandir, which has branches all over India. These schools have a specific cultural agenda of the promotion of 'Indian' Hindu values of education, which is explained as Hindu values in their organisational website. There are 400 students enrolled in the school coming from nearby areas. It primarily caters to the lower-middle-class groups in Banaras. The families are primarily engaged in petty businesses, that is, running small retail shops and private services. Apart from common public events, they also celebrate some of the Indian festivals in the school by organising *prabhat pheri* or morning marches. They follow government prescribed textbooks for main subjects and use supplementary books provided by their trust. A primary-school teacher, Sangeeta, talked about the ideas and techniques of learning in the 'Hindu' tradition which are now being repackaged in modern schools such as, emphasis on physical training, handicrafts, relating with nature by making pedagogic tools out of leaves, vegetable cuts, etc. She also recounted the significance of the teachings of Indian leaders like Vivekananda in current times.

The medium of instruction is Hindi. When I inquired about the language that students use in the playground and elsewhere, the principal asserted that they make sure that students use proper language in school. He also added that they lay special emphasis on the learning of English to ensure quality of education to everyone in the school. One of the office staff, sitting in the same room added that they have been able to attract students because of the assurance of quality education and an increasing concern among parents about the loss of Indian values among children such as respecting one's elders. The school teaches '*sanskar*' or values which are lacking in English-medium school kids.

Moonbeam School, Sigra

This is a completely privately funded coeducational school with English as the medium of instruction. It is a high fee-charging and reputed school of Banaras with several branches all over the city. The monthly school fees range from ₹1,500/- onwards. There are around 2,000 students in the school and the majority of them are from the upper-middle-class families. Their parents are either self-employed or are high-ranking salaried officials in government or private sectors. The school has a formalised and hierarchical administrative structure. The school is managed and controlled by the Managing Committee, the Principal, the Vice-Principal and the Rector. The school has several academic departments and has designated heads for each department. Apart from the compulsory teaching of English and Hindi, Sanskrit and Urdu are offered as optional languages. They also have a Department of Foreign Languages that offers French.

I met the rector of the school Mr Avasthi, who informed me about the school curricula which follows instruction in English language. This norm of speaking only in English is strictly enforced by teachers on students by imposing fine on violation. He, however, believed this to be a practical need of the time where people have to be seen as smart which necessarily include 'being fluent in English'. In his capacity as administrator, he had to reject many qualified applicants for teaching positions because of this very lacuna. Interestingly, he admitted to using a mix of Bhojpuri and Hindi at home, but forbid such usage at school. He is very clear in his mind that parents are paying such high fee with an expectation that their children would pick up English in school. Such clarity about the purpose and the perceived role of the school helps him to reconcile with the contradiction in his own practice.

Similar conflicts in attitude towards language were seen in my interaction with Ms Geetavali, the senior Hindi teacher. She admitted that Indian languages make us more comfortable with each other which is why whenever students get a chance they speak in Hindi. Even her students reportedly told her that she sounds strict and *kathor* (strict) while speaking in English, but much softer when she speaks Hindi or even Sanskrit. The sense of colonial superiority is still attached with English whether people really like it or not. In public, people are often ridiculed for wrong use of language which would imply not just the wrong usage of English language, but also using a correct form of another language, the use of which is considered uncool for a particular context. She recollected an incident in which some students were making fun of a student who used the Hindi term *peelia* for jaundice.

Nanak English-medium School

There are two branches of this school in the city run by a Gurdwara trust. Both the schools offer education in the English medium for boys and girls, catering to the middle-class families of the city. The principals of both the schools categorically clarified at the beginning that the school is not specific to the community of Punjabis or Sikhs and is open for all, and no prominent signs of community affiliations were visible in the bigger school which looked like any other private funded school.

SCHOOL 1

The smaller branch with provision for classes till standard 10 is located in the city adjacent to the Tegh Bahadur Gurdwara. The school shares its campus with another bigger school, Gurunanak Khalsa Hindi-medium girls school. This school is run in one of the floors of the building of the bigger school. The students were described as coming from 'mediocre' class and from diverse backgrounds including Hindus, Muslims as well as Sikhs because of its location, which is close to the pockets of Sikh and Muslim weavers' settlement. In occupational terms, most of the students came from families of petty business owners or were engaged in private salaried jobs. The school fee was ₹350 per month.

I noticed that students' religious affiliations were marked in the attendance register of a teacher under the heading of 'caste'. When I asked about its significance for school activity, the teacher did not elaborate much and said it is just for information of their background.

When I enquired about the different language varieties used by students in their class and outside class, she emphasised that they make sure no one uses any 'foul' language or abusive words within school premises such as *sala* (a derogatory term used in informal contexts). Her idea about any local variation of language was directly related to the use of 'foul language' which needs to be curbed at the school.

Most of the teachers were women and held temporary positions in school. I interacted with one of the senior teachers, a

Punjabi woman married in a north-Indian family. She described the school as a very disciplined school for girls' education. She saw Punjabi students as being the majority group in the school, followed by other Hindu groups and some Muslims from nearby areas. She described the parents as very demanding in their expectation that students should become fluent in English after joining the school. She said most of the time teachers have to use Hindi for students when they can't follow what is being taught. In informal settings, mostly Hindi and Punjabi languages are used in this school.

School 2

The school has a bigger campus, building and staff members to look after the school. It is located at the outskirts of the city bordering on the rural areas. Because of the bus facility and provision of hostel for girl students, they were able to attract students not just from the city but also from the rich farmers of rural areas. Apart from the rural–urban divide, the students came from diverse occupational backgrounds. Majority of them were from the Hindu community. The school administration maintained that they believe in the principle of *sarvashiksha* which means education for all.

The majority of the teachers are middle-aged women from the city. Though the medium of instruction is English, in classroom instruction, Hindi is liberally used. The informal space of the school mainly uses Hindi as the common language. One of the teachers of Hindi complained that the students who join the school in later years have to struggle to come at par with older students.

Reena, the English teacher of the school, complained about the strange use of language in the city and how it hampers the learning of the English language. Because of their backgrounds, students find it difficult to understand, let alone use, English. Sunita, the Hindi teacher, maintained that there are a number of errors which inadvertently creep into the written and spoken use of Hindi, the major ones being the influence of the local dialects.

Noorjehan Girls' School

This school is a privately funded English-medium school for girls' education, located in Revaritalab, a prominent settlement for weavers in Banaras. The school building appears distinct because of the light green painted high walls that separate it from the surrounding clusters of small dwellings. The inside space of the school appears dark by the absence of natural light and open space. The school has a physically enclosed *aangan* (courtyard) which is used by the students for play. The girl students wore salwar kamiz and a few women teachers covered their head.

The school is run by a committee, chaired by Mr Mohammad, a college teacher by profession. Though it is a high school for girls, it also has the facility for education of boys up to the upper-primary level. The school primarily caters to the Muslim families of the area that are engaged in the Saree trade as weavers or are small-scale businessmen. But the teachers come from both Hindu and Muslim communities. According to the principal of the school, a senior lady who was wearing burka inside the school, the school caters to educational needs of families from nearby areas, mostly Muslim families from lower- and middle-income groups.

Mr Mohammad took over the conversation about the school and its catchment population. They taught Hindi and some Arabic, in addition to English. The medium of instruction is English, but Hindi is used by teachers and students alike. He also added that most of the students use a different variety of language at home which is neither Hindi nor Urdu. This is specific to the weavers' population in Banaras. It has developed in Banaras due to its history of intermingling of various kinds of people for trade purposes, which included merchant Hindus and Muslims. He gave me examples of mix of words from different origin such as *daddu* (grandfather) and *izad* (to invent), borrowed from Bengali and Persian respectively. Many Bengali Hindus converted to Islam which leaves trace of Bengali words such as *dada* (grandfather in hindi, also used in Bengali to refer to elderly brother) and daddu. He also cited Abdul Bismillah's novel on the weavers of Banaras which has used the same variety for majority of its characters.

It was interesting to know that, in his view, students who had the ability to write and speak 'Hindi' were doing better than the rest. The contrast with the other two English medium, private schools suggested that there is disconnect between a school's formal and informal cultures. The everyday life of school functioned in Hindi which was neither the language of instruction at formal level nor the language which the majority of its students used at home.

The school also faces the serious problem of a high dropout rate at the secondary levels. The girl students would drop out at large numbers in higher classes. The school administration believes that this is because it is primarily a school for girl students from Muslim families, where many of them marry early in their life. Mr Mohammad attributed this trend to an absence of role models other than that of being a housewife, a role which was the norm within their closed circle. The few girls who cleared their high school examinations would get admitted in other mainstream, Hindi-medium all-girls' schools in the city.

Madrasa Dar-ul-Uloom

This madrasa is located in Ausangunj, the heart of the weavers' settlement in the northern part of the city. I visited it on a Sunday morning, it being the only school open on Sundays among the ones that I visited. High walls and an imposing entrance gate put it in stark contrast to the extremely narrow lane outside. The madrasa was set up in 1892 and caters to almost 400 students. It runs in separate shifts for boys and girls. When I reached the school, the girls with their headscarves on, were heading for their shift. A branch for the higher education of girls has also been started and is run separately in a different building opposite the main building of the madrasa. As per the school-in-charge, it was popular among Muslims and steadily progressing. They had 16 teachers with the necessary qualifications and many madrasa-educated teachers. They had appointed lady teachers specifically for the girls' section. In his opinion, the madrasa can be compared with any other school in Banaras as they teach all the subjects. The *only* difference is that they train students in *diniyat* (religiosity) and the medium of education is Urdu.

One of the former students of this madrasa, now a teacher in another school, commented that disadvantaged and poor children are generally sent to the madrasa and further claimed that they are also more oriented towards religion, than the rich. Yet one could claim that most of the students attend because the education is almost free. The madrasa even offers scholarships to some students. Textbooks are given to the students for free under a government scheme set up specifically for madrasas. Only few rich families send one of their children here to get some *dini* education. It has also expanded its base in the field of girls' education. Now girls are taught up to *aalim*, the degree level.[11] They have also introduced subjects such as English, Hindi, Computer Science, etc. Computer Science is offered for free to all girl students. Most of the students from this madrasa shift to other mainstream schools after Class 5. The rest continue with the madrasa and obtain *dini* education. Such madrasas continue to be the popular option for the poorest among Muslims, with or without strong religious leanings. These are the institutions which give compulsory training in Urdu, a language which otherwise has a shrinking support from government. I also learnt from my interaction with their organisation committee members that some bigger madrasas are undergoing transformations in two important ways: first, by making provisions for the education of women up to the high school level, and second, by responding to the mainstream school-market through measures such as initiating training in computer education, making use of grants from the state government for procurement of free books, etc. These big madrasas often feed into the mainstream educational system by supplying students at the upper-primary level. Fewer numbers of students continue to the higher classes.

These are few examples of schools in Banaras, diverse in terms of students' composition, school management, sources of funding, media of instruction and affiliation to state or other organisations. Because of the central role of the state in setting the school curriculum, the alternative institutions are relatively marginalised. My objective is to explore the conflicting claims over the curricula of schools in Banaras. I found little variation in the formal curriculula of these schools in terms of state regulation, including even the madrasa schools. However, each school seemed to have its own distinct character in terms of its organisational affiliation and the students that it catered to. One could also discern significant change in school cultures even within the category of English-medium private school, with regard to the variation between their formal identity as English medium and their actual practice of English inside school. Similarly, within the category of Hindi-medium schools, one could see variations in terms of infrastructural support, students' composition and organisational and ideological differences of the schools that we examined.

While making observations about the school's link with communities, gender segregation deserves special mention as a characteristic feature of the schools of Banaras. Interestingly, at the outset, the segregation is more obvious in the Hindi-medium schools than in the English-medium schools because majority of the Hindi-medium schools in the city are all boys' or all girls' schools. This could be another remnant of the historical past of the city which was an active site of struggle between colonial and community models of education.[12] In Banaras, we have seen the emergence of several senior-secondary-level schools specifically meant for women such Vasant Kanya Inter College, Arya Mahila Inter College, Durgacharan Girls College, Khalsa Girls School, Agrasen Mahila Vidyalaya, etc. These schools sought to impart 'modern education' to women while keeping the 'Indian' ideal of femininity intact.

I conclude by saying that schools in Banaras present a diversity of forms which cannot be neatly categorised in terms of their relationship with the state, nor can be explained through their medium of instruction alone. Religious, caste and gendered norms of community cut across these categories of government and non-government schools and English- and vernacular-medium schools. These issues necessitate an alternative to the framing, based on division of schools catering to the metropolitan English-speaking elite and the regional Hindi-speaking elite or to the older division between Hindi-speaking Hindu elite and Urdu-speaking Muslim elite. Rather, one can look for a more contextualised examination of school and its relation with varied ideologies of education. Only then can we gain insight into the conflicts over what is prioritised in the school as knowledge and as legitimate identity over other forms of knowledge and identities. The school which I had the opportunity to study in greater detail and far more systematically for the above purpose was Hind Kishor Higher Secondary School, HKHSS, located in a busy commercial centre in northern Banaras. HKHSS is an example of a Hindi-medium private school catering mainly to students from the backward classes, and from lower-middle- and middle-class families from Hindu and Muslim communities. A detailed study of the school actors, sites and practices which present the school as a site of conflict between several identities is presented in the next chapter.

Notes

1. For difference between reading cultures in indigenous and colonial model of education pertaining to study of literature, see Kumar (2005b).
2. For a detailed discussion of the political economy of Banaras in the pre-colonial and early colonial periods, see Freitag (1989) and Bayly (1983).
3. For example, organisations like Theosophical Society and their prominent leader like Annie Besant set up important college for education in Banaras. This college emphasised a certain kind of education which was 'modern' yet imbued with oriental values. Later, as per their teachers this college was used for setting up the Banaras Hindu University which stood for modern education with Hindu worldview.
4. Kumar (2005d) has written about the development of a pan-Indian nationalist form of education, as a resistance to the colonial education. This was finally culminated in Congress' Wardha scheme of education in 1937. The ruptures within a seemingly uniform nationalist response, particularly from the Muslims league's perspective, have been discussed by Oesterheld (2007).
5. Minority schools, here, refer to the madrasas of the city with their own affiliations to institutions other than the state. Some of these are Deobandi, Barelvi, Ahle Hadith, etc. Some madrasas have affiliations with the state as well such as the Uttar Pradesh Madrasa Board.
6. The variety has also been for literary purpose in recent times by Abdul Bismillah in his *Jhini Jhini Bini Chadariya* (2008). Also refer to Goswami (2011) for a detailed account of multiple aspects of Ansari identity.
7. It was set up by the students of Queen's College, Banaras, in 1883. Early membership of the Sabha represented people from the Brahman, Khatri, Rajput and Baniya caste-groups. One of the pioneers of modern Hindi was Bharatendu Harishchandra, who hailed from the aristocratic merchant community of Banaras. Refer to King (1989) and Dalmia (1997).

8. Mr Mishra, currently teaching in the University in the same city, recollected these episodes as part of his student life in the same institution in the 1970s. He remembered how, many students from the University actively participated in the drive to 'Banish English' from Banaras. Even as English is not a language of common use anywhere in the city, but many shopkeepers would have their hoardings in English to attract the large number of tourists which that would flock to the city from various parts of the country.

9. Many other regional languages coexist in Banaras in their own residential pockets.

10. Brass (1974), King (1994) and Dalmia (1997) have looked at the larger historico-political scenario, while scholars such as Pai (2002) and Ahmad (2002) have examined the fate of Urdu in the language education policies of contemporary India.

11. A degree awarded by Madrasa Boards which is equivalent to the Bachelor of Arts.

12. One of the dilemmas faced by the nationalistic elite during the colonial period was to delineate the role of Indian women in the process of nation building. The elite who shaped the nationalistic discourse on education were attracted by the promises of Western education for their men, but sought to protect women from its corrupting influence. In this discourse, the ideal of the Indian woman had to play an important role in the construction of a distinct national identity, which would be free from the vices of Western materialism. How the nationalistic intelligentsia dealt with this problem led us to an interesting history of the construction of modern institutions with 'traditional' gender norms (Chatterjee 1989; Kumar 2000).

4

Between Standards and *Mohalla* Location: Hind Kishor Higher Secondary School

Ye to mohalla ka ek standard school hai.
'It is a standard school of the neighbourhood'.

—Anwar, 32, weaver, resident Narharpura

This expression indicates the position of HKHSS in the educational market of the city and in its immediate locality, as the one which enjoys a higher position vis-á-vis other smaller schools in its immediate surroundings but only a modest place in the overall hierarchy of schools in the city. In other words, the school presents itself as a standard school of the mohalla, or neighbourhood, as compared to the other private schools and the government-aided schools in its vicinity, and caters to the middle-income families located at the heart of the commercial city centre. The speaker, a weaver, gave examples of two other schools in the neighbourhood which would charge lesser fees and attract children from lower-economic backgrounds like his. He commented that only the rich loomowners of Jaitpura could send their children to HKHSS. In the eyes of the people in close proximity to it, the school has a reputation for being a good school, which is beyond the reach of people from a working-class position.

Contemporary studies on the school and its communities suggest that the relationship between the two is shaped by both the demographics of its neighbourhood and by the larger institutional context in which the school is placed (Arum 2000). The larger and common context is provided by the state policies, the policies of the local administration, political struggles, the school-market and so on. The local context is provided by the neighbourhood characteristics, school demographics and local power tussle. While the school is influenced by the common context provided through the norms of the state such as government prescribed curriculum, its location in education market of the city influences the actual implementation of the common curriculum. The actors involved in the implementation of the official school curricula at the school level are also tied to communities and institutions other than the national and the official. These differentially located actors and discourses of identities play a role in maintaining and sometimes challenging the official school discourse. The objective of this chapter is to explore the nature of a locally embedded school, by examining both the commonality and uniqueness of the school in its structure and practices from close quarters, to understand how actors, particularly school administrators and school teachers are negotiating the conflicting norms of the state, the school-market and the local community.

Locating HKHSS

HKHSS is a Hindi-medium[1] private school affiliated to the Uttar Pradesh Board of Education. The school is located in Lohatiya Gali, a busy commercial lane in the northern part of the city (Kotwali Ward of the Varanasi Municipality). This lane connects one of the three important weavers' settlements in Banaras, the Alaipura–Jaitpura area, to the main market area or *chauk* in the city. The lane bustles with the mixed sounds of metal workers working on aluminium sheets and those of the vehicles moving through it (Figure 4.1). It is lined with wholesale shops of iron goods and plastics and some small general merchandise stores. Lohatiya market, literally, means the market for iron goods. On the remaining three sides, the school is flanked by a government aided college for boys, a government city hospital and commercial and residential settlements in narrow lanes (Figure 4.1).

Social Organisation of School Space

The administration of the school is managed by the Hindustan Welfare Trust, set up in 1966, by a lady from the well-to-do Bakhtiyar family to start 'modern' and secular education for people in Banaras. Mr Bakhtiyar, the nephew of the founder, is currently occupying the post of school principal as well as the chairperson of the trust. His wife holds the chair of the manager. The family which owned it and set the guidelines had the highest degree of control over school affairs. It is a completely private funded school and never received any government aid. The Bakhtiyar family represented, in many ways, the fading high culture of the Urdu-speaking Muslim elites in Banaras, a minuscule minority in this Hindi heartland.

The current management has a two-tier structure of authority. The second tier consists of some senior teachers and non-teaching staff, who help in the management and realisation of the objectives set by the first tier. The rest of the teachers of the school come next in the school authority structure and mainly follow the instructions given by the first two set of people.

This constitutes the majority of teachers who are low paid and hold minimum control over school affairs. These teachers, as we examine later in greater detail, stayed in the school only for short periods of time. There are other marginal actors, further lower in rank and hierarchy such as peons, cleaners and helpers, essential to the everyday needs of the school but with negligible or no control over the functioning of the school. The older workers among them are allowed to admit their children in the school with a fee waiver.

The school has seen many changes since its inception and has grown in scale. From a modest beginning it has turned into a full-scale senior secondary school. One of the senior teachers, Rajesh, who had been working there for the last 15 years, talked about the changes that the school has seen over the years:

Now running a school has become a business ... the founder was an
idealist and didn't aim at making profits. There has been a shift during
the time of our current principal. He has always been very advanced.
Competition was fierce and the school also grew up to the senior-
secondary level.

In a way, the school has only recently become a fully commercial
venture and was actually set up with the intentions of serving the
local community. The current principal is seen as an efficient and
strict administrator by the school staff and parents of the students.
His childhood was spent in Allahabad and he received most of his
education in that city. He holds a postgraduate degree from the
University of Allahabad. He takes regular rounds of the school to
see if things are going well. Because of his reputation and absolute
authority over school matters, these rounds are also the times when
teachers want to look busy in their work. The power dynamics of
a private school and the insecurity of jobs held by teachers there
make them particularly vulnerable to the supervising gaze of the
school administration.

Mr Bakhtiyar comes across as a self-proclaimed *nastik* (non-
believer) because of his secular education and as someone who
is keen on learning about progressive education. By 'progressive'
he also referred to his liking for 'left leaning' literature and participation in organisations such as Shaheed Bhagat Singh Samiti.[2]
In the educational context, he occasionally referred to literature
pertaining to innovations in the field of education carried out
by individuals and organisations such as David Horsburgh and
science-based organisations like 'Vigyan Parsar Samiti'. During my
visits, he often discussed with me his interests and efforts towards
introducing reforms in the methods and curriculum of the school
and the problems of education in India, in general. For example, he
is completely against the idea of corporal punishment to students
and expected his teachers to engage in 'creative ways' with children.

For the educational needs of his two sons, he sent them to
a reputed Catholic school in Banaras. The particular school has a
high reputation among the city schools for its academic standards
and gaining a seat in the school is considered a matter of prestige

for families. As part of their Muslim identity, these boys would also learn to read the Koran in Arabic at home. In his view, the maulvis who come to teach them are not very knowledgeable about this world as they are not exposed to modern sources of knowledge. Sometimes, his sons try to make fun of them because of their traditional ways. In these ways his own identity was constructed in contradictory ways in various domains of life, as a strict educational administrator and someone who is keen on reading about progressive education, as a political person with leftist leanings, and also inheriting the religious legacy of his family.

He would also bemoan the loss of the cultural assets of older times such as customs, rituals and the value of literature and poetry which run in the family tradition. The practice of Urdu language still forms a very important part of the same cultural world for him. His source of learning fine Urdu expressions and picking up vocabulary continues to be this small cultural world, in which everyone including his servants uses Urdu. However, that cultural world is no longer seen as robust and is showing signs of decline. He compared the children of his childhood days with the present-age children and he felt that they were missing out on some of the finest elements of that legacy. The current generation of children are not able to pronounce even common words like *keema* properly. Many other words are dying out because no one uses them at all. His father, in one of his visits, joined us in this discussion and he shared his despair at the waning practice of literary Urdu among the current generation of youth. He described that once he had to judge an elocution competition in Urdu in Allahabad and ironically none of the participants were actually speaking in Urdu in his view. The current generation uses a language which is much closer to Hindi; due to lack of exposure to literary expressions, which one can gain either through family heritage or by reading Urdu literature. In these ways Urdu appeared to be an essential part of the exclusivist culture of high nobility among Muslims, which very few other families seemed to have access to.

Sara, the principal's wife, was the manager of the trust that ran the school. She was brought up in Allahabad and she had come to Banaras only after her marriage. Recounting her experiences in both the cities, she expressed her belief that Allahabad had a sophisticated city culture because of its educated population, which was missing in the city culture of Banaras, marked by the rustic language of Banarasi. Coming from a middle-class family of a different city, she narrated an incident of culture shock when she saw the parents of some students coming to the school dressed in *lungi*.[3] School, in her view, represents a formal space where certain norms regarding conduct, dressing, etc. have to be followed. The cultural world of her upbringing prepared her for a relatively easy entry into the world of educated upper-class Muslim family, but it did not prepare her to deal with the population that this school catered to, the lower-class segment of Muslim population. The popular culture in the city of Banaras is known to be based on informality and carefree attitude of people in general and Ansari weavers in particular.[4] Even as she holds the managerial position and is involved in school affairs, most of the important decisions regarding academics and the administration are taken by Mr Bakhtiyar and are implemented through various committees of senior teachers. The Bakhtiyar family is assisted by two individuals working as office staff, Amresh Singh and Rajni, in the functioning of the school.

The school has two sections (Figure 4.1). The primary-level classes run in the newly constructed part of the school just near the school entrance. The classrooms and the principal's office are located in an L-shaped building. The building overlooks the sand and clay ground, which is used for the morning assembly and sports by both the junior and senior sections. The morning assembly usually consists of the performance of a devotional song in Hindi, followed by the national anthem. The practice of newsreading is also followed sometimes. One of the senior teachers presides over this daily performance. During this time, students stand in queue, in order of their height in the playground overlooked by the principal's room. After the morning assembly, students start for their classes in queues but this order is maintained only for a short while, that is, until they are within the teachers' gaze. Teachers also head towards the staffroom located just against the main

Figure 4.1
Map Showing the Layout of Hind Kishor Higher Secondary School (Not to Scale)

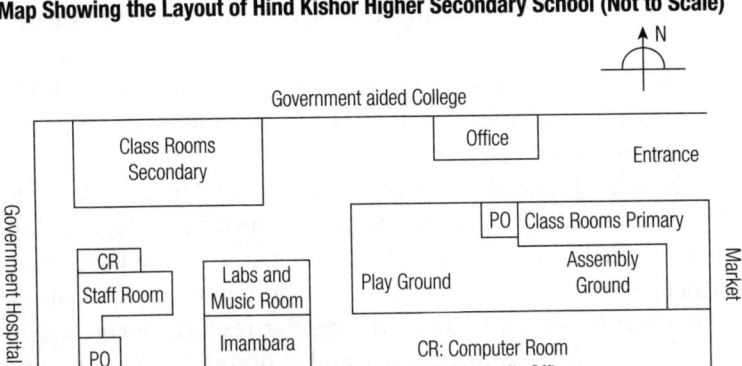

Source: Author.

building where classes are held. These rituals are an important site of examining how the disciplinary efforts of the school are maintained by the school authority in organising the physical space and students' bodies. However, students standing at the back rows of the assembly and some teachers can be openly seen violating the norms in various ways, not participating in the singing, changing their positions and sometimes chatting in lowered voices.

The secondary and higher secondary sections run in an older building, separated from the primary school by a corridor and another school building. The older and the bigger structure is a three-storied building which houses all the classrooms of the upper-primary and secondary sections. The school classrooms are medium-sized and generally overcrowded, with the number of students per classroom sometimes crossing 40. Neither the teachers nor the students seemed to be much bothered by the claustrophobic size of the class. Most of the classrooms have only one door and two windows and are ill-lit as there is no provision of cross-ventilation and most windows face a high wall which separates the school from the campus of a neighbouring college.

The seating in the classrooms are arranged in 3–4 columns of desks and benches, facing the blackboard and the teacher. Such an arrangement of a classroom sets hierarchical relations between the teacher and the students in which the teacher takes full control over classroom activities and minimises the scope for equal participation.

The school time on an average day is divided into 6–7 periods of 40 minutes each which are allocated to specific subjects and to the concerned teachers. The subjects ranged from the Languages, Science, Mathematics, Social Science, Computer Science, Games, Drama and Music. Apart from the regular teachers, a counsellor, a sports teacher, a music teacher and a drama teacher are also appointed on part-time basis.

The second building which overlooks the main building is smaller in size. It is a cluster of rooms including the staffroom, computer room and another room for the principal on one side and other smaller rooms and labs on the other side. The staffroom is always abuzz with activity and chatter. Morning times in the staffroom are generally busy with teachers heading to their respective classes to take the attendance of the students. It also offers the only space of some freedom and recreation where they can sit and chat about school and the world outside. The school incharge sits in a separate enclosure with a set of steel almirahs acting as barrier between this space and the rest of the staffroom. This space is also used by the teacher incharge to meet visitors and parents.

Adjacent to the staffroom is the computer room, where 6–8 computers are kept for the use of the students. Both the rooms are connected by a small verandah with benches, where the peon and other helpers sit. The benches are also used by the students who come to the computer room for taking off their shoes as it is prohibited for students to go inside the computer room with their shoes on. Taking off the shoes at the door step of a computer room is a common activity which is seen even in some computer coaching centres. Partly it is due to the aura around the 'knowledge' associated with computers, but mainly it has to do with the high cost of purchasing and maintaining computers in a low-end private school. The computer teacher of the school also explained to me that dust and dirt are strictly avoided as these are thought to be damaging the computers.

The staffroom on the other side is connected to a lobby of three rooms used by the teachers to keep their belongings, meet students for some specific tasks, etc. The first floor above this cluster of rooms houses the music room and the science labs with bare minimum equipment for actual experiments. The school does not have enough space for a library.

The residence of the school principal is behind this cluster of rooms. A small and narrow corridor adjacent to the staffroom leads to the ancestral residence of the Bakhtiyar family. The mown, green lawns, fountain and marble-floored whitewashed ancestral property are in stark contrast to the old and discoloured school building in the front. The principal has another office where he sits during the afternoon session of the secondary school. This room is connected to the staffroom on one side and opens on to the garden of his house on the other. It would afford him the convenience to stay connected with both his family and the school.

Spatial organisation of this school follows some common patterns found in other schools. Like other schools, one can see that the physical space of this school is divided on functional basis between the academic and administrative units, that is, between the administration, teachers on one hand and between teachers and students. Again, classrooms, computer room, etc. are demarcated from the area of play and the school space is separated from the private residence of Bakhtiyar family while sharing the same premise. The idea of space is also imbued with relational understanding of positions occupied by various actors in different field (Bourdieu 1985). The area marked as office for the school principal and of manager, is positioned differently from the other office staff. The Principal's control over school is visible in the fact that he holds two offices—both at the eastern and western ends of the school campus. The eastern-end office is near the school entrance and is decorated more formally and meant to meet visitors to school. It also helps him watch over the school assembly and other such gatherings. The western-end office is adjacent to the school staffroom and closer to classrooms. Within staffroom, one teacher is given supervisory role over others with the help of reorganisation of space. The menial staff of the school has to sit in the concrete benches out in the open verandah. Even within the classroom space, the teacher's space is accorded a centrality in relation to children. All these arrangements are based on principle of hierarchy and supervision. Among children's seating arrangements, formally no such demarcation is seen but in practice segregation is followed between boys and girls.

However, the clear-cut demarcation and separation of space does not always work as neatly as it appears and there are areas of overlap between these boundaries. For Bakhtiyar family, the division of private space of residence extends and overlaps into the public domain of school. Particularly the Principal's room falls in between the two from where he can exercise his authority and remain within the reach of his family. The second area of overlap is at a symbolic level. The school maintains a carefully cultivated image of a secular school completely avoiding any display of sign of any religion, as the majority of its teachers and students come from Hindu families. However, the presence of an *Imambara*[5] within the residential premises of the principal's house brings uniqueness to the school, which can unfold another dimension of their lives which is not accessible to other participants of school life.

The Principal's room overlooks the family Imambara. It was established by Mirza Kamran Bakht (an ancestor of Mr Bakhtiyar) and the principal claimed it to be the most beautifully maintained in Banaras with the sacred *mitti* (earth) brought from Mecca. This Imambara becomes a major site of activities during Muharram. The school remains closed on these occasions. Even as he claims to be a non-believer, he was placed in the paradoxical position of being the head of the family which patronised an *anjuman* for the Shia Muslims.[6] I happened to witness one of the gatherings of their anjuman (a society or club) in their family imambara. He would not participate in these gatherings himself, but would help in the arrangement of the community feasts, etc. The members of their anjuman would gather for performances and rituals on the occasion of Muharram. Muharram is considered a very important event in the life of Shia community which involves the tradition of collective mourning. Such an occasion was bigger in scale and his father would come from Allahabad to Banaras during those days and take charge of the management along with his wife. This space lies at the border of the school zone and the residence of Bakhtiyar family and is regarded as a sacred space. Occasionally, school allows some Muslim students to offer prayers on Fridays but the number of students actually making use of it is very small.

It is interesting to see that the boundaries between the public and the private, and the secular and the religious are maintained by the school, but there are times when they become porous and fluid.

Students' Socio-economic Profile

The school has a small catchment area. The students come from an average distance of 1–2 km from the school. Since the school does not offer any transport facilities to the students, most of them come on foot or by bicycle, and some on hired cycle rickshaws often shared by 4–5 students.

This school caters to the middle- and lower-middle-income group families. We have seen how it has a higher reputation among the neighbourhood schools, like Adarsh school in the vicinity which charges ₹150 as school fee. In this school, monthly fee ranges between ₹250–350 for the primary–secondary levels. However, school expenses include much more than fee. As PROBE Reports of 1996 and 2006 have shown, both government and private schooling involve additional expenditures for parents. These items include expenses on books, stationeries, transport, uniforms and private tuitions. Similarly in this school, parents have to be able to incur all the additional costs that private schooling involves, some of which may be optional such as costs of participation in extra-curricular activities, picnics, school excursions, etc. Only a few students are admitted at a subsidised rate, usually the wards of the teachers and the support staff.

There were 650 students enrolled in the school in 2006–07. The number of students whose families were engaged in some form of small trade varied between 50 and 70 per cent of the total students in different class/grades. Of these, the majority are from families involved in the Banarasi saree and allied industries. Others belong to the families of petty traders and small shop owners. Only a small section of students are from families where parents were engaged in salaried services in the public or private sectors. Since the school is situated at a busy commercial area and caters to the families staying in the nearby areas, most of the students belong to the traditional trading castes but have shifted to newer means of livelihood.

The major caste groups present in school are Jaiswal, Agrahari, Yadav and Vishwakarma. In the school area, the Jaiswals were traditionally engaged in selling liquor and were known as Kalwars. Now, they mostly work as petty traders of cement, groceries, etc. Similarly, some caste groups like the Telis who were traditionally engaged in the occupation of oil pressing have also moved into petty business by opening grocery shops or cement shops. The Vishwakarmas were earlier known as Lohars or blacksmiths in the same area while the Yadavs are those dealing with milk supply. All these caste groups have adapted urban ways of living and have now engaged in different occupations. Few of them can be seen in the service sector, that too mostly in private sectors because of the limited expansion of service sector in the city. Majority of these groups are now self-employed.

Table 4.1 presents the percentage distribution of students from Classes 6 and 7 in different occupational groups. The occupational clusters presented in Table 4.1 serves the purpose of classifying dominant occupations of students' families as identified by them and the teachers. The clusters were not homogeneous and had several layers within. For example, the cluster of the saree and allied industries included those who owned power looms and sold some of the finished goods on their own and supplied the rest to the sellers, those who owned looms and also worked on those, one designer, one dyer and one *zari* (golden thread used for embroidery) maker. The cluster of the other self-employed included small shopowners, grocers, betel leaf sellers, iron goods sellers and so on. The category of government employees included, among professionals, a lawyer,

Table 4.1
Percentage Distribution of Students from Hindu and Muslim Communities in Four, Broad Occupational Clusters

Community	Saree & Allied Industries	Other Self-employed	Service (Govt.)	Service (Private)	Others	Total
Hindu	19	52	10	15	4	100
Muslim	82	6	6	6	0	100
All	35	40	11	11	3	100

Source: Based on fieldwork (2006–2008).

a veterinarian, a district officer and teachers of government schools and colleges.

The school strikes as catering mainly to the low-caste groups with a majority of the students belonging to the other backward class (OBC) category. Table 4.2 presents the percentage distribution of 65 students from Classes 6 and 7 in different caste categories.

It is an unusual school among other Hindi-medium schools in Banaras in that it provides facilities for the co-education of boys and girls. However, the number of girl students in this school starts declining as one moves towards the higher classes. The school has an overall skewed proportion of girls to boys ranging

Table 4.2
Percentage Distribution of Students among Boys and Girls, and Hindus and Muslims, in Each Caste Category

	Boys	Girls	Hindu	Muslim
General	20.90	2.99	20.89	2.99
OBC*	50.75	16.42	44.78	22.39**
SC	7.46	1.49	8.95	0.00
All	79.10	20.90	74.63	25.37

Source: Based on fieldwork (2006–2008).
Notes: * includes Sunars, Yadavs, Telis among Hindus and Ansaris among Muslims.[7]
         **Ansaris among Muslims.

from 30 per cent in some classes to as low as 10 per cent in some others. The presence of Muslim girl students in this coeducational environment is a noteworthy feature of this school. However, their numbers also shrink drastically at high school level. As compared to a strong 25 per cent representation among the girls till Class 8, their percentage drops to negligible levels in higher classes.[8] Teachers also confirmed that Muslim girl students followed a general trend of dropping out at the high school level. The teachers attribute this to the lack of concern for higher education among Ansaris in general and for girls' education in particular.

The school has a mixed population of Hindu and Muslim students. The proportion of Muslim students varied from 20–25 per cent during each academic year. Interestingly, most of the teachers, except the Urdu teacher, overestimated their proportional representation among all the students. These students were from the Ansari community.[9] It is important to note that the majority of Ansari population in Banaras does not have access to modern schooling facilities because of their economic condition and their traditional engagement in the occupation of weaving which demands their engagement in the craft from a tender age.

> *Agar aap bunkar ke bacche hain to aap nahi parh sakte ... Ye kala aisi hai jisme bachpan gawana padta hai ...*
>
> 'If you are child of a weaver, then you cannot learn to read ... It (weaving) is an art in which one has to sacrifice one's childhood ...'
>
> Noor Muhammad, 55, dyer of silk yarn

The school has 114 students from this community which is 18 per cent of the total strength and more than 90 per cent of the total number of Muslim students in the school. Nearly all of these students' families are engaged in the Banarasi saree and related industries. However, the Ansari students of this school are not from working-class population. They are from the relatively better-off families of big master weavers or small traders who could afford to send their children to private schools like HKHSS.

Teachers' Work in a Private School

The school has a floating population of teachers. There are a total of 25 teachers, of whom only one-third have continued for more than five years in the school. During the course of my visits from March 2006 to February 2008, I met different teachers for Hindi, English and the Sciences every year.

The majority of the teachers are high-caste Hindus. A striking feature of the school is that high-caste Hindus, especially Brahmans, constitute the majority of the teaching staff, while there are only a few students from the same caste. According to a senior teacher, this pattern is a result of the strict policy of school in which they recruit teachers only on the basis of merit and not *sifarish* (recommendation) or reservation. It is pertinent to mention here that government schools are expected to follow certain regulatory norms for recruitment of teachers. These recruitments are through public notice which notify about availability of posts, necessary qualification and pay-scale details. Like other government services, teaching positions are also reserved for SC, ST and OBC category. In public discourses surrounding reservation, a typical middle-class and upper-caste response posits reservation system in government employment as essentially against meritocratic ideal of bureaucracy. In contrast, private sector avenues are not under government regulation to enforce norms of reservation in recruitment. The senior teacher, while commenting on the caste profile of the school teachers was alluding to the same notion of 'merit' which is not spoilt due to the system of reservation. In other words, the notion of merit is always uncritically associated with the upper-castes and the private sector jobs. Nepotism or favouritism is also seen as associated with the bureaucratic set-up of the government organisations.

The only Muslim teacher of the school, Abdul, comes from the Ansari community and teaches Urdu. He is from the well-known religious family of Nomanis in Banaras. He takes pride in the fact that his is among the few Muslim families in Banaras, who are engaged with higher education. Theirs is also among the few to be using 'pure Urdu', unlike the majority of the Muslims in the city.

His father was a renowned scholar of Islamic history. After him, his elder brother followed his path and now holds the important position of being the current *Mufti* or community leader of the Muslims associated with the Gyanwapi mosque. Mr Abdul received early education from a madrasa and later went on to study Persian and Urdu in Aligarh Muslim University (AMU). However, later developments in life and his marriage with a Bengali-Hindu woman, made him turn into an atheist. He lives separately from the family that he was born in, with his wife and two daughters, one of whom studies in the same school.

There are just six woman teachers and only two of them are teaching at the secondary level. Renu Verma teaches computer science and also assists in some official work of the school. She is a postgraduate in sociology and has completed a certificate course in computer applications.

She has been with the school for three years. She left the school when she got married. Another lady teacher, Ms Srivastava, teaches Hindi. She is a Science graduate and a trained teacher of Hindi. She is from Meerut and had shifted to Banaras 10 years ago when she got married. She still finds it difficult to adjust in Banaras because of her dislike for the place and people. In her view, people in Banaras are uncouth and the language they use is crude and full of slang. Her husband works for a public insurance company. Her mother-in-law is a retired school principal of a reputed convent school for girls. She is very conscious about her son's education who was studying in an Army school in Banaras. She joined the school in 2008 but left in 2009 in favour of a more reputed English-medium school in the city.

The monthly salaries of the teachers range from ₹1,500–3,500 for most of them, which varies according to the seniority and the amount of responsibilities shared in the school. For example, the senior teachers are involved in additional tasks of guiding and supervising the new teachers, managing the school events on daily and periodic basis.

A senior teacher from primary section, Samir, seemed to be inspired by the new child-centric teaching methods. During one of our conversations, he mentioned his use of primary-level textbook poem *Naav Chali* ... from *Khushi Khushi*, Hindi text-book for Class 2, and how he used the same to teach young kids in his class. This book was not the usual textbook for the designated class; it was published by Eklavya in Madhya Pradesh. The Principal shared the book with him to see if it can be used. He used it to teach a new poem and also improvised it according to the needs of his students. He is given the position of the teacher incharge of the primary section. Ironically, he is also involved in saree trade on part-time basis, which he attends to after the school hours. He believed that in the school, he is able to make a mark for himself in a relatively lesser period of time, referring to his status as the teacher incharge of the primary section. He finds his teaching job more rewarding in terms of earning him positive self-esteem.

The school, however, is not able to retain many teachers like Samir. Such teachers, though fewer in number, would share relatively more power in the school as they are part of the managing committee that is formed to run the everyday affairs of the school, and also direct other teachers to do the necessary tasks. However, as is evidenced in case of Samir, even that power and position is not sufficient to enable them to run their family from the salary and they have to supplement their income from other sources. This trend of teachers being employed elsewhere after school hours is a common phenomenon among young male teachers of the school.

Another senior teacher of social science, Ramsaran, has a rural background. Many such teachers come to Banaras for higher education from rural hinterland and rent a room and stay back in the city in search of jobs. He has a postgraduate degree from BHU. His 5-year-old son is also attending the same school. Every day, he travels around 20 km on his motorbike to and from the school. The school has rewarded him by appointing him as the new incharge of the secondary school with a hike in his salary. He, unlike many of his other colleagues, claimed that teaching was a fruitful job and that creativity lay in one's attitude towards one's work and not in the nature of the job. His recent promotion to being the incharge of the secondary school has made him a relatively powerful person in the hierarchy of the school administration.

One afternoon in the staffroom, many teachers were busy correcting copies of the mid-term examinations during which a discussion on teaching profession unfolded, mainly among the male teachers. The discussion took place between Dube, Dhiren and was later joined by Ramsaran.

Dube, a teacher of Mathematics, looked tired while sitting in the staffroom. He complained that he was the only teacher for the senior section and as a result he had to take all the classes from Class 6 onwards and had no time to rest like others. He was particularly unhappy about the fact that in spite of his qualifications, he has to teach below Class 9. He had recently submitted his PhD in Statistics in the Central University and also worked as a part-time instructor in a coaching institute in the city. When he found most other teachers sitting and correcting copies, he remarked that it was a complete wastage of time and there was no creativity in school teaching. It was only a clerical job. His is clearly a case of underemployment where his aspirations and his actual position in educational sector are in mismatch. This is worsened by the low-paying nature of his job and the usual drudgery which is involved with teaching. He confesses that, being a PhD candidate, it is below his dignity to teach students of the upper-primary level. His lack of engagement with students' progress is evident in his confession that he finds it a waste of time to evaluate the answer sheets of school children. On this remark, Ramsaran, who is sitting close by, intervenes and says that one can consider the work clerical and if one *wishes* he can also do something innovative in the same work. Ramsaran, being a senior teacher and section incharge, is not countered by Dube who is relatively new to the school. However, Dhiren, another senior teacher who teaches social science responds to Ramsaran. Dhiren says, unprovoked, that he is not afraid of working hard but not for something which is *routine* and *clerical*. Pointing towards me, he says, 'I can do research all my life.' At this point some students come to meet Ramsaran and he gets busy and the discussion stops.

This episode, which initially appears about perception of teaching as a vocation, turns out to be a pointer towards the more deep-rooted structural issue of the vulnerable position of a low-paid school teacher in a private school. The disagreement over the perception of teaching as a 'clerical' or 'creative' job is more a comment on their dissatisfaction with the *conditions* of teaching rather than on *teaching* per se. This is corroborated from similar expressions of dissatisfaction of teachers about their current status as a 'low-paid' teacher.

Later, when I probe further about his views about the profession of teaching, Dhiren explains to me that he is bitter about his profession because he does not find any dignity in the life of a school teacher. He finds his own situation worse than that of manual workers who are not expected to present themselves as middle class. He feels so because of his meagre salary as school teacher which has a 'false' social status attached to it but leaves him in a worse off position than that of a daily wage earner. He spends most of his time earning money through private tuitions. In the mornings he has to leave his home early and return late after completing his school work and evening tuitions. He confesses that in those moments of tiredness and low living conditions, he feels more like an animal and not a human!

The lower range of salary is a major issue faced by all the teachers, particularly the new ones. In order to cope with it, most of the new male teachers are involved in private tuitions and coaching centres to compensate for their low income from the school. Most of the new and young teachers, both men and women, use this school as a platform till they are eventually absorbed by some better-paying schools. They often express their dissatisfaction with their current jobs. Majority of teachers are not satisfied with their current job and are always keenly looking for newer and better job avenues for a variety of reasons.

This helplessness of being a low-paid teacher while being expected to be a part of the middle class is more clearly articulated by a non-teaching staff, who manages the accounts and empathises with teachers as well as school administration for their tight budget. When some construction work was going on in the school, while discussing about the daily wage workers, she brings in the idea of teachers' payroll all of a sudden.

Reema: workers make good amount of money on daily basis ... it is just that they cannot save and spend everything in alcoholism. Now they earn ₹150 everyday. Here they (school staff) don't earn that much. Most of them get ₹100 ... not even that much. Everyone's pay varies. This is because the school is not aided ... it is *swa-vittaposhit* (self-financed). If it were aided, all our scales would be fixed. Now all expenses are managed through students' fees. After giving everyone nothing much is left. Even if we increase the fee by ₹10, the parents start making a lot of noise. Parents do not understand.

In this case, unlike Dhiren's outburst, Reema presents a more factual statement about the teachers' pay as being much lower than that of the daily wage workers, and also describes the financial constraints because of which it happens. For many young job aspirants, it is the government sector which seems to offer better opportunities than the private sector. Reema also feels that if this school was aided by the government, only then will their problems be solved. Here, the school is seen as limited in its capacity as a private school, tied to a particular type of client population.

The perception about private and public sector jobs also frequently showed up in the teachers' conversations about insecurities of job market. In HKHSS, one common topic of staffroom discussion among the male teachers is the sharing of information about the various competitive exams conducted by the state. It is interesting to note that the teachers of this school do not seem to be lured by the upcoming surge in the service industry in the metropolitan areas. These teachers are from low economic backgrounds, having attended the vernacular mode of education, and do not see themselves as getting entry into the private sector jobs in metropolitan centres. It is important to note that private sector does not mean the same for people living in a metropolitan world and those in the smaller cities. For these teachers, the metropolitan private sector, which is growing very fast, is seen as something beyond their reach. They rely more on the jobs created by the government sector and keep appearing in various competitive exams.

'They (the private sector) salute only the rising sun, not people like us... It is the government which has space for people like us.'
—Dube, 32, Mathematics teacher

These teachers in their late 20s and early 30s refer to the new generation of smart youngsters as the rising ones who have the necessary capital and skills to appear for interviews in private sector jobs in the big cities. In contrast, they are unsure of such skills which make them feel wanted only in government sector jobs which still relies on written exams for its recruitment processes.

In all these episodes, the despair among teachers is evident because of teaching being a low-paying and insecure job, particularly in the context of a non-elite private school that caters to lower-middle-income groups. Ironically, it is this sector which is often propagated as the one that has seen 'mushrooming growth' and is supposed to employ a huge segment of educated population, and also as the sector which is winning over the expensive government schools which "over-pay" their teachers.

School Curriculum and the Teachers' Role

Another common concern expressed by teachers is that of frequent changes in the syllabi prescribed by the school, especially in the social sciences. The school is affiliated to the UP board which prescribes its own set of textbooks, but now the school is gradually moving towards an affiliation with CBSE. For primary sections, it has already done so. CBSE board schools usually prescribe NCERT textbooks which set the curriculum for other state boards.

LaDousa (2014) has pointed out that Board affiliations carry a sense of status for various schools just as medium of instruction, whereby, Hindi-medium government schools affiliated to the UP state board are often seen as low status, while private English-medium schools affiliated to boards such as CBSE and ICSE are considered high in status. This school is also in the process of shifting its affiliation to CBSE board from UP board.

The school management committee, which includes few teachers, in recent years, started emphasising that NCERT books should be used as far as possible for future shift. NCERT has come up with revised curricular framework in 2005 which brought many changes in the focus and approach of all textbooks. The most visible changes are in the field of social science education (Batra 2010). However, these changes are not always welcome by teachers at the ground level because there is no provision to involve teachers at any level during the preparation or even at the stage of dissemination of these textbooks (Ramachandran 2005). Such changes, however well-intentioned they might be, exclude school teachers, particularly the private teachers in non-metropolitan circles, and bring forth tensions and conflicts over the 'right curriculum' in their classrooms.

One afternoon during our staffroom discussions, Dhiren was reading the new History textbook prescribed by NCERT. Sharma, the senior English teacher was sitting next to him. The following is an extract from their conversation.

> Sharma: The UP board is now following the NCERT and it has degraded the quality of history books in the UP board. In our time, we had more substantive knowledge of history than the new generation. International politics and Indian history are now all mixed up. The new generation is completely confused and they do not know anything. Parents are only interested in their children's performance in Mathematics, English and Science.

> Dhiren: Nowadays, whoever writes derogatory things about Hindu kings and glorifies Akbar and Aurangzeb is called secular. The trick is to learn to abuse your own culture and religion. The new *samajwadis* (socialists) reside in books. If you don't abuse the higher caste people, you will be termed a casteist. The biggest threat to India is from such socialists.

Secularism and socialism are terms loaded with political meaning in the school educational contexts. In recent times, the rewriting of textbooks of History and Civics for schools has become a topic of public debate between different ideological groups in academia and in the public forum (Advani 2009; Batra 2010; Bhattacharya 2003). Similar strands of debates about how the past history and future vision of the nation-state is to be presented in the school textbooks, also concern one of the teachers in the school. The other teacher, however, is more concerned about the confusing nature of changes in the syllabi. Here, we see a gap between the objectives of textbook writing and the perspective of the teachers of History in this school.

As ordinary teachers in a private school they have little control over deciding the content that they are supposed to teach in the classroom. A change in syllabus leaves an already ill-prepared teacher with a sense of helplessness and very little control. It also instils in the teacher, a sense of insecurity over what he/she feels is his/her domain knowledge. The absence of any in-service training programme to keep them engaged with the new debates in education, let alone involving them at any stage in selection and preparation of teaching material, makes the concerns even deeper. At this point, it is important to bring in the historicity of the role of the teacher in post-colonial societies. As K. Kumar (2005c) has pointed out, from the colonial period, the social status of a primary- or secondary-school teacher has been relegated to a low position. This was a result of the overall move towards the bureau-cratisation of education and the centralisation of control over the content and methods of teaching. On the one hand, it severed the close ties that a teacher shared with the community. On the other hand, his/her position was reduced to that of a low-paid government employee placed below the rank of other educational officers in the overall bureaucracy/authority structure, with no role in setting the curricula and how it is to be transacted and evalu-ated. Teaching, then, became a service devoid of any intellectual engagement on the part of the teachers. Even now, their role in the syllabus making, deciding the content of school textbooks or setting the examination pattern, is very low. The school teachers find the syllabus alien and fail to understand the rationale behind the new textbooks and also the reforms in pedagogy. In such situations a school like HKHSS, in its efforts to become more competitive in the local school-market by switching to the NCERT syllabus and without making necessary provisions for their training in the new curriculum, its philosophy and its pedagogic aspects, inadvertently denigrates the authority of the school teacher.

Authority and Resistance

Even as the school teachers are placed low in the overall educational hierarchy, the school space is not to be mistaken as without any resistance to the notions of education and teaching methods. The teachers' and the administrative staff quite often diverge in their opinion on academic matters, and even as the administrative point of view prevails as official school culture, it is resisted in many quarters, if not openly, in a discrete manner.

The school principal feels that the biggest obstacle in bringing reforms in the teaching and learning environment of a school is the lack of 'motivated' and 'dedicated' teachers. He also complains of the flux of teachers from his school knowing well that this school is paying the teachers less. Still he maintains that if teachers are motivated and committed towards teaching–learning process and well-being of students, they can improve the teaching–learning methods. He thinks that it is because of the uninspired teachers that all his ideas of student-friendly education are not being implemented in the right spirit in the school. He discussed with them his idea of non-corporal punishment to students and asked them to motivate students through positive rather than negative stimulation. He has also appointed a full-time counsellor to deal with the troubles of students. Unfortunately, majority of teachers are either indifferent or do not understand the very idea. He gives example of a teacher with whom he had a difficult time.

One of these teachers, quite senior and 'knowledgeable' in the principal's assessment, believes that it is not possible to discipline students without giving physical punishment, because if they (teachers) do not punish students, the students might think of them as their servants! This statement echoes the predicament of the colonial school teacher whose position is 'meek' in the overall system and yet wants to cling to the little authority that he enjoys in school (Kumar 2005c). Understandably, only a few teachers participate in these 'reform' methods of the principal. The teachers who are part of the school management committee include both the primary and secondary school incharges, Samir and Ramsaran.

This proximity of a few teachers to the school authority brings in certain dynamics of power play and resistance among school teachers. The staffroom discussion on the issue of teaching profession, discussed previously is one such encounter, also brings in the dynamics of status differentiation among teachers in school and how they cope with their respective positions. In that situation, one teacher being promoted to a supervisory position over the other is viewed as a representative of the school's administration and does not evoke response from the junior teacher. This duality of role for the teacher with higher authority brings benefits as well as tensions in his relation with other teachers. The disagreement over the perception of school teaching, in this case, presents one expression of the same conflict. The tension is also evident in the other teachers' strategy to deal with this situation. For example, in the absence of the teacher, in the staffroom, a few take a jibe at him by saying *yahan to sab Rambharose chal raha hai*. It is important to note that *Ram Bharose* is a common Hindi expression which means 'in trust/faith of Lord Rama', the Hindu deity, but it is also used to describe a state of affair in which people have no control whatsoever!

To a great extent, therefore, Principal's ideas about teachers' lack of interest in his view of education holds true, however, for reasons different than what is simply termed as 'lack of dedication and commitment'. The teachers, given their position in school hierarchy and overall position in terms of class and status, are least interested in carrying out any such modestly reformative ideas about a child-centred learning. For example, in staffroom discussions, the teachers frequently cite, with a sarcastic tone, what they considered as the punch line of the school administration— *Bacche ki bhavnaon ko samjhe* (understand the viewpoint of the child).

The school administration, thereby, fails in implementing its 'child-friendly system' of learning. Such a system puts the onus of teaching and learning on the teachers, who are expected to be sensitive to the emotional and cognitive needs of children. Any kind of labelling of success or failure of students should be avoided at least in primary level. This is also mandated under the RTE Act 2009 and Sarva Shiksha Abhiyan Programme pursued by the Indian state at national level, which follows a 'no detention' policy for students. Because of this policy, the teachers lose their 'power to fail' the students on the basis of what is written by them during exams.

It is often argued that it is very difficult to maintain a high level of motivation among teachers, unless one gets support from the community or has strong teaching values as driving force (Khora 2008). The economic profile of the city is such that there are few industries which could absorb the educated youth of the city, other than the traditional handicrafts industries. Teaching in the private schools is the commonly available job for the educated youth of the city. However, it remains a low-paying contractual job without any social security.

It is interesting to note the feeling of despair towards the job of teaching among private school teachers, because most of the literature on 'problems' of school teachers in India have focused on government school teachers and their lack of motivation (Majumdar 2011; De et al. 2011; Ramachandran 2005). Often, the government school teachers are cited as being irregular and unmotivated in their work even if they are structurally and culturally constrained to perform their work (Ramachandran 2005). In recent years, the concept of low-cost private schooling has gained ground in urban and rural areas. Lowering of salary and contracting of services, are quite often offered as the solution to the problem of accountability that plagues the government schools in the developing world under 'the accountability regime' of new models of public management (Madan 2012; Jain and Saxena 2010).

In private schools like HKHSS, the position of the teacher is weak in terms of economic rewards, security of tenure and social prestige. There is very little support on part of the administration to equip them with necessary training and resources to improve their work. Additionally, they have almost no control over the teaching and learning processes. Most of the male teachers in this school would bank upon earnings from coaching centres and tuitions, which are an added burden on their daily working hours. Given the situation, they cope by minimising their efforts on their part in engaging with teaching in the school. They find ways of avoiding going to class and discretely mock the school authority. Whenever they get a chance, they would switch to better-paying jobs.

The situation reflects a structural problem with the profession of teaching in Indian education system, which is caught in a double bind. The government schools are widely criticised for being dysfunctional and one of the reasons attributed is that the government teachers are not considered responsible enough in their work, thus lowering the overall quality of education. As a panacea to the same, it is suggested that service of teachers should be 'contracted' and must be made accountable through strict supervision and control. In recent years, regular positions of teachers have become negligible adding to the overall drive towards recruiting undertrained contractual teachers for schools. However, low pay scale, economic insecurity and uncertainty of future together take a toll on the desirability of the teaching profession. Lower social status of a teacher, adds to the overall grimness of the scenario. A different approach to make teaching more accountable and joyful would be to promote an alternative to the accountability regime, a new approach which promotes 'the processes of building commitments and cultures among teachers' which yields social, emotional and cultural rewards for engaging with teaching as a critical and creative pursuit (Madan 2012).

Organisation of School Life

The organisation of school life, both in terms of daily routines and annual events provide important clues of school life. Sometimes, a close examination of the rituals of the school bring out the conflicting ideologies and tensions within the school culture (Thapan 1986, 2014). An examination of the rituals organised on daily basis such as performance of the national anthem in the morning assembly can also serve as an entry point to examine the celebration and embodiment of the making of the nation in everyday life (Benei 2009). Some other events are temporally arranged throughout the academic year, so as to remind the school community of the landmark events in a year. Events such as Independence Day and Republic Day may also invoke performance of nationalism. This school, like others, organised various events in one calendar year. Some of the events were common public festivals celebrated in all the schools of the city, such as Independence Day and Republic Day, annual function of the school and parent–teacher meetings. There were some celebrations which were specific to

HKHSS, such as classroom decoration day and Shahadat Diwas, or the Martyr's Day of Bhagat Singh. Through these events, the school constitutes a certain image of its ethos in the eyes of its participants as well as the outsiders. We examine a few of these events to get a glimpse of how the school life is organised around these events. This exercise may provide clues to understanding the school's position through visions of modernity, progress, citizenship education and gendered norms of community. All these events are carefully marked in the school calendar and project a certain image of the school which is constantly guarded and maintained by the administration. For example, classroom decoration day is a day which involves students' participation in decorating their respective classrooms through their own creations. For one full day, the classes remain suspended and students take time out to decorate classroom walls with posters, paintings and chart papers and display scientific-models made of cardboard. A designated guest is invited to assess their creations and towards the end of the day prizes are distributed. This is meant to enhance creative pursuits among students. Of similar events, two important ones are being described here to examine how the school's position is constructed in the local school-market through the twin ideals of social mobility and commitment to nationalism. Both these ideals are important in constructing and projecting the image of a competitive school committed to training of the students in skills useful in employment market and in common civic values like citizenship educations. I am focusing on celebration of annual day (held in January) and Independence Day (August) for this purpose.

Modernity, Mobility and School Success

One important component of the school image is that of a growth-oriented modern school, which promises academic success in state-level exams to its students. It emerges strongly in the presentation of its annual report during annual day celebrations.

The annual function, celebrated in December–January, is a major event to project and celebrate such an image of the school.

The school formally showcases itself to a wider audience by inviting the press and some special guests. All those students who are involved in programmes or work as volunteers prepare in advance for the event. Every teacher is expected to work towards a cultural show with his/her team of students. So, all the students and teachers are expected to actively participate in the organisation of the event. The parents of the school children constitute the main audience along with some invited guests from city representing different fields such as education, politics, theatre, etc.

> I would like to briefly present the vision and Annual Report of the school.... For the past couple of years, our school has been producing 100 per cent results in the Board Examinations of Classes 10 and 12. The percentage of first-division holders was 70 for Class 10 and 95 for Class 12 (in 2005–2006).... We are also trying to get CBSE affiliation for the school and also to change it to the English medium. Next year, we will have separate classes for the English medium up to Class 7. We have introduced counselling and career-oriented programmes. We have come out with a News Bulletin and Admissions Alert services to orient students towards a better future.... In the current mechanical system of education, where the student is overburdened with studies both at school and at home, it is important to make provisions for his/her all-round personality-development through his/her involvement in extra-curricular activities and social affairs. We have worked a lot in that direction.
>
> Bakhtiyar, 43, School Principal

The speech presents an emphasis on the theme of success and mobility of students through this school. The school proclaims absolute success in the examinations conducted by the UP Board. The school also presents itself as aware of the necessary skills needed for success in the job market such as English and working actively towards its provision. It also creates an impression of a child-friendly learning atmosphere through emphasis on extra-curricular activities for them such as music, drama, classroom decoration, sports, etc., and in the hiring of a professional student-counsellor. All these proclamations, particularly about child-centric learning, are high in rhetoric rather than in their actualisation in real school setting due to financial constraints.

All these projections are meant for the audience, mainly parents, and to keep them assured of their choice of this very school for their children. The whole notion of packaging and showcasing the school in the best possible light is an important strategy in the educational market. If educational field is conceived as a market just like other commodities, then parents become the consumers of this good (Ball 2003). In a market economy, survival of a commodity amidst rivals is ensured only when existing consumers are satisfied with the product and new ones are lured towards it. However, the vision of schools in educational market is not constructed only on simple economistic logic. There are counter narratives of schools as a place for learning of good citizenship values. Towards this moral obligation, it has to again assure the audience that students learn the necessary virtues for future participation in modern civic life.

In a way, school is presented as trying to maintain a fine balance between the two pursuits, to prepare students for future success in educational market, and also to make them virtuous by turning them into good citizens by exposing them to nationalistic ideals, such as Bhagat Singh, someone who died at a young age for the nation's freedom.

The Chief Guest for the occasion, a Professor from a university, made special mention of aims of education as cultivation of citizenship education through commitment towards national figures like Bhagat Singh.

I am very happy to hear that Mr Bakht's school is doing so well … it shows in their results, building up infrastructure, working towards getting grants for the school …. Mr (the principal) helps not just in building good values among the students by reminding them of Bhagat Singh, but by also making them successful in the future….

One has to become a good citizen … and schools have to work in that direction… the fight for independence of this country was the biggest school … we became citizens beyond (the category of) caste, and of Hindu–Muslims … we became *Hindustani*. Everyone, including the old and the children were educated in that mission. It was the magic touch of Mahatma Gandhi which mobilised the masses … that was education.

Professor Chatterjee, 58, University Professor

The extracts of these two speeches highlight two different ideals of education. On one hand, and particularly in the principal's speech, frequent references are made to values such as competitiveness, guarantee of good results in the board examinations, a career-oriented approach, necessary training in English, extra-curricular activities for the children, etc. On the other hand, and particularly in the guest's speech, a different ideal of education emerged where he emphasised on the idea of a form of citizenship education which goes beyond the narrow ideas of caste and community. Even as he acknowledges the significance of success in exams, he puts a premium on virtues of an engaged citizen's life, which comes from a commitment to the larger cause of the nation. The two themes of commercial success along with moral virtues of citizenship education are not necessarily seen as contradictory by either of the two speakers. However, the principal's main audiences are the children and their parents, and he is more directly addressing to their anxieties about future, while the guest being a university professor is delivering his own ideals of nation, not necessarily taking the local gathering of Varanasi as his audience, but presenting a grand nationalist narrative for the community of educators. These twin ideals of education, at least in their presentations, seem to coexist with each other.

Celebrating the Nation

In a 'secular' state, schools are expected to prioritise national identity over other forms of identity by promoting patriotic feelings among students.

Independence Day, celebrated on 15th August is the day when the symbols and ideals of the nation are remembered, created and enacted by schools all over India. The meaning and interpretation of these ideals are formally enshrined in the constitution and spelt out by the state bodies like the judiciary. However, the processes through which the commonly understood meanings are communicated and recreated at school level can best be understood in a performative context (Benei 2009). Celebrating Independence

Day by following some common rituals by the various actors associated with the school is a collective act, an exercise which produces and reproduces the meaning of Indian nationhood. Everything, from the use of colour and sounds on this day distinctly declares the purpose of the day as a celebration of the nation. On this day, children dress up in white uniforms, city streets are lined with white powder, teachers and other staff also dress up in white or in colours close to white. However, these diverse actors draw on different discourses to interpret the meaning of the same rituals as brought out in the celebration of the Independence Day in this school.

When I reach the school in the morning, the school has a completely different feel to it from other days. Rather than heading to the classrooms, I move to the assembly ground where students from both senior and junior sections, along with the teachers, are gathered in a more relaxed form than usual days of assembly. Patriotic songs from popular Hindi movies are played through a loudspeaker ordered on rent for this very day and installed on the school playground. It is also seen as a day of relaxation and freedom from the daily chores of school activities, class, attendance, tests, etc. Students are seen happily enjoying themselves with their friends before and after the main ceremony began, some of them having the special tricolor ice creams for this very day, another unusual sight in the school.

With the arrival of the Chief Guest, Mufti of the main Mosque, the formal ceremony begins. He comes dressed in sparkling white kurta and pyjama and a black and white headscarf. The Principal is invited to start the session beginning with the garlanding of portraits of Gandhi, Nehru and Bhagat Singh, and the unfurling of the national flag hoisted with a lot of effort. The students perform their PT exercise to the disciplined drumbeats. After that, the Principal addresses the students. Later, the chief guest's speech follows. The chief guest's speech is in complete contrast to that of the principal. While the Principal made use of common Hindi, interspersed with English and Urdu, the chief guest's speech is more of Persianised Urdu. Formally, the programme continues with the performance of songs, dances and skits by the students. One of the plays, written and enacted completely by students is based on the idea of Indians versus foreigners and eulogises the tradition of hospitality among Indians. The selection of a religious leader as chief guest on Independence Day lends special meaning to the usual turn of events. His dressing up and the choice of language for speech marked an unusual presence in this school, because the school otherwise carefully avoids display of any religious symbolisms. In my conversations afterwards, majority of the students did not remember what he said, partly because of the indifference and mainly because of the exclusive use of Urdu language. The Principal, in later conversations, explains that the particular person enjoys a special status in the city and is held in high regard because of his interventions in the situation of Hindu–Muslim conflicts in the city. When I pointed out the incomprehensibility of his speech, the principal felt his status demands such a speech. In other words, he has to use such language precisely because he is a distinguished person and his audience expects him to speak in an exclusive way. We know how cultural 'distinctions' play an important role in the game of status differentiation in the field of art, culture and education (Bourdieu 1984). The greater the incomprehension for ordinary people, the higher the status one gains in their eyes.

However, not everyone shares similar views of the chief guest's position in the city. One of the teachers expresses his disagreement with the choice of speaker through a sharp polemic. Without singling out the current guest, he remarks that all *deshdrohis* (traitors) are invited as chief guests to this school. He recollects how during the previous year, a political party leader who was caught in a controversy for hurting the religious sentiments of the majority Hindu community was invited as the chief guest. The teacher's interpretation of nationalism and vision of community relations is strikingly different from that of the principal. The students, however, are unaffected by such matters on this day. Most of them did not remember the content of the speeches because of their discomfort while standing in the harsh sun. As soon as the programme comes to an end, they rush to collect their sweets, the major attraction of the day for them.

The aforementioned vignettes from the annual events of the school indicate how the school becomes a site of production, reproduction and projection of values and identities of modernity, and an emphasis on nation through patriotism. These are constructs which are deeply contested and differentially valued by various actors. Even within a school, the conflicting discourses of nationalism and visions of mobility come to full display in these settings. The school principal takes pride in the secular and modern credential of the school vis-à-vis others, while the same moves are interpreted differently by some other actors.

Gendered Norms of Schooling

One entry point into similar conflicting discourses of communities in school is through an examination of gendered codes that organise school life and access to the same. In patriarchal societies, gendered norms of sexual segregation aimed at controlling sexuality have found various expressions such as restricted access to schooling, *zenana*[10] mode of separate school for girls, gendered socialisation within school, low retentions in school after puberty and gendered school choices. (Chanana 2001; Dube 1997; Goswami 2015; Manjrekar 2003). In the history of school education in Banaras also, we have seen such concerns affecting the school curricula in girls' schooling (Kumar 2000). This school was different from other schools, in catering to lower-income groups and providing at least a common space for schooling to both boys and girls. However, a close examination reveals the underlying practices of proper conduct expected from boys and girls.

In the school, the students share a common space but also remain segregated along gender lines. The common spaces are manifested in practice of common classroom and courses, within school and also created some common space for girls and boys to mix outside the formal domain of the school such as, during picnics, annual excursions, annual days, etc., yet the school would reinforce segregation in overt and covert forms. The classroom seating order was such that students sit in several rows and in 2 or 3 columns facing the teacher and the blackboard. The girls would usually occupy one column of tables and benches. Such physical segregation of the girls and boys extend to informal spaces as well, during games and at lunch time. There are few, mixed groups formed during play. During sports hours, girls would be seen playing badminton amongst themselves.

The school administration follows some specific codes which restrict gender mixing, thus maintaining the local norms of gender segregation. One afternoon, when I was in the office, I saw a queue of boys with scared faces before the senior teacher Shankarlal. They were summoned because they had mehndi on their hands. The teacher scolded, bullied and threatened to rusticate them from the school. He also kept ridiculing the boys:

> *Ladki ho kya? Ye dekhiye, ye mehndi lagaye huye hain.*
> 'Are you a girl? Look at him! He has applied mehndi'.

Later, he explains that the manager (the principal's wife) is annoyed at the boys who applied mehndi and had instructed him to discourage them from such practices. They fear that this might be a way of the boys to attract girl students. They feel a need to be cautious in such matters because theirs is a coeducational school. The incident also led to a discussion within the staffroom during which Nirmala, a junior Hindi teacher, intervened and commented that it was because of the festival of *Teej*, during which male members of the family, including young boys apply mehndi. She adds that it is anyway an auspicious sign and should not be punished by the school. This suggestion is laughed at by Shankarlal, while most of the other teachers remained silent.

This incident presents the different discourses of community regarding bodily adornments and its implications for social life. A dominant discourse is that in a modern school, students are supposed to dress in neutral ways so as to avoid any reflection of community affiliation. There are many studies which have reported on school cultures of discipline on bodily adornment by students (Thapan 2014). Another discourse is based on community-specified gendered norms of conduct which suggest that in patrilineal society among both Hindus and Muslims, intermingling of the two sexes should be avoided after girls attain the age of puberty (Dube 1997). HKHSS is a senior secondary school and it faces the twin challenge of accommodating both the set of expectations of neutrality as well as enforcement of community specific gender norms. Its enforcement of 'neutral' dress codes of physical appearance on children is actually backed by the community-specific concern to discourage sexual attraction between girls and boys in the school. Finally, the school followed community-specific gender norms by extending its regime to regulation of their bodily adornments. In its practice, it suppresses another community-specific practice of applying mehndi in hands which is acceptable at home but not in school and that too for boys.

The students are regularly instructed about how they are expected to dress up in culturally and sexually neutral ways. If probed deeper, these 'neutral' norms would have turned out to be deeply gendered and are meant to maintain the local norms of avoiding the mingling of girls and boys beyond a certain level, while maintaining strong binaries of gender. In this particular incident, the teacher used a special tactic of shaming the boy by challenging his masculinity. The school, thereby, creates a common space for both the sexes to interact in a school situation in an otherwise segregated societies, but does not seek to challenge the norms of segregation and strict notions of masculinity and femininity.

Languages in School: Presence and Absence of Official Languages

At first glance, it appears that the vast majority of students in this school come from a monolithic Hindi-speaking group and some from homogeneously Urdu-speaking families. However, as we take a more plural conception of Hindi and Urdu, we uncover diversity within the categories of Hindi and Urdu, which challenges the rigid notions of the boundaries around these standard languages. Drawing on the empirical work on language varieties in North

India (Grierson 1967; Kachru and Bhatia 1978), I assume Hindi to be a loose group of several language varieties.

I tried to inquire about the students' *ghar ki bhasha/bhashayen*, or languages of the home, and avoided the term mother tongue, so as to explore the variety of speech used outside the school. The term mother tongue remains ambiguous with changing definitions, and it often conceals rather than reveals a diverse and complex linguistic scenario where people report a high variety as their mother tongue (Annamalai 2001). Therefore, when I asked students about the languages they speak at home, I asked them about both bhasha and boli, or language and speech. I tried to further ascertain if their variety of Hindi at home is different from the variety used in the school. The data on the students' linguistic backgrounds reported here are based on the students' identi-fication of the popular as well as the standard ones. These responses were mainly collected in the school, but wherever possible, I also examined their language-use in the family setting. A majority of the students reported more than one variety used at home. This is because they often speak in different varieties with their relatives from the villages or other towns, friends from the mohalla, etc. Nonetheless, the categories of scheduled and 'non-scheduled'/ popular languages shall be used to explore the linguistic diversity of students and juxtaposing it against the state-defined categories. This approach leads to questioning of the convention of collecting information, which creates and imposes superficial divides that do not necessarily exist. Particularly, in the context of North India where linguistic boundaries are drawn along religious lines, it is interesting to find that children's reporting of language don't necessarily fall in the same line, when probed deeper.

The figures presented in Table 4.3 indicate the diverse linguistic repertoire of the students from two classes. It is significant that they lack exclusiveness in the official sense of linguistic identity. One must point out that these reported varieties are not necessarily significant in terms of linguistic categories per se. The objective is not to essentialise the categories as more genuine but to use these labels or markers to examine the processes of boundary-making pertaining to languages and the corresponding group relations

Table 4.3
Students' Reported Language Varieties According to Religion in Non-exclusive Categories

	All (65)	Hindu (48)	Muslim (17)
Scheduled Languages			
Hindi	60	48	12
Urdu	9	0	9
Only Hindi	15	13	2
Others*	2	–	2
Popular/Non-scheduled Languages			
Bhojpuri	12	12	0
Banarasi	10	9	1
Bihari	5	5	0
Urdu–Hindi/Hindi–Urdu	5	0	5
Others	1	1	–
Bhojpuri Only	–	–	–
Urdu–Hindi/Hindi–Urdu Only	3	–	3

Source: Based on fieldwork (2006–2008).
Note: *There existed isolated cases of Marathi and Punjabi speakers.

and, finally, their implications at the school level. Boundaries are assumed to get drawn, redrawn, transgressed and negotiated in a plural/diverse setting so as to define groups in different contexts (Barth 1969; Lamont and Molnar 2002).

It is clear that the students use various labels to describe the language varieties used at home. Apart from reporting the more common standard languages such as Hindi and Urdu, they also named several other varieties such as Bhojpuri, Banarasi, Bihari, Dehati, Theth, Kharibhasha, Khariboli, Urdu–Hindi/Hindi–Urdu, etc. It is important to note that during my initial interaction with the students, the majority of them reported Hindi to be their mother tongue and denied using any other language variety. Only students with specific regional affiliations had different languages to report such as Marathi, Bengali and so on. One can explain the initial denial partly through the common perception that Hindi is inclusive of all the varieties spoken in the city. However, the denial may also be because of the diffidence associated with the use of a popular variety like Banarasi, as it is not considered to be a respectable language. To explore the according and denial of legitimacy to different language varieties, responses were collected over a long period of time and from a small group of students (65) in and outside classroom settings in the school and, in many cases, substantiated in family settings.

In the aforementioned distribution, the number of Hindi speakers dominated, with 62 out of 65 students, both Hindus and Muslims declaring it as one of the speech varieties used at home. Out of these, however, just 15 students reported that Hindi alone is their *ghar ki bhasha*. For majority of students, there is no name to describe what they used at home, and it is just Hindi. However gradually, they start telling me about how the language of the elderly at home or relatives from the village is different from the Hindi used in the school. Then, they begin mentioning Theth, Dehati and Julehti,[11] along with more known varieties such as Banarasi and Bhojpuri. Much later, they also admitted that they enjoyed speaking Banarasi occasionally with their friends or siblings at home and even in the school.

Muslim students report both Urdu and Hindi or Urdu–Hindi as their language. No one reports Urdu alone to be the language of use. Some of them also mention Banarasi as their home language. Here, the contrast between the social class of the principal and the Muslims students is apparent. Among the Muslims, Urdu is apparently spoken by those belonging to the culturally rich high-class Muslims, while the majority apparently speaks Julehti/ Banarasi/Urdu–Hindi. Those who actually practice these would, however, use a loose term like Urdu–Hindi rather than Julehti. Sometimes, it is also referred to as *aiyo jaiyo wali bhasha*, the language of *aiyo* and *jaiyo* instead of the more genteel *aaiye* and *jaiye*. The latter terms are used in honorific tone for the common verbs 'come' and 'go'.

The Principal and the Urdu teachers also believe that access to Urdu as a cultural resource and as part of the family heritage is not available to the vast majority of Muslims in Banaras. The Principal exemplified his account of the difference between the high variety of Urdu and lower-class Urdu which is closer to Kashika[12] (Banarasi) than Urdu. He gave the example of a sentence: *Bhuyian pe suttee rahe* or 'I was sleeping on the ground'. In Urdu, there are different words used for earth, such as *zameen* rather than *bhuiyan*, and the use of the latter word suggests the influence of local varieties such as Banarasi or Kashika. This clearly indicates that students are exposed to a mixed repertoire of speech which is not exclusively divided along religious lines as is commonly believed.

The pedagogic implications of the same will be explored later, while here we focus on the significance of students' population and school administrator's ideological leaning in shaping the school policy regarding language of education, through their negotiation of the official mandate of language teaching.

Languages Offered at School

A majority of schools in Uttar Pradesh and in Banaras offer Hindi, English and Sanskrit languages at the secondary level (refer Table 3.2). HKHSS offered Hindi, English and Urdu. Hindi and English are compulsory languages for all, while Urdu is offered as an optional subject at the upper-primary level. The option of Urdu seems to have been an important pull for several Muslim families in the neighbourhood. Specific periods are allotted to Urdu, which are also open for non-Muslim students, but this choice is rarely exercised. In 2006–2007, Urdu as an optional subject was placed along with the other optional subject, drama. This arrangement effectively meant that Muslim students opting for Urdu cannot go for the drama classes. When I inquired about the arrangement, the school administration cited some problem in time planning, because of which Urdu and drama were allotted the same periods, virtually leading to a segregation of students on religious lines.

Sanskrit is conspicuously absent from curriculum. Sanskrit is taught only as a part of the Hindi curriculum by the Hindi teacher. The UP Board of education has made Sanskrit a necessary component of Hindi, the first language of the state. We have seen how language politics in Uttar Pradesh has polarised Urdu and Sanskritised Hindi as two different languages belonging to two different communities. The principal of the school has a very clear stand on the issue. He criticises the neglect of Urdu by the government of India and promotion of Sanskrit, which in his view is a dead language. While reacting to the drive towards the Sanskritisation of Hindi words, he commented

> *Banaras ko Varanasi aur aspatal ko chikitsalay bana dene par bhi log Banaras aur aspatal hi kahenge ... Sanskrit is a dead language... Usko pata nahi kyu jinda rakhna chahte hai...*
>
> 'Even if Banaras is named Varanasi, and (hospital) is named *chikitsalay*, people will continue to call them Banaras and *aspatal* only... Sanskrit is a dead language... Don't know... (they) want to keep it alive...

This statement expresses the principal's take on the conflict of the Sanskritised Hindi names with the popular ones used in Banaras. He mocks the futility of the attempt made by the administration to change the name of the city, and other such words of common use towards more Sanskritised variety remote from linguistic repertoire of people. He elucidated how people subvert these measures by choosing not to use such official terms. He also believes Urdu to be a popular language and not restricted to Muslims alone, but forming a part of the daily interaction of everyone, as against Sanskrit which has few speakers in present times and is being kept alive only because of the government's support.

These discourses shape and influence the options of the languages offered by the school administration to its students. We do not see the official TLF and the regionally common practice of offering Sanskrit as the third language in this school. Such arrangements are indicative of the complex dynamics of educational market which can't be explained through recourse to the simple economic logic of market or to rigid official frameworks. In this case, teaching of a language like Sanskrit also means an additional cost for the already low-budget school with no promise of significant returns, while Urdu is a language worth investing in because it has won them a clientele of a section of relatively better-off Muslims, who would prefer to send their children to a modern school which offered Urdu over a madrasa. The option of Urdu as one of the subjects gave the school an important advantage over other schools.

One can further examine the issue by asking why Urdu was offered only as an optional subject even if the school authorities were convinced that it is a more alive and popular language than Sanskrit. Giving Urdu the same status as that of Hindi and English would have been possible only at the cost of damaging the secular image of the school that it has carefully maintained. So, Urdu is offered as an optional subject, open to everyone in principle, but in practice only the Muslim students opt. This arrangement does not affect the modern and mainstream image of the school adversely and also attracts students from a specific community. However, in practice, it also reinforces the affiliation of Urdu with Muslims, something against which the school Principal wishes to take a principled stand.

The option of Urdu offered by the school suggests how a private school administration negotiates the official framework of TLF and exercises important choices regarding the languages to be taught in the school. While being a modern administrator, the Principal also represents a tradition of Muslim elite whose cultural capital included Urdu and who resist the Sanskritised version of Hindi. However, he is not able to challenge the segregation of students on religious line which has resulted in loss of symbolic power of Urdu in contemporary times.

Conclusion: Negotiating the School-market of Banaras

The person incharge of the primary section, who is one of the senior teachers, claims that the school is perceived as a 'semi-English-medium' school because it is striving for a complete shift towards English-medium instruction in all classes.[13] This is partly a result of all the efforts put in by the school to carve out a space for itself in the school-market of Banaras that we have examined in this chapter. However, all these strategies of projecting a growth-oriented modern school image fail to attract students from all over Banaras like more prestigious schools do. The school remains localised in its outreach. Barring a few exceptions, all other students come from the nearby areas ranging from 1 to 2 km. Some of the students leave the school after Class 5 or Class 8 for more prestigious schools in the city. It is also constrained in its resource base to attract qualified teachers, retain them and provide them with sufficient training and other resources for better engagement in teaching–learning activity of school. The learning environment that the school proclaims and seeks to create, demands a considerable investment of resources, time and energy on the part of the entire staff and students alike. However, its position in the overall school hierarchy restricts the chances of realisation of the same, reducing it to a local school for the lower-middle class.

The ownership of the school by a Muslim family, and one-fifth of the students (23% in 2006–2007) from the same community, made it a good case to examine the cultural politics of language and community in a city that played an important part in the construction of Hindi nationalism in pre- and post-independence India discussed earlier. Through our reflections on the school practices, it is made clear that notions of modernity, nation, gender and community identities, remain contradicted because of the demands of the competitive school-market on one hand and the demands of the 'provincial' community it is associated with on the other. With a school population so diverse, and operative logics of the school always being redefined it functions as a school which while adhering to the logic of private school-market in the city also fulfils the community needs in its own way.

Notes

1. The school has been trying to convert itself to English medium. They had already tried to get recognition in 2005–2006 for their junior section under the name of Albert Educational Institution. In 2010, the school was finally changed to English medium. The important implications of this development could not be included here and the author intends to address this issue in her future work.

2. Bhagat Singh is a nationalist icon in Indian history. His name has recently been mired in controversy because both the Right-wing nationalist groups as well as communist party of India claim him to be their iconic figure. The organisations run in his name are often seen as progressive circles which come together to discuss political issues and also act as reading circle.

3. Casual lower garment used by men in North India. A particular variety is associated with lower-class Muslims who are seen in the streets of Banaras wearing it along with a cap and vest.

4. For details of popular culture in Banaras see N. Kumar (1998).

5. An Imambara is a building or a room for congregation of Shia Muslims of a particular anjuman or a society particularly during the period of Mohurram. *Tazias* or floats which are taken out for procession during Mohurram are also kept there.

6. A religious group based in the mohalla among the Shias of Banaras, of which the Bakhtiyar family is the patron.

7. Even as UP government lists Ansaris among its list of Other Backward Caste groups, not all identify themselves as one. This was brought out in a discussion with the school Principal, where he suggested that among Muslim population people still find it beneath their dignity to identify themselves with a caste category. This was evidenced in the fact that for many government assistances, even after announcements, these students would not come forward. However, slowly this trend is changing and some people have started claiming the benefits.

8. The parental construction of these issues would be discussed later in the book.

9. The Ansaris were referred to as the 'bigoted Julahas' in colonial times, and as constituting the provincial community as compared to the metropolitan one in post-colonial societies (Kumar 1998, 2000, 2008; Pandey 1989).

10. Zenana means of women or pertaining to women. With reference to education Zenana system refers to a form of schooling in which women were educated while maintaining their segregation from men. Refer to work of Dube (1997); and Chanana (2001) for details.

11. *Theth* here refers to 'typical of Banaras', *Dehati* refers to the rustic language and *Julehti* is the language of the Julaha or weaver.

12. Sanskritised name for the language of Kashi, that is, Banaras.

13. In recent years, attempts were being made to run the school in both the media till Class 5 and eventually in all the grades.

5

Educational Strategies in Changing Language Market

Hum daal me jitna ghee dalenge utna hi swaad ayega ... Usi tarah hum medium class walo ke liye HKHSS ek accha school hai ...

'The more *ghee* (clarified butter) there is, the better the *daal* (lentils) tastes ... Similarly for people like us from the medium class, HKHSS is a good school ...'

—Pandey, 40, father of Amar

This quote is by Mr Pandey, who works as an agent in an insurance company. He makes a qualified assessment of the school he chose for his son Amar, because it fits the budget of people like him.

The qualification comes from its accessibility to the middle-income-group people like Mr Pandey who cannot afford a more expensive school. In the school-market, affordability for parents plays a very crucial role and it is linked in various ways to the notion of proximity of the school. The notion of proximity and distance has both physical and cultural dimensions to it. The most prestigious schools tend to be the most distant ones, both physically and culturally.

When education is understood in a wider sense, family, workplace, neighbourhood, market areas and popular cultures emerge as important sites of learning languages and work cultures, besides school; for, these sites give us a chance to explore the alternatives to the standard language cultures of Hindi, English and Urdu imbibed by the students. Cultures learnt in such sites may or may not converge with those practiced and preferred in formal school space. To understand the points of convergence and divergence between learning cultures of family and school, the concept of middle class and its associated cultures are often employed. The commonality of learning cultures at school, with middle-class cultures at family level, is an area which has seen extensive research in educational studies. Many among them have also been able to point towards the role played by language ideologies in these contexts. In the Indian context, it is argued that English language is perceived as an important marker of middle-class identity and is actively sought after as a vehicle of social mobility for entry into the gated community of the middle class. Many studies have shown that the educational decisions arrived at family level play an important role in the same direction. A majority of these studies have exclusively focused on upper-middle-class families from professional backgrounds and settled in metropolitan centres.[1] Even as the employment records estimate that the number of people employed in professional or service-class is a very small proportion of the actual workforce, the large majority of workers continue to be employed in the informal sectors of economy with minimum social security provisions.[2] A major problem with the use of the category and concept of middle class to understand educational experiences is its heterogeneous composition which makes it difficult to define. Its application in an urban context like Banaras, largely reliant on informal sectors of economy, and which does not show full integration of labour market and symbolic market as is presumed in many industrial societies, presents further challenges.

To understand the educational strategies of families which aspire to be the part of 'the mythical middle class' in India, while being trapped in the informal sectors of economy, we need to unravel the various meanings of the term middle class for them. We use the tropes of formality and informality both in terms of work cultures and in terms of language-use to explore such meanings. It will help us to understand not just the aspirations which are specific to a particular form of economic activity, but also to a form of communicating, which accompany the formal domains of work and schooling.

This chapter is based on my field interactions with parents, particularly mothers and other relatives in families associated with HKHSS. One major objective of the exercise is to examine their linguistic practices, preferences and educational strategies against the changing dynamics of labour market in Banaras. From the fieldwork, it emerges that people continue to rely on a variety of networks and make use of different language varieties in different domains, even as there seems to be a transition towards preference for more standard varieties like Hindi and aspiration for learning English. Such practices, preferences and aspirations for good schools and associated languages can be explained through the occupational variance between the salaried classes and those self-employed in 'traditional' business, along with parental education rather than blanket conceptualisation of middle class and their preference for English education in contemporary India.

Middle-class Identity, Prestige Language and School-choice

The conceptual category of class is often used in the literature on school education to discuss the inequality of accesses, differential school experiences and educational mobility. In particular, the term 'middle class' and its easy familiarity with school culture is considered of great importance in describing the reproduction of social and cultural inequality. However, the category of middle class is mired in conceptual haziness which makes it particularly difficult for empirical investigations in Indian context.

First of all, the problems accrue because of a shift in emphasis from defining middle class as indicating objective social positions (Wright 1985) towards a more subjective understanding of the term as referring to a set of 'practice' and 'performance' (Fernandes and Heller 2006; Foley 1992). Here, it is important to note that class should also be viewed as an identity which is constructed discursively (Ball 2003; Ortner 1998). When we examine class as an identity, it helps us analyse various ways in which people identify themselves as middle class irrespective of their objective social position in terms of measurable index of income and consumption pattern.

The term middle class lacks precision when used in the political and economic context of India. Many studies have documented the rise of a middle class in the developmental state of post-independence India, as represented by technocratic professionals employed in public sector and a miniscule private sector. In more recent years, many others have examined the rise of a 'new middle class' propelled by the economic reforms of 1991 and a boom in the IT sector jobs. However, both the old and the new category of middle class together constitute a small and miniscule proportion of total working force. Further, entry in these circles is extremely limited for the majority of the population. Still their presence and weight in policy discourses, media discussions and market projections appears hugely disproportionate to their actual existence. Satish Deshpande asserts that the mismatch between the actual and claimed strength of the middle class makes it sociologically significant and must be explored to capture the critical, multidimensional role of the middle class in India (2003).

Deshpande (2003) conceptualises the category of middle class in three ways—as articulators of hegemony of the ruling block; as the class most reliant on the production and reproduction of cultural capital; and as constitutive of producers and consumers of dominant ideologies (2003, 139–42). His last formulation conceives of a division in middle class in India in relation with their role in circulation of dominant ideologies, with upper middle class acting as producer and lower middle class as consumer of dominant ideologies. Similarly, Beteille (2003) suggested that while examining the heterogeneity of the people, it is more useful to talk in terms of 'middle classes' rather than a singular category of middle class in India.

Drawing on Marxist understanding of 'contradictory class locations' of the middle class and echoing Deshpande's proposition, Fernandes (2006) argues that the petty bourgeoisie, that is, small property owners and merchants do not fit the definition of middle class as per the considerations of production and dissemination of dominant/hegemonic ideologies. However, since their property is rarely sufficient to provide material support for the next generation, the class practices of the petty bourgeoisie often mimic those of the middle-class proper (Fernandes 2006). She develops the idea of 'middle-class practices' through which those who are excluded from the 'middle-class proper' in terms of objective positions try to build up their own identity.

These followers constitute the bulk of the population and are mostly employed in the informal sectors of economy, with minimum provisions of economic and social security. There have been very few sociological studies which explain class relations in the informal economy-dominated, urban centres of India. One such attempt is made by John Harris (2011) where he finds it useful to differentiate within and between the categories of middle class, informal working-class and permanent wage workers. Harris (2011) defines middle class as referring to those

> disposing of significant cultural capital—which may consist of identities (in terms of caste, community, region) and competences—(linguistic, educational, or other social skills including facility in English)—and who have some property or relatively well-paid salaries or professional employment. Informal-working-class, on the other hand, refers to subalterns (rather than the articulators of the hegemony of the ruling block) and who do not dispose of significant cultural capital, and who also lack the advantage of protection through regulation by the state of their terms of employment or occupation. (447).

This class may also include the section of petty bourgeoise which is also exposed to the vulnerabilities of market shifts.

The political–economic context of Banaras is, numerically speaking, dominated by informal sectors of economy, and what Harris identifies as the informal working-class. And yet during my visits to the schools of Banaras, it was the term middle class which was most frequently employed by the school staff to describe the clientele of students that most of the schools cater to. However, there were various formulations of the same term depending on who is using the term and for whom.

For example, in HKHSS the neighbouring family of Ansari weavers viewed the school as catering to the (relatively) 'rich loomowners' families' and not to the 'ordinary workers', given the amount of monthly fee charged. Here the school seems to cater to the better off sections of people coming from a specific industry. Ordinary people who are not rich enough to send their children to a better quality private school have to rely on government schools or less expensive private schools of the mohalla for their children's education, until they become ready for work or for marriage. Here the distinction of class is made with reference to a 'traditional occupation' like weaving industry in which some are better off than the others.

There is a large segment in the borderland area of the middle and lower classes who seek better educational opportunity for their children, and for whom the choice of a right school is a step in the right direction. Some of them hesitatingly identify themselves with the middle-class category. For example, an insurance agency worker, whose son is studying in HKHSS, refers to the school as catering to 'medium-class families' like theirs. Here, medium-class refers to people occupying a median position in relation to all others, neither rich nor poor, making varied choices of schools ranging from low-fee-charging aided schools to moderately-high-fee-charging private schools. Such schools, as well as the families associated with these occupied a middle position and, therefore, are seen as catering to 'medium-class people'. This notion of being located somewhere in the middle of the class spectrum is extensively employed by people whom social scientists would consider as located in lower-class positions or at best in lower-middle-class position.

Apart from this idea of a median point, the sense of middle-class identity is also hinged on the distinction between 'business-class' and 'service-class'. If we examine it from the perspectives of the school staff and teachers who are employed at school, majority of the families associated with the HKHSS are identified as belonging to the 'business-class'. The school teachers, in particular, do not have a very positive evaluation of the category of business-class vis-à-vis the 'service-class' people who are few in number. This distinction was maintained on the basis of difference of occupations and of associated cultures between the two kinds of groups. The pedagogic implications of the same in terms of school experience would be explored later in the book.

Such complexities make the task of formulation of a clear understanding of the relation between class identity and schooling chances, and experiences of various groups increasingly difficult. However, this messiness of social world that one encounters in trying to make sense of how people identify themselves and are identified by others in terms of their class and social status is essential to an understanding of schooling in India. The literature on middle-class choices regarding schooling in India has tended to focus on 'high-prestige schools' or English-medium schools to explain the educational strategies of the emergent middle class, particularly in the post-1991 period. Vaidehi Ramanathan, in her work on English- and Vernacular-medium divide, shows how the chasm between the two worlds is maintained by differentially training them for success at college life and through gatekeeping mechanisms of high-prestige colleges (2005). Very few studies have focused on lower middle classes or 'informal working-class' or the fringes of the 'mythical middle class' who are the followers of the dominant ideologies or are in the process of becoming followers. One noted exception is the study of David Drury (1993) conducted in Kanpur city. He employs the notion of 'class fractions' to discuss how various groups within middle class employ various strategies to gain access to schools that they consider worth investing. His account provides a story of differentiated access to limited educational capital as well as how families negotiate with the terms set by the schools. LaDousa (2007) identifies the newly emerging middle class and their perceptions of Hindi- and English-medium schools of the north-Indian city. He highlights the conflicting interests within the broad category of middle class between a section who identifies with and whose aspirations are set at the global and pan-national level and those at the regional–national level. He aptly sums up these sections in the title of his recent work 'Hindi is our ground English is our sky' (2014). The current chapter is based on my understanding of the relation between class identity and educational strategies, particularly among the lower-middle-class or informal-working-class segment engaged in informal sectors of economy in Banaras through my exploration of families associated with HKHSS. Some of these people are firmly grounded in the Hindi world and looking for venturing out to the world of English education, but majority of them are still making an effort to construct their middle-class identity by grounding themselves first in the form of Hindi which is respected in a school like HKHSS, with a realisation that it may or may not lead them to be a part of the much coveted but elusive 'middle-class' circle.

These observations are based on my interactions with family members in an attempt to socially locate these families and understand their perception of languages and education. These interactions are supported by preliminary information about their family through my interactions with students in school and my participation in the parents–teachers meeting in school. I am exploring perceptions of families from varying occupational backgrounds regarding their work, their language-use and the relevance of schooling for their social mobility aspirations. Most of these families are either self-employed or are working in some private firms in unregulated sectors. Only a few families are involved in secure salaried jobs in organised sectors, namely, as school teachers in government school or college. Both because of the heterogeneity of their employment profile and the nature of work in the informal sectors in Banaras, it is difficult to classify these families in clear categories of middle class and/or working-class to explain their choice of this particular school. Instead, occupational variance and educational background of parents emerge as the more important factors to explain their relationship with the school.

During interviews, everyone used their own styles of Hindi. Given the gendered division of space and work in these families, I mostly ended up talking with the women, young and old, and with few men. This might have limited my understanding of language-use patterns at workplace across communities and caste groups, but enabled me to probe into the gendered nature of socialisation of children into the right language-use patterns within family.

Variance of Occupation, Languages and Educational Capital

The number of ways in which identities of class, religion, region and gender interact with each other in a given context helps to understand the educational choices exercised at family level. Occupational profile of families assumes special significance in this context, because the choice of schooling and the kind of cultural resources including languages that a child has access to are influenced by the parental occupations. In Banaras, small-scale industries in informal sectors predominate and service sector is rather limited in providing employment opportunities. In school, the two terms of 'business-class' and 'service-class' are frequently employed by the staff and teachers and, at times, also by parents. My visits to students' families sought to examine their relationship with school education across generations, and also to examine their home context and pattern of language-use. The relationship of work, socialisation, language-learning at home and schooling experience has been examined by many scholars from different perspectives (Heath 1983). The home cultures tend to have influence on language literacy among people from different class positions. S. B. Heath's work among the three different neighbourhoods and the language-learning patterns at home revealed the differential styles of communication among ethnic communities from working- and middle-class backgrounds (Heath 1983). The differential communication styles also have implications for how these families exercise their educational strategies with respect to school choice (Reay 1999).

My interactions are organised around three kinds of families based on their occupations—those engaged in Banarasi saree; those who have moved to other kinds of business; and those who are in service sector. Majority of the families engaged in saree industry tend to come from Ansari community, and because of the specific character of the industry and its association (or lack of it) with formal schools, such families have been discussed in greater detail. The other kind of families are in a phase of transition of moving away from the saree industry and joint family structure.

The third set consists of the service-class families which represent a smaller segment in the students' population, but its analysis is important to understand the dynamics of educational strategies in the given contexts.

All the 17 families are settled residents of the city except five of these who migrated to the city in past 10–15 years from rural areas of eastern UP and western Bihar. The rest are settled in Banaras for many generations and live in joint family settings. The families include both Hindus and Muslims, involved in small-scale trade and service-based occupations. Among these, nine are self-employed as small traders, suppliers to retail shops and shopowners. In every family, it is the men who look after the family business, supported by elder sons, while women stay at home and provide carework for children and other family members.

The production system especially in textile industries has moved from being person-centric to family-run enterprise, but does not yet follow a corporation model with modern forms of managerial controls (Jaiswal 2012; Varman and Chakrabarty 2007). It involves many aspects of work such as bleaching and dying the silk thread, designing, weaving, supply of raw materials, supply of finished goods, selling to the retailers, etc. In a way, in spite of the changes, the industry continued to be the major employer of people in the city (Refer Table 3.2).

There are men who were absorbed in this industry as workers even though it could not provide them sufficient support for a comfortable living.

> Every Ansari in Banaras is born with the skill of working in saree trade. There are hundreds of works in the business of Banarsi saree, colouring, embroidery, designing, weaving etc. But now it is difficult to make ends meet in this business. You get *dal roti* not anything else, not even sufficient to get *chutney*... (Noor, 35, weaver)

The worker clearly makes a strong expression that even as the industry continues to provide him with the bare minimum for survival, it is not sufficient for even slightest of expansion in needs. The industry is still seen as the natural destination for families from varied class positions. It is important to note that the Ansari families that I visited come from better off economic background who can afford the school expenses of a private school like HKHSS. This is not the case with other Ansari workers who live in a more vulnerable position, particularly in the wake of stagnation in the industry.

Among these business families, some have been engaged in the work for generations, gradually upgrading themselves within it from the status of master weavers to the small-scale traders. Others are in the process of transition and exploring new avenues in readymade garment industry, embroidered clothes, etc. because of the market shifts. Many of them talk about a phase of stagnation in saree business caused by a lack of demand for products and diminishing returns in the trade. Workers or weavers are the worst affected in this trend as they could manage to earn just ₹300–400 for a week's work. The schemes announced by the state government in support of the industry never reached the weavers and the small traders. All the benefits are garnered by the rich loomowners.

I interacted with five families from Ansari (Muslim) community and one from Jaiswal (Hindu) family who were engaged in saree industry as their primary occupation. These families stay in narrow lanes of Alaipura, Jaitpura and Kachhibagh. These locations are known primarily for the settlement of weavers, many of whom now run power looms. The open space outside the lanes is used for drying the dyed threads to be used for weaving. Their houses are typically a multi-storeyed building in which the ground floor is used as factory space where hired labourers work on power looms, sometimes with the help of generators. The customers are shown samples of Banarasi saree at the ground floor with the help of the hired staff or more usually a young man from the family. A narrow staircase usually leads from the *aangan* to the upper floors where the women folk of the house manage their domestic world and meet guests. These houses and the conversations therein resonate with the noise of power looms. I am usually taken to the upper floors for talks about family with the women. The Hindu households also have arrangements similar to the Muslim ones, living in joint family set-up and engaged in saree trade. Unlike the

Ansaris, they do not directly employ workers or own power looms. They purchase readymade products from small- or medium-scale weavers and supply to the retailers.

Among these families there is an interesting pattern of language-use which is a colloquial form of language specific to the mohalla, and is described to the outsiders like me as a mix of Hindi and Urdu.

In Nazma's home, her aunt clarified me that though they are Muslims they do not speak Urdu. Urdu is spoken by very few, highly educated people. What they use at home is a hybrid variety of Urdu–Hindi at home. This was a common description of their language in all the Ansari households.

> Our language is different from others. It is odd. It has Hindi, Urdu and all kinds of words in it. This is spoken among Ansaris. Some call it *julehti*. It is not used by other Muslims like Pathans. We use it at home. I don't like its use.
>
> Nargis's mother, 32

> It is a *dehaati ilaka*. People speak the language of *ailu gailu* … At home they speak Hindi–Urdu mix among themselves. In which 75 per cent of the words are in Hindi and the rest are Urdu.
>
> Salim's father, 37

Interestingly, the Hindu families settled in these lanes and engaged in the saree business have similar views about their home language and talk about its shared features with the language of Muslims.

For example, in Puneet's family, a Jaiswal family, settled in a mixed neighbourhood of Hindus and Muslims they use a common language, a hybrid of Hindi–Urdu.

> Our most of the business dealings are with Muslim clients. They call each other *miya*. But the difference between the two languages of Muslims and Hindus is very less, not more than 20 per cent … Within Banaras, Hindi is the normal language … and with the *karigar*, we use Hindi–Urdu mix. At home we speak Banarasi and Hindi … This is a Muslim locality so the style is a bit different … 20 per cent language is different … If you go to Ausangunj from here the language will change.
>
> Puneet's father, 40

So in these families, both Hindus and Muslims, the home languages are also used at workplace for communication across class and community. It is understood that one has to be flexible enough to learn the language of others in business. Here, it is also important to note that the distinction of work and home is not so strict in this trade where family is the unit that is managing the business. In a majority of the cases, spatial separation is not maintained as one's residence also serves as the place of business.

Similarly, these common languages are also used in neighbour-hood areas within and across communities. When Puneet's father described the use of Banarasi and Hindi at home he also mentioned his neighbourhood. The mohalla presented an interesting case of inter-community speech in a mixed neighbourhood where 'Hindi–Urdu' or Banarasi is used between the two communities.

Though the Hindus and Muslims maintained difference in identifying their speech as slightly different from that of the other, they also believed it to be not significantly different. For example, the only difference Mr Jaiswal could refer to was the use of certain words like *Ammi* (mother), *abbu* (father) among Muslims which is not prevalent among Hindus.

The business of Banarasi saree calls for different kind of skills, and social and cultural capital which are not necessarily dependent on modern schooling in the same way as in other occupations. The amount of time and energy that one has to invest in the trade seems incompatible with the modern schooling, which presumes a separation between work-life and school-life for a long duration of one's life. For this very reason, those engaged in this trade, partic-ularly the Ansaris, who are more engaged in weaving rather than trading, were seen as averse to modern schools and more reliant on madrasa or Maktabs from mohalla (Kumar 2000). Gradually, these families are moving towards more modern forms of schools beyond their own mohalla. Schooling, and to a limited extent, higher education, are now being seen as symbols of modernity and gaining legitimacy in their social circle.

In Ansari families, the choice of the school over the madrasa is made only in recent generations. Most of the older siblings, both boys and girls, now in their 20s, have all been to some madrasa school for 5–8 years. In all these families, in spite of the continuity of their traditional occupation and widespread stereotyping, some changes are visible in their relation with formal education.

The younger generation in these families, the younger siblings, are moving to non-madrasa schools and sometimes, to English-medium private schools. Almost every family seemed open about sending their younger sons for higher education, a luxury which is not given to the eldest son. They also seemed open for investment in education in supplementary forms like tuitions, etc. Apart from these changes in preference of schooling, some gender norms are also changing where girls are being sent to a school like HKHSS which is a coeducational school.

Saba's mother feels amused at the way her daughter dresses up in Western clothes and goes for school picnic along with school friends including boys. This was unthinkable in her childhood when she was attending all-girls madrasa school.

A few girls are also being sent for higher education without challenging the norms of gender roles in the community. This trend may be attributed to the changing norms of the marriage market which now demands that women be educated up to a certain level so as to be able to look after the education of their children.

In one household, I was introduced to Razia and Nazia, college-educated unmarried women in their early 20s. They were the only college-educated women in their entire family and kin-network. They studied in a madrasa to complete high school and then shifted to a women's college in the city. Their elder sister, Nargis, was married off much earlier, just after completion of her primary-level madrasa education. She also went to the same madrasa for her education. Besides learning Arabic and Urdu, she learnt all the subjects that a regular school would otherwise offer. She felt that the family environment was not suitable for women's education in her time and things have improved for her sisters, but some issues exist even today.

Earlier there were not many schools for Muslim women. It is only recently that 'National College' started its separate shift for women.

> Our people would start talking rubbish about educated women. My
> sisters who are the most educated (in the community) could have gone
> for even higher education after completing their graduation. But they
> were not allowed because it may cause problem in their marriage.
>
> Nargis, 33, mother

These moments of change, however sluggish they might seem, are
not without their tensions. Very few would send their children to
the English-medium schools in the city or allow their daughters
to continue in a coeducational school beyond secondary schooling. Daughter's education is still a luxury which can be afforded
only by a few, and has to be achieved while following strictly gendered norms of control and security. For these families, the sites
of education are plural and not restricted to schools alone. The
alternative sites of family, workplace and community norms of
education were sometimes in conflict with the school education
and adjustments had to be made accordingly. For example, having
made the transition to school education, these families continued
to arrange for private instructions in reading of Koran along with
school subjects such as Science, Math and English.

However, not all 'business families' have a similar experience
with school education. There are other families who are going
through a phase of transition from traditional joint family business
to newer occupations which are less dependent on kin-networks.
Their future aspirations for social mobility are more closely tied
with career prospects and training in formal education of their
sons, as compared to the Ansari families. For this reason, they
are more invested in 'better school education' and are more open
in exploring good schools for their children. These families are
also making a clearer shift from their home language Bhojpuri–
Banarasi to Hindi, especially among the younger generations.

Saurabh lives in a residential colony in Nati Imli, where his
father and four uncles lived together along with their families.
They are engaged in small separate businesses of their own. They
moved out from Jaitpura, the weavers' settlement area, two decades
earlier when they closed down the saree business. All the brothers
now have their own general stores.

Both the parents of Saurabh's are from Banaras and they went to schools till Class 10, but they are very concerned about their son's future education. Even as they speak Bhojpuri with their parents, they maintain Hindi in their communication with children. Saurabh's aunt, much younger and more educated than his parents, is stricter in her approach and insists that her children should at least use English words even at home and they should be punished if they fail to do so.

Similarly, Madhuri's family has also moved on to the business of supply of embroidered clothes from saree industry. Madhuri's mother comes from Jaunpur and is very critical of the Banarasi culture and language. She has two daughters both of whom are pursuing education in the city but she feels that the city life is not suitable for their proper education. Madhuri's sister just finished her college education and was planning to get into University education for better job opportunity. Her mother is always concerned about the mohalla culture where the boys roam around till late evening and tease the girls who return a little late. Back in Jaunpur, her family members were into service and everyone was well educated. Banarasi *bhasha* or language also used by her in-laws, is uncouth and rustic to her taste. These families showed more concern for education, more policing of language-use than the families we discussed earlier.

The families in service sector present a very different home environment. They invariably live in rented houses, having moved from their family of origin and settling near the workplace. They are not involved in any form of business, lack necessary capital, skills and connections, and therefore must rely on school education for creating opportunities in life. In these service-class families, just like in the business-class, men are employed and women manage the domestic world. Out of eight such families that I visited, only two of them are occupied in regular government positions as teachers in schools. The rest of them are employed in private shops or work with insurance agencies. The parents have come from nearby villages to settle in the city for work. The city with greater employment opportunities and educational options provided them with hopes of mobility in the future.

Amar Pandey and his family lived in a rented room in a large house. His father works as an insurance agent. They come from the village of Gopalgunj, with poor rail and road connectivity, yet they visited their village every year. His father studied in Banaras and obtained his postgraduate degree in Sociology from the University. He looked for teaching position in school or college but was unsuccessful and now works in the private sector. He feels he could not secure a government job because of his weak social connections in the city. His teachers did not support him like his other batch mates from the city. His wife is from Azamgarh and is schooled till Class 10. She tells me that they use Bhojpuri when in village but not with their children. Amar's father is very strict against its use in their home in Banaras, so the children have not been able to pick up Bhojpuri at all.

Those employed in regular teaching positions of government schools or colleges are envied in a city with limited job opportunities. One such family is of Rajesh and Rakesh, the twin brothers, who are considered the brightest students of their class in the school. They are also more visible on other platforms of school activity through their participation in elocution, recitation, drama, etc.

Their family lives in a rented house. The family is nuclear and consists of their parents and an elder sister who is studying in an all-girls Hindi-medium college. Their father, Mr Jaiswal, is a school teacher of a government-aided Hindi-medium school. I met him during a parent–teachers meeting in the school and later in their home.

The father's family was settled in Banaras and made the transition from business to service category much earlier. He obtained his postgraduate education in Science from a College in the city and started working in a government school. His wife was only educated till high school level. This family, unlike those in private sector jobs, is supported by a regular monthly salary, but more importantly, is also equipped with better cultural resources for school education. Theirs is the only family that keeps some literary books at home and the father shows the same to me with great pride. In this family too, everyone used Banarasi at home, but the children speak among themselves in Hindi. It is important to note that unlike other parents, Mr Jaiswal, , who is also a teacher in a government school, claimed an ease of switch between not just Banarasi and Hindi but also between Hindi and English.

The city, as a centre of education and occupation, attracted migrants from nearby rural areas. From the aforementioned accounts it is not possible to generalise about social mobility patterns and educational pursuits in the city, as my interaction was limited to the families associated with a particular school. However, given the social profile of students of the school, we get glimpses of the shifts taking place in occupational structure, and educational values at family level of a very important segment, the informal working- class and the lower middle-class. What emerges very strongly from the aforementioned narratives is the difference of occupational background and parental education from similar class positions, and how these are connected to the ease with particular language varieties and preferences for others.

Language-use Dynamics and Mobility Strategies

There have been great changes in Banaras. Earlier everyone would use Bhojpuri. Only the educated few would speak in Khadi boli and very few, say 1 per cent would speak in English and even fewer spoke good English. Now, there is a trend towards increased use of Khadi boli by everyone and now young children are speaking in English.

Mr Jaiswal, father, 45

In all families, it is interesting to note the shifts in the language-use pattern particularly across generations. This shift is least visible in case of those engaged in saree trade. In almost every family the language of use at home or extended family is different from the standard Hindi or Urdu. This is common for both Hindu and Muslim families and those engaged in service and in business sectors.

The difference between speech practices of Hindus and Muslims is not clearly articulated, only vaguely spelt out in terms of use of address words like *ammi*, *abbu* and suffix like *ailu* (coming), *gailu* (going) among Muslims instead of *Ma*(mother), *Bauji* (father) and *aili* (coming), *gaili* (going) in case of Hindus.[3] Among the Ansari families, contrary to the common assumption that they have a distinct identity and language of their own, they claimed to use a hybrid variety which they call Urdu–Hindi, a form of language not very different from Banarasi used by Hindus engaged in the same occupation. Some even tried to apportion their language in terms of Hindi and Urdu words which is an indication of how categories of Hindi and Urdu continue to dominate mental conceptions, but not necessarily use of language, especially in mixed neighbourhood settings and in contexts of inter-community trade relations.

Another important point which needs to be emphasised is the difference between the speech of lower-middle-class Muslims from Urdu, the latter is valued much higher but is not practiced. 'Pure Urdu' is clearly seen as an exclusive cultural resource, but its practice is not necessarily increasing in families. Even in upper-middle-class families like that of Mr Bakhtiyar, the school principal, we saw a decline being experienced at use of Urdu among younger family generations. It is important to note that initially some Muslim students identified their home language to be Urdu in school context, but later at home they come across using Hindi–Urdu and some version of Banarasi. Urdu, at best, deserves respect, and is seen as being used by the maulvis or college-educated people. It is not to suggest that it serves no purpose in their cultural world. One mother suggested that she learnt some Urdu in her madrasa and she still values that knowledge and sometimes makes use of it but is incapable of using it in everyday practice.

On the other hand, use of standard Hindi is visibly on rise among families from both service- and business-class segments. Within one family one can notice the use of a mix-repertoire, particularly in joint families, where the young ones are actively encouraged to speak in Hindi while the elderly are still using the home variant. Along with the increasing preference for standard Hindi, one notices an emergent 'sense of shame' towards home languages, especially among those who are moving away from their traditional occupation and seeking jobs in more formal sectors. It is a trend which is sometimes pronounced vocally and sometimes expressed in subtle forms. It also has a gendered nature which has a bearing on educational strategies, a theme to be discussed in detail in later sections.

English, on the other hand remains a distant yet desirable cultural resource for most of them, and gradual shift towards use of standard Hindi in all the domains seems to be a stepping stone in that direction. In a nutshell, from being a city of differentiated language-use, we can see a gradual shift towards use of more standard languages. In north India, English and Hindi are considered as valued languages at the national and regional levels, respectively (Brass 2004; LaDousa 2005). However, in the lower-middle-income segments that this study caters to, the shift is more visible towards standard Hindi, even when a large population engaged in a very different occupational culture continues to organise their work-life without relying much on standard language cultures. The pronounced desire for a better future definitely seems to be connected with training in English, albeit only for those who are exploring their future in non-traditional industries and service sectors, and are already educationally and occupationally mobile.

Rather than the category of middle-class, the occupational cultures of a class segment is crucial to understand how the family's schooling decisions and experiences are mediated by ease of language-use. The ease of shift from home language to the standard language, as and when required, is a great resource as is evident in case of Mr Jaiswal's, the government school teacher. This resource came to full display during parents–teachers meeting in the school, in which families participated quite differently from one another.

It was quite common to see the elder brothers, young uncles and in few cases the elderly sisters to come to the schools for the meeting meant only for parents. This became subsequently clear that parents of a majority of students were constrained due to scarcity of time and the necessary confidence needed to encounter school personnel. Only some parents had ease in terms of communicating with teachers. Most disadvantaged on such occasions were the few women from Ansari families who turned up for the meeting. Their lack of familiarity with a coeducational school, made it really difficult for them to communicate with teachers.

Nevertheless, they collected report cards and listened to whatever the class teachers had to say and also shared a few concerns if the teacher was a fellow woman. People like Mr Jaiswal were exceptional; because being a teacher himself, he had a familiarity with school culture. He claimed a superiority to the young subject teachers, and would always prefer talking to the more senior ones and to the school Principal with whom he could interact in English. As we will discuss later in the book, this easy access to different repertoire of speech, has many pedagogic implications for children at school in many ways.

One can argue that the occupational cultures prevalent in the family of students and parental education have bearings on a family's engagement with formal schooling. Nevertheless, in all families, people make explicit reference to the hope of better learning, both in terms of schooling and of the valued languages, especially Hindi and English. Their educational strategies in this attempt are different from the overt forms of extensive parental work related to school education, as in case of professional-middle-class families, also termed as 'concerted cultivation' (Lareau 2002). The parenting strategies in these families are revealed in their efforts to make children more refined, keep them away from the morally and linguistically polluting effects of the surroundings, rationalising school-choice and in some cases, managing support system for schools.

Parenting Techniques, Educational Strategies and Status Management

In our discussion of occupational clusters, we find that the sites of learning can be plural for many families where the cultural ideals and values to be learnt in different domains can be contradictory in some cases, and consistent in others. Use of language is one area where the consistency and conflicts between school culture and family culture is clearly demonstrated in these families. Gendered division of space and labour is another area of activity which faces an inconsistency between norms and practices at home and in modern coeducational school. Both these areas have implications for relationship with formal schooling and call for critical investigations of parenting techniques in family setting. Existing literature in this field suggest that these techniques are more employed across class predominantly by women rather than men.[4]

One common concern which is expressed in all these families is the need to use a respectable language. Through the use of polite and gentle language one can earn social honour, but it entails other more significant benefits, not always clearly articulated in business-class families. In a changing economic context of occupational shifts to the new labour market which is more integrated with standard rather than native/localised/neighbourhood languages, switching to standard varieties is always more rewarding. At family level, we can discern a variety of educational strategies employed to achieve this end of learning better languages. In this project, mothers played a very important role by both carefully protecting their children from supposed contamination and regulating their language-use patterns. This strategy is closely linked with the sense of shame with local languages, which is expressed in a more pronounced way by the married women whose lives are invariably shaped by compulsory migrations to a new cultural world after marriage. Many of these women devalue local speech as impure and crude variants. They always projected a distance from such crude variety by claiming that it is spoken by someone else in the family or in the neighbourhood but not by them. These concerns add to their attempt at protecting their children and their speech from getting spoilt. Many women used terms like *dehati* and *latthamar* to describe the local language variety of Banarasi and complained that it is disrespectful, vulgar and abusive in nature. All of them favoured their language back home as being much softer in comparison to the city language.

This trend is also visible in case of Ansari women who articulate such disdain in a more nuanced form and resist their familial compulsions of extensive use of Julehti form of Banarasi. For example, Nargis's mother said that the Language-used by the Muslims in Koyala bazaar, where she lived before marriage, was a better variant of Urdu compared to the Alaipuria's language. She also complained about her inability to check the same in her family.

> We can't stop its use among our children because they keep listening to it everywhere. The women of the house, however, don't use abusive language the way men use it. They keep using *abe tabe* in their language.
>
> Nargis's mother, 32

Women in patrilocal settings are expected to adjust to a new setting and adopt new ways of living, speaking and being after marriage. The cracks within these adjustments become visible when they express their nostalgia for their maiden homes and disdain towards things at in-laws' family, including the speech style. The devaluation and sense of shame with local languages find an expression in their use of protective strategies in and outside the family.

Another polluting threat is posed by mohalla influence from which children's speech is to be protected and regulated. One major preventive mechanism is to keep their kids away from mohalla. The social space of mohalla or neighbourhood is associated with informal cultures such as playing at street, gossiping among peer groups in Banarasi and its other varieties. So the perceived threat of the mohalla influence is very pronounced among mothers, and is articulated through preference for and disdain for other language varieties. Everyone complained against their neighbourhood as lacking in mannerism and speech of educated people. Since people in mohalla speak in local language, they restrained their children to play with them. For example, one of them suggested that she regulates her children's play-habits by motivating them to play inside the house rather than go outside. She arranges indoor games for this purpose. The threat from mohalla also gets imbued with a status distinction which is caste based and gendered.

> We don't let them pick the local language from the neighbourhood children. They play inside the home only. The locality people are from *neech jat*. They are not concerned about education.
>
> —Shivani's mother, 38

Mohalla is otherwise viewed as a common space where different communities interact. This is also a space where common tongues such as Urdu–Hindi and Banarasi are used by older generations and the younger ones too. However, it is also seen as a space which posed threat to the security of grown-up girls. So the polluting threat of mohalla operated differently for boys and girls. For girls the protection is needed all the more because in their case the perceived threat of pollution is physical as well as symbolic. These regulations are selectively employed and are aimed towards a certain end.

For example, Nargis' mother cited security concerns for her grown-up daughter, and the distance from home as the main causes of her decision of changing the school for higher classes. She was concerned about the safety of her daughters because the second shift of her current school would close at 5 pm.

> 'I am very scared for my daughter. The school closes at 5 pm when it starts getting dark in winters. For girls, it is unsafe to come back to this area then. The other day, we heard that somebody's daughter had got kidnapped. Can't you ask the principal to change the timings of the school?

Several such strategies are used in all the families to control the socialising pattern of children in order to make them more refined and cultured. These processes were deeply gendered in nature, both in terms of direct engagement of mothers and in their being differentially targeted at boys and girls. Overall, these are processes of boundary-making through which a sense of high moral status is achieved among peers within community and sometimes beyond their immediate social universe.

Apart from these more generalised steps towards gaining high status, many families engaged themselves in more direct and specific forms of educational work for children. Steps are taken to ensure that for children right kind of learning support is provided at home. Some of these measures included finding a good school, using one's social network to help them in gaining admission and arranging for private tutors.

All these families provide for some or the other form of school support for the children, but only a few mothers suggested that they actually helped with their children's homework. This is because most of the mothers are not educated beyond secondary level of schooling, so they do not feel confident in helping their children. For example, Nargis's mother helps her daughter in homework but due to her limited exposure to schooling, she restricts herself to subjects such as Urdu and Hindi with which she has some familiarity through her madrasa education. For other subjects, a private teacher, a married Muslim woman is appointed who comes on a daily basis. Other families also report that they keep tutors to help their children in subjects such as Math and English. This trend is noticed in all types of families from both the communities and occupation types.

In comparison to arranging for a tutor, thinking about the right schooling for children is a more difficult exercise for which not all families are equally equipped with necessary resources. Majority of families have some kind of assessment of the overall schooling market in Banaras and the relative position of HKHSS. In Ansari families, with the least exposure to school education, only few family members like elder siblings showed familiarity about school position, while in service-class families and other families, the parents have a clearer position of the school vis-à-vis other schools, and have some ideas about the quality of teachers.

Madhuri's mother has a more comparative perspective of various schools in Banaras. Their two daughters studied in a private English-medium school with higher fee. In her view, the school had high standards as compared to any Hindi-medium school in the city but because of her husband's illness both the daughters were temporarily shifted to a Hindi-medium all-girls' school. However, soon enough, Madhuri was sent to HKHSS to improve on her studies.

> HKHSS is a better school because they are regular in taking classes. *Parhai* is good there. Teachers have some control over students and because of their influence the children finish their work in time.
>
> Madhuri's mother, 38

This account shows how financial contingencies take their toll on schooling experience of children even in families where mothers are relatively more engaged. It also suggests how notions about quality of schooling are constructed around medium of instruction, teacher regularity as well as projection of school discipline.

Most interesting accounts emerged from the joint family set-up of Saurabh, where each family unit came up with varying estimations of proper schooling. Saurabh's mother sent him to a neighbourhood school which was found to be bad in terms of discipline. In their quest for an English-medium school, his family finally settled on HKHSS because they thought it would be difficult for him to move too quickly to an all English-medium school. So HKHSS serves the purpose of a transit school before he could be sent to a better English-medium school.

His young aunt however, was more forthright in her complete endorsement of English-medium schools. All her children are being schooled in English-medium schools. The elder son is in St. Johns Mehrauli, a reputed convent school in the city, while the two younger daughters are attending Dynamic Public School, a more local English-medium school.

In such families, parents' choice of school depends on medium of schooling, along with the school's reputation. They believed that such choices are important in making a difference in the children's future. The younger generation of parents, themselves better educated than the older ones, believes that times have changed and now Hindi-medium schooling does not equip one for employment in contemporary times. Ironically, however, all these families settled on one school for their children's education which was Hindi medium. Also none of them claimed familiarity with English language on their own but were ready to invest in the same with the help of private tutors or coaching, and in some cases planning to educate their sons in English-medium school. The only exception with regard to use of English language was Mr Jaiswal, father of Rajesh and Rakesh, who also worked as a government school teacher. He is confident in his own usage of English and flaunted it well. His estimation of the current school was positive but with concern about the declining number of students and retirement of good old teachers from the school.[5]

I speak in English with the 'modernised' and those who can speak in it. Earlier, there was an English teacher (in HKHSS) with whom I would always talk in English. Now I often talk to Bakhtiyar ji. I keep discussing various affairs of the school with him.

The experiences and concerns of the Ansari family were of a different nature. While expressing their future plans for children, these families relied less on formal education alone and more on their own social connections in and outside trade. It was also because of a pragmatic awareness about the stiff competition for jobs in service sector, where they stand little chance from other families with greater investment in school education. Formal education at higher level, therefore, is not considered with much seriousness. Some form of skilled training which might be useful for trade is considered more reliable along with the social network necessary to access the same. For example, Karim's father is planning to send his son to Bangalore to stay with his cousin for a computer diploma course in desktop printing and publishing, in the hope that it may help him in future for using computers for designing.

In all these families, with varying forms of engagement with schooling for children, parents formulate the idea of good school in varying ways. For a majority of them, good school meant a formal site where the serious business of education goes on, which calls for investment, financial as well as social. Most of them, particularly mothers, assumed extra vigilant role for their children in matters of education by proscribing certain languages from their immediate use and making provisions for private tuitions. In some families, the same child was to learn Koran reading skills and spoken English at different time slots from different teachers. Other families were more invested in promoting the formal school culture in family and actively planned for their children's, particularly sons, future in the formal education market.

Conclusion

The aforementioned narratives suggest that these families constitute a heterogeneous category, tied in various ways to the informal economy of the city on one hand and formal schools on the other. One can find enormous variations in their social–economic–symbolic worlds which make them value different cultural resources depending on the context, namely, Banarasi or Urdu–Hindi for trade and for interaction with the elderly and the neighbours, but standard Hindi and English for their children's future. Among them, service industry jobs are socially more coveted but scarce in nature. The languages associated with such occupations are likewise considered high in prestige as compared to the popular languages, particularly in the wake of changing dynamics of labour market.

Following Bourdieu's conception of fields and capital, we argue that particular forms of languages and schools are valued differently from different vantage points in multiple fields (1985). Each of these families though attached to the same school, belong to different social–cultural worlds and had different ways of interacting with the school. Their expectations from and dependence on schooling, particularly in terms of upward social mobility, also differ from each other. Families with varying occupational backgrounds hold different levels of educational aspirations as is reflected in their strategies of education. Parenting, and particularly the social process of mothering, plays an important role in the social mobility and reproduction of class and status identities. Women from different families appear to be more sensitive to cultural differences of language-use and corresponding status boundaries. They also more actively participate in their children's educational goals. This is a peculiar characteristic of parenting strategies among middle-class families, which helps them succeed in reproducing their class and status privileges through intense investments of time and resources. The less successful ones in this picture, even when they are equally invested in parenting strategies, tend to come from families engaged in traditional occupational settings. It is in these setting that the values of education at family, community and workplace come in sharpest conflict with those of modern schooling.

In this study, Ansari families constitute such a contested sphere of learning for their children where women are expected to marry and men are expected to take reins of *karobar* (business). However, one can clearly identify a trend towards learning of standard languages in which modern schools play an important role. For many of these families there are transitions from madrasa to non-Islamic schools, all-girls' to coeducational schools, from less expensive government to more fee-charging, private schools and from Hindi-medium to English-medium schools. These transitions have a clear trajectory which can't be reduced to a singular narrative of modernisation of education and standardisation of speech. Rather the trend can be viewed as a net effect of all the steps taken to preserve, protect and promote certain cultures over others in a given context. Choosing a school like HKHSS is also to be understood in a similar context.

Nambissan, in her recent work (2010), has reviewed how different middle-classes in India make use of strategies to reap educational advantages. The lower middle-classes and the families of the first generation of school-goers also employ similar strategies and have aspirations towards acceptance into a wider prestige community through schools.

All these examples help us to understand the relations of the students' families and the communities with the school. Most of these families talked about the schools with reference to their children's futures. The school was viewed as creating opportunities for the future through better career prospects. It also provided hope for inclusion into a wider and more prestigious community through training in certain appropriate skills. One important skill for that is the command over the languages valued in the employment market as well as in the community in which membership is sought. In nation-states, these languages tend to converge into each other. In north India, such valued languages at the national and regional levels are English and Hindi, respectively (Brass 2004; LaDousa 2005). Some of the aforementioned families made explicit reference to the hope of learning these valued languages, especially English, through schools and modern education, in general. HKHSS, as a modern school, in its structure and practices, provides them one such space for learning these languages. In the next chapter, we will focus on the school space and processes of learning languages in the school.

Notes

1. Refer Kamat (1985), Waldrop (2004), Donner (2005) and Chand (2011) for study of middle-class strategies for schooling, which are primarily based on professional service class families in metropolitan settings. For notable exceptions to this trend, refer to David Drury (1993) and LaDousa (2014).
2. Arjun SenGupta committee report on Unorganised Sector (2007) estimates informal sector to employ 92 per cent of total workforce in India.
3. The respondents claim of such variations not just in the line of religion but also in terms of mohalla in the city. A detailed examination of the actual form of speech was beyond the scope of the current work. For details of Banarasi language-use, refer Simon (1998) and, refer to Goswami (2011) for multiple dimensions of Ansari identity.
4. Refer to Lareau (1985), Reay (1996), Ball (2003) Byrne (2006) and Nambissan (2010) for middle-class strategies and Panda (2015) for working class parenting strategies in Indian settings.
5. But very soon he shifted his sons Rajesh and Rakesh from HKHSS to a reputed convent school of the city. His daughter continued to study in the all-girls Hindi-medium school.

6

Boli ka Prasaar, Shuddhata ka Prachaar: Spreading Speech, Propagating Purity

Apan ma ke doodh me mati ka mehek me jo suwaad ba bidesi zubaan me na ba.

'The taste of mother's milk ... the fragrance of earth ... cannot be attained in a foreign language.'

Hariram, 64, Bhojpuri Compère and Songwriter

In the above quote, Hariram, a Bhojpuri writer, draws a striking imagery by referring to the authenticity of fragrance and flavours of nature in its pure form. For him, his language of the village—Bhojpuri, retains the purity, in comparison to which everything else fails. In my search for an authentic Bhojpuri voice in the city, I met him at his home. He comes from a village—Serwan, which is around 70 kms away from the city. After his education he gets a job with the All India Radio Station and settles down with his family in the city. His residence in the city for past 40 years does not seem to have affected his use of Bhojpuri. He also believes that it is possible to maintain Bhojpuri and Hindi simultaneously. However, it is pertinent to note that he is able to maintain both the languages because in All India Radio, he could use Bhojpuri in his professional capacity as an announcer. This overlap of personal and professional interests is very rare for people from other walks of life.

In a very different setting of school, one very senior teacher of HKHSS remarked while commenting on the various forms of Hindi used in Banaras

Boli ka prasar ghar se hota hai aur shuddhata ka prachar skool se hota hai.

'Common speech spreads from the home and purity is propagated by the school.'

Shankarlal, 59, Hindi teacher and School in-charge (till 2006)

In these words, the teacher summarises the different realms of activities for different forms of language. Here, home can be associated with boli or speech while school as an institution is assigned the task of maintaining *correctness* of form. In Bourdieu's seminal work (1976b) on language and symbolic power, schools and teachers are viewed as gatekeepers of the standard varieties of language and contribute to the tacit acceptance of the same by even those who might not be using it. In a social context where language markets are multiple and disparate, schools are sure to be implicated in cultural battles of different kinds. In this work, the focus is on teachers and students, their conception of languages and how they adhere to and negotiate the language curriculum in school. The languages which are part of the school curriculum in HKHSS are Hindi, English and Urdu but the school actors also make explicit reference to and make use of popular varieties in school. This chapter examines the processes through which the official language curricula is transmitted and negotiated at school. I am focusing on the construction of Hindi vis-à-vis popular varieties of Hindi, the growth of English and the receding extent of Urdu. It also explores how schooling processes contribute to the reproduction of dominant ideologies of class identity, with specific reference to the language economy of Banaras.

Shame, 'Culture of Education' and Notions of Correct Language

The understanding of parental concerns about good and bad forms of language help us to understand their strategies towards preservation and promotion of some over others in a family setting, where sources of learning are much more diffuse and plural. Similar distinctions between crude and refined forms of language figure more centrally in the teachers' discussion about language and students. They quite frequently refer to the different forms of languages used in the city, and have clearly set notions about their differential status. While describing their use, teachers also refer to the different occupational sectors, associating specific kind of language-uses to certain kinds of work.

We have seen how the cluster of Banarasi saree industry is based on a different system of production and functions on a different kind of skill set. In the accounts of teachers, Hindi, which is seen as associated with bureaucratic services in government sector, may not be used and valued in the same way in this industry. This is brought out in my interaction with several teachers, particularly Mr Samir, a teacher who also works in the industry to support his family. While comparing the two worlds, one of Banarasi saree and the other of the school, he brings in the notion of differential sense of honour in these different jobs. In his estimation, he enjoys a higher status in his job of being a school teacher. He also suggests how this sense of honour is closely related with the practice of positively or negatively valued language varieties in two different spheres of activities.

> *Mujhe bada ajeeb lagta tha jab bunkar log abe tabe ki bhasha bolte the ... Mai padhai ke mahaul se wahan adjust nahi kar pa raha tha... Yahi karan tha ki mai bijness me bahut jyada safal nahi ho paya ... Skool ki naukri se mera ghar nahi chal pa raha tha isliye maine bijness shuru kiya ... Ghar walon ka mujh par dabao bhi tha ... Skool ka kam mai pasand karta hu ... Bahut jaldi maine apne liye yahan ek jagah bana li ...*

> (I used to feel strange when weavers would use the language of 'abe, tabe'... Coming from the field of education, I was not able to adjust there... For this reason I have not been very successful in business... I started the business because I could not earn enough for my family from my job at the school... I also felt pressure from my family members... I like my job at the school... I have made my mark here very soon...)

Being a teacher in a school, a place where Hindi is spoken, he finds the kind of language spoken in the saree industry crude. This sense of honour, associated with a particular use of language, is then transposed to his personal experience and self-worth in his job as a teacher. It is interesting to note that, in comparison, even though teaching is a low-paying job, he feels more comfortable in it because of the sense of respectability attached to the school and the kind of Language-used in the school. Here, the school is seen as representing a training place for high culture among middle- and lower-middle-class families, and the language variety associated with it is considered more respectable than the other locally practiced varieties. Being a part of two different cultural worlds, he faces the dilemma of conflicting values.

Other teachers also referred to *Banarasi boli* as a crude form of language as compared to Hindi. Use of *Gaali galauj* (abusing/calling names) is reported to be a major feature of Banarasi by most of them. They also suggest that its use is declining with the wider spread of schooling and emphasis on the value of 'good' schooling in the city. The package of 'good schooling' usually includes training in standard languages such as Hindi and English. The school, as a workplace for adults and also as a place of learning for children, emerged as an institution associated with standard language. Official languages are usually taught in the school and used in formal sectors of economy and in government offices. In this sphere, the use of Hindi bestows the social prestige that comes from its being a part of the formal sector, the modernising nation-state, and the new forms of service, professions and industry, rather than being part of the older handicrafts- and pilgrimage-based work of Banaras. The linkages of education with the labour market make school Hindi a coveted language associated with education and employment opportunities, over other varieties of Hindi.

On the other hand, the language of the informal economy which is not strongly tied with schools, is the language which brings 'shame'. The sense of shame is also reported in context of a gradual move towards Hindi in the households where earlier the language of common use would have been Banarasi–Bhojpuri. Describing the overall shift towards Hindi in the city, the school teacher talked about the feeling of shame with the use of local varieties.

Parents apne baccho ko acche skool me bhejna chahte hai jisse bolchal me fark aya hai ... Gaali galauj me kami ayi hai ... Ab teen saal ke bacce bhi khariboli bolne lage hai ... Pahle Banarasi me hi sab bacche bolte the tab ise bolna bura nahi mana jata tha... Par aaj padhe likhe logon, 'next generation' ke samne ham nahi chahenge ki mata pita ya bacche Banarasi me bole... Banarasi me ab jhenp shuru ho gayi hai... Ham sahaj nahi rahenge...

(Parents want to send their children to good schools, which has brought a change in general speech ... The use of slang has decreased ... Now, even three-year-olds have started speaking Khariboli ... Earlier, everyone used Banarasi ... Then it was not considered bad, but today we would not like it if our parents or children speak in Banarasi before those who are educated and belong to the 'next generation'... Now, shame is there in Banarasi ... We won't be comfortable ...)

—Samir, Mathematics teacher, HKHSS

Apart from the decline in the practice of a language, it also suggests a decline of the cultural traits usually associated with it. The fact that the speaker doesn't feel comfortable in his/her own language before the educated others, suggests that there is a sense of shame vis-á-vis the new community of the educated 'next-generation' people.

Amidst such changes in language-use pattern in the city, teachers construct their notions about students, their families and engage in tacit classificatory processes. Some anthropological studies of literacy practice have demonstrated how different communities have different socialisation patterns, and how these are not valued similarly in school (Collins 1988; Heath 1983). These studies do not necessarily assume a Deficit-model to explain difference in pattern of language-use on the basis of class; rather, they provide thick descriptions of language socialisation process at home and in schools. Recent approaches have more clearly moved beyond the assumptions of a Deficit-model implicit in the older studies, but continue to uphold the significance of teachers' evaluation of students' social identities through labelling, tracking and stereotyping practices (Reay 2010). The teachers in HKHSS are also engaged in similar acts of labelling and classifications. They hold opinions about students' speech pattern and believe that only few students come from family backgrounds where 'respectable form of speech' is used. In fact, they quite actively indulge in identifying students by their use of language. This emerges as a common trend in all kinds of teachers irrespective of their subject expertise.

Amar: *School me to har tarah ke bacche aate hai par ye school me restriction laga hua hai isliye wo sirf Khariboli hi bolte hai ... Otherwise wo bhi jab school se bahar nikalte hai to wo bhi Bhojpuri jo Banarasi–Bhojpuri hai wo hi use karte hai ...*

(**Amar:** All kinds of students come to this school, but because of the restrictions they speak only Khariboli ... Otherwise, when they get out of the school, they also use Bhojpuri, which is Banarasi–Bhojpuri ...)

Dhiren: *Yahan jo karib 80 per cent bacche hai wo local Banaras ke hai kyuki high school tak hai to Banaras ke hi bacche hai aur wo Bhojpuri ka use bharpur karte hai...ghar aur bahar ... School me teachers ke sath jo hai wo Khariboli ka use karte hai ... lekin wo bhi shudhta utni nahi ho pati ... 95 per cent shudh karne ki koshish karte hai par usme Bhojpuri ka put rah jata hai ... angrezi bolne ka koshish karte hai ... lekin 95 per cent ke bad jo 5 per cent bachta hai usme Bhojpuri ka put milta hai ...*

(**Dhiren:** 80 per cent of the kids here are local residents of Banaras because the school is upto the high school level ... and they use Bhojpuri liberally ... at home and outside ... In the school and with the teachers they use Khariboli but they cannot make it pure ... Their efforts at purity succeed 95 per cent but the effect of Bhojpuri remains ... They also try to speak English ... but the remaining 5 per cent is influenced by Bhojpuri ...)

For Dhiren and Amar, Hindi/Khariboli and Bhojpuri represented two major linguistic markers of the students. In the above discussion, it is implied that if it was not for school environment, students would be using their own language of home which is Bhojpuri and not Hindi. It is also suggested that the students invariably fail in their efforts to conceal the effect of Bhojpuri in their language-use.

All the older teachers mention one or the other way of identifying students through their language-use, in terms of their class, regions, occupations and castes positions. For example, Abdul, the Urdu teacher in HKHSS, employed an elaborate classification scheme by identifying students' family occupation, class, religion and location in Banaras through their language-use. In his estimation, the majority of Bhojpuri–Banarasi-speaking students are lower- and middle-class Hindus. Then, there are the Banarasi–Julehti-speaking Ansari Muslims, a small proportion of Hindi-speaking middle-class Hindus and very few students from Urdu-speaking Muslim-elite families.

According to the teachers' classification, there are two languages used by the majority of students. One is Bhojpuri or Banarasi–Bhojpuri, used by the majority of the Hindus in Banaras, especially those living in the old commercial–residential settlement, pakka mahal, of Banaras. The other group which he describes in much detail is the Ansari weavers. Their language is sometimes called Julehti or the language of the Julahas. In his view, it is closer to the language spoken by the Agrawals, the Hindu merchant caste, because of their common connection with the saree industry. In his view, the influence of Urdu is negligible among the students. *Khalis* (pure) Urdu is spoken by very few Muslim families in the Chowk and Dalmandi areas. Abdul took pride in belonging to one such family in which Urdu is still practiced.[2] Samir, the teacher in HKHSS who also works in the saree industry, however, disagrees with Abdul's contention that the Hindus and Muslims share their speech. He believes that although mutually intelligible, there exist some difference in the varieties used by the Muslims and the Hindus in the same trade.

Most of the teachers, thereby, constantly engage in identification and classification of students on the basis of their family backgrounds, in terms of occupation, religion and *mohalla* location. On the basis of their discussions and through my interactions with family members, we can estimate the relation of the social boundaries of class, occupational clusters and religion with cultural boundaries of language in case of this school and the school population in the following diagram. In Figure 6.1, both standard and popular language varieties have been arranged on the basis of class and occupational background of people and religion.

Figure 6.1
Schematic Representation of Language Boundaries by Class, Occupational Groups and Religion

Class/Occupation	Hindu	Muslim	Prestige
Upper-middle-class Middle-class Cultural elite	Hindi	Urdu	High
Lower-middle-class Petty Businessmen Working-class	Bhojpuri/Theth/Banarasi Urdu–Hindi/Hindi–Urdu Julehti/Dehati		Low

Source: Self-drawn by author.

Common perception of the prestige of language is also given. It comes across that the languages which are considered high in prestige, are most frequently associated with either upper-middle-class or middle-class service professionals who can use Hindi in their everyday interactions effortlessly or as associated with the cultural elite. The latter association is usually made to distinguish the superiority of some Muslim families over others in terms of their access to cultural resources, because we have seen how the two families in the school which claim to use Urdu are seen as coming from very different class background, but both are united by their access to a culturally valued resource. On the other hand, languages associated with the lower-middle-class groups, both Hindus and Muslims, and with petty businessowners are considered low in prestige.

It is interesting to note the various ways of boundary-making even as people describe their imprecise non-standard variety of home languages. Depending on the context, boundaries get drawn or redrawn to highlight or mitigate locational-, regional-, religious-, generational- and class-based differences. Quite often the boundaries overlapped and sometimes are drawn quite sharply against others. There are regional variations in the speech variety used at home. So quite often in a family, the language varieties of the wives differ from that of their husband's family. There is also an awareness of speech variations even within the city. Such as how Banarasi varies from mohalla to mohalla, namely, how Ansaris from two different settlements Lallapura and Alaipura, speak differently.

All these boundary making exercise reinforce some classifications while transcend the others, depending on the context. Here, we are more concerned with classificatory schemes of teachers which also have implications for students' learner identity in school context. It is important to distinguish between learner identity and social identity of a student and one need not be collapsed into another (Reay 2010). However, as studies conducted from school and home mismatch framework argue, teachers quite often mix these two and label students as 'good' or 'bad' on the basis of their social class (Lareau 2004). But as Reay (2010) argues, social identities cannot be neatly transposed onto learner identities, there being varying degrees of inconsistencies and overlap between the two.

In this school, teachers talk about students, reflect their assumptions about the students' family backgrounds and, inadvertently, connect the same to their estimation of a student's performance and suitability/adaptability in the school. This discussion most frequently emerge during discussions of academically 'poor' students but also emerge, though relatively less frequently, in discussion of 'good' students. The following two excerpts indicate how teachers share their perceptions about business families and service background families.

Most of the business-class people cannot spare much time on the studies of their children. They can afford to keep tutors but they don't know about their children's progress.

—Reeta, 42, English teacher

Yes, parents' education and profession influence the behaviour and the languages used by the children. The children of educated parents, who are concerned, tend to do well. Take the example of Prakriti, who is the first-rank holder in her class. Her father works in the press. One can see the traits of willingness to learn and improve, and the competitiveness in Prakriti. Though her family is not in a financially very good condition, they have the culture of education. Then there is a daughter of a computer engineer in the school. She is also doing well.

—Reema, 35, Social Science teacher

The first example, while devaluing the 'business-class people' also mocks at their inability to convert their economic capital or wealth into educational credentials. The second passage alludes to an important notion of 'the culture of education'. The 'culture of education', is seen as related with fathers' occupations, that is, middle-class white-collar jobs. When the same teacher is asked if these good students are always from service background families, she answered in the affirmative, after some thought. Then, she adds that some students from business families are also cultured such as some girls from the Marwari community. They know how to behave. She is critical of the families coming from the Yadava caste, saying that they do not use proper language. Teachers' construction of learner identities of students are coloured by their estimations of students' occupational background and, sometimes, through their caste and community affiliations.

In both the cases, there are common assumptions and expectations from students coming from middle-class 'educated' families and students coming from 'business-class' families. In this context, business-class families refer to families employed in traditional occupations in Banaras, such as the saree and allied industries, and other self-employed petty businessmen.

Construction of Hindi vis-á-vis 'Local' Varieties in the School

The school alters the language practices of students to some extent, and the majority uses Khariboli at school, even if they use some other variety outside the school. However, their Khariboli is not as pure as it should be. There is a notion of *shuddhata* or purity in the language. The influence of Bhojpuri is seen as bringing impurity into Hindi. In the official discourse of the school, varieties like

Banarasi/Bhojpuri are seen as deviations from Hindi and are to be kept at a distance from schools.

Defining School—Hindi

The Hindi teachers define appropriate Hindi in terms of the grammatically correct use of the language. They observe that the practice of Hindi in everyday life in Banaras is heavily influenced by the local varieties. They often point out the errors and mistakes committed by students because of the influences of the languages used outside the school. Such errors are either grammatical in nature or are in the form of an illegitimate mix of sounds and words with Hindi. There is a complaint that such influences are noticeable in the speech of the students. A female Hindi teacher of the school considered the local influence on the students' speech as 'backward'.

Jab hum skoolon me padhate hain, tab bachho ka jo ghar ka class hai kahin na kahin ubhar ke aa hi jata hai ... Kyuki jab kapiyan check karte hain, to kai bar likh dete hai jaise ki 'ketna parha hai' ... 'ae' ki matra aur is tarah ke local shabd bhi unke aate hai ... Jaise ki bahut shudh Khariboli me wo kabhi kabhi Bhojpuri ka luk de dete hai ... Mera matlab Banarasi–Bhojpuri ... Jo sahee nahi lagta hai ... Khariboli hai, padhai ke purpose se to khadi hi honi chahiye usme local shabd acche nahi lagte ... Thoda sa backward lagta hai ... Jitna Hindi unhe shudh likhna chahiye utna shudh wo likhte nahi hai...

—Shashi, 35, Hindi teacher, HKHSS

(When we teach in schools, then the family backgrounds of the children come up in some way ... Because when we check copies... (they) sometime write 'ketna parha hai'... The use of the sound 'ae' and similar local influences are seen... For example, in pure Khariboli, they will give the impression of Bhojpuri ... I mean Banarasi–Bhojpuri... which does not look good ... Khariboli is meant for education, so it should be used like that ... There should not be any use of local words ... It seems a bit backward ... They don't write as pure Hindi as they should ...)

She distinguishes between the varieties such as Banarasi–Bhojpuri and Khariboli, the latter is referring to the appropriate version of Hindi to be used in the school while speaking and writing. Again, the presence of influences from the former is seen as deviation from Hindi. Such influences indicate backwardness, while the Hindi which is the school language is a symbol of modern education, and thereby, of progress. Her definition of the appropriate Hindi, therefore, is contingent on the identification and devaluation of the local influences of Banarasi–Bhojpuri. This form of Hindi then becomes the norm to be followed in various activities of the school.

Textbooks and Classroom Norms of Hindi

A school is one of the institutions that helps in constructing the norm of Hindi through its curriculum and practices. There are several other institutions such as literary bodies and textbook committees which have played a role in setting the norm for Hindi in pre- and post-independence India (King 1989; Rai 2002). It has been argued that they have helped in constructing a norm of Hindi that tends to be a highly Sanskritised version. In the case of Uttar Pradesh, Sanskrit is a necessary component of the Hindi curriculum in school education. We know how textbooks play disproportionately important roles in Indian schools. The kind of Hindi that sets the norm for school practices is the textbook Hindi which tends to be highly Sanskritised. Some of the older teachers did express concern over changes in the content of the curriculum during the course of their teaching careers.

> The course in Hindi has changed. In our times, it was interesting but now it has become dull and uninteresting. We would read Tulsidas, Kabir and Soor in our course. But now, since 2000–2001, we have new books in which there is more emphasis on *azaad nagma* and *mukta chhand*, or free verse.
>
> —Jafar, 52, Principal, Municipality School

Alok Rai (2002) in his *Hindi Nationalism* has described the gradual decline of Brajbhasha as the major language for writing poetry in Hindi, when Khariboli was established as the standard language of Hindi prose. The Khariboli form of Hindi excessively relied on Sanskrit root words and set the norms of textbook writing for schools.

In one of the Hindi classes that I attended, a poem, *Shakti aur Kshama* (power and tolerance), by Ramdhari Singh Dinkar is being discussed.

Kshama, daya, tap, tyaag, manobal
Sabka liya sahara
Par nar vyagh Suyodhan tumse
Kaho kahan kab haara?
…
Sahansheelta, kshama, daya ko
Tabhi poojta jag hai
Bal ka darp chamakta uskey
Peechhey jab jagmag hai.
…

Forgiveness, sympathy, sacrifice, grit,
Everything was tried
But fiendish Suyoudhan
Could not be defeated.
…
Tolerance, forgiveness, sympathy
Is valued in the world
Only when it is backed by
The glory of power.
…

The text quoted here is an example of literary Hindi and needs to be explained by the teacher in its proper context. But, it is only a particular variety of literary Hindi replete with words which are highly Sanskritised such as *kshama* (forgiveness), *nar vyagh* (tiger), *darp* (pride), etc. The Hindi teacher identifies another text which she finds unsuitable for children in terms of the use of the language. But, these texts provide the model or norm of Hindi to be followed in the school. We have discussed in previous sections, how the drive towards the use of the Khariboli form of literary Hindi from the use of Brajbhasha was an institutionalised attempt in north India. Interestingly, one can also see countercurrents of a movement towards the more 'rustic' use of language in recent times (Dalmia 2003). Krishna Kumar (2001), in his analysis of classroom Hindi has argued that the language in textbooks is set with a political agenda such as routinely portraying the Muslims as foreign within an official realm of secularism. Such texts, because of their remoteness from a child's lived experiences, fail in rousing the child's imagination in terms of creative use of language.

Classroom Order and the Learning of Hindi

The process of the normalisation of Hindi is realised through several mechanisms as part of the routines of the school. For example, in many of the Hindi classes that I attended, reading out extracts from the textbooks was an important ritual followed by both teachers and students. A student is made to stand in the classroom and he/she reads aloud a passage from the given text. The teacher often corrects or helps the student to read out the difficult parts. It was a matter of pride for many students to do this exercise with a minimum of interruption from the teacher and fellow students.

In another Hindi class, the teacher, Nirmala, begins the class by explaining the meaning of the text and asking the students to write down the same in their 'rough' notebook. She reads out a couple of lines and then explains the same. The students look very anxious in their attempt to note down every single word uttered by her. They get confused when she changed the sentences while repeating. She scolds them all for writing too slowly. There was some confusion among the children about what to write when she explained and dictated simultaneously.

Explanation and dictation are two different processes which are learnt by students during the course of their schooling. But in practice, they have little distinction as students are anxious to note down every word uttered by the teacher. Reading the textbooks and explaining the content are an integral part of the classroom teaching of Hindi. In all the classes, the onus is on the teacher to explain the content to the students. The teachers take complete command of the content by reading the passage, identifying the difficult words for the students and simultaneously explaining the content. Explanation often means paraphrasing the textbook's content in a language which they thought was easier for the students and suitable for a Hindi class.

Here, writing or taking down notes is an activity that keeps the students engaged and maintains order in the class. The student–teacher relations are formal and impersonal. The teacher and students are minimally engaged with the text in this process of learning, in which the teacher gives the readymade explanation and the student notes it down accurately. In some classes, students are noting down all the sentences spoken by the teacher, verbatim. During this ritual, students are easier to manage, but remain completely passive in the classroom interaction. Rarely does one ask a question about the subject.

During the same class, though the text referred to a famous episode from the epic *Ramayana*, there is only a casual reference made to it. The students made references to the ongoing TV serial *Hanuman*, but it is not taken up further by the teacher. Time is a precious resource and is not to be wasted on distractions from the main text which has to be covered during the allotted time period. The issue of pedagogy and identity are also linked in a crucial way in which an essential component of learning a language is to encourage independent thinking in the same language, which is completely missing from a majority of the classrooms here. We hardly see criticism as an accepted part of the school's discourse. Rather, there is an overt emphasis on the need to maintain order. The two activities carried out in the language classroom are reading out aloud from the textbook and learning and writing the difficult words and their meanings.

Reading in a flow is a skill which is a necessary component of all language classes. It is also used in various ways in the class-room setting. It can be used to maintain order in the class, along with other more direct techniques of controlling the students. In such cases, reading ceases to be an activity of learning to use and appreciate the language. The following scenario describes the same teacher taking her next Hindi class:

> The teacher heads for her class upstairs. This is a bigger and noisier classroom. I come in and sit on one of the side benches, which some students had put near their benches to keep their bags on. They keep moving from their places and are curious to know what I am writing. A wooden duster is continuously used to tap on the table and to keep the class in order. Class monitors have to struggle and quarrel with other students. When the teacher enters the class, she cautions the students to be quiet and the class continues in the same noisy mode. Some students continue to crack jokes and quarrel with each other. One student starts reading aloud from a story-book. Once the reading starts, the class comes back to order. But at the slightest pretext, they start shouting again. The student keeps reading even when the teacher leaves the classroom to talk to another teacher who is at the door. When the chapter is over, the students are confused as to what to do next. They get back to making noise and playing pranks on each other. She comes back to the class and asks them to write the 'word-meanings' of Chapters 9 and 10 as home-work. The class ends there.

In the aforementioned episode, the students are managed in a language classroom without any engagement with the Hindi language, as such. No attempt is made by the teacher to make the students interested in the text. Students, consequently, remained detached from what was taught in the class while blindly following the ritual of reading. The mechanical practice of reading in this case only achieved temporary order and is reduced to being a substitute for supervisory authority. Students also tend to learn the passive acceptance of authority. In the process, language-learning is also reduced to a mere following of the teacher's directions and the completion of the given task. Any creative engagement with the language is rarely seen, neither on the part of the teacher nor that of the students.

Normalisation of Hindi

Reading aloud is also rewarded at other platforms of the school. During school events, students are often required to make a presentation in the form of elocution, recital of a poem, etc. When the teachers are given the task of preparing students for the occasion, they prefer students who are good at reading and speaking. Here, being good at reading not only requires the ability to speak in a flow, but also the ability to speak the correct version of Hindi. Speaking Hindi free from the influence of local varieties is continuously rewarded during the routines of the school. Such a conception of Hindi is also internalised by the students in their ideas about formal school practices like evaluation. They have an idea of what was the appropriate and desirable way of writing an answer that could be rewarded.

Me: *Tum log jab sawal ka jawab likhte ho to kaun si bhasha me likhte ho?*
(When you write answers what language do you use?)

Shivam: *Hindi me, aur baki subject jaise English, Maths, Computer ye sab English me likhte hai.*
(We write subjects in Hindi and, English, Math and Computer, we write in English.)

Me: *Kabhi apne ghar ki bhasha apne skool ki copy me likhte ho?*
(Do you ever write in your home-language in your copy?)

Rajesh: *No, Ma'am.*

Me: *Kyu?* (Why?)

Rajesh: *Nahi likhte hai wo kyuki wo hota hi nahi hai … matlab … jaisa ab prashna hoga waise hi na likhenge.*
(We don't write because … it is not done … meaning … we will write according to the question, won't we?)

Prem: *Kyuki ghar ki language me koi koi me bahut antar hota hai.*
(Because in some home-languages, there is huge difference from the school language)

Me: *Kya antar hota hai?*
(What kind of difference is there?)

Prem: *School me ekdum sahi prakar se answer likhte hai...*
(In school, we write in the correct way.)

Nitin: *Aur agar Bhojpuri bhasha likhenge to number kat jayega. Aur
number kat jaye ga to ... jitna bhi result hoga sabme fail hi hoga.*
(And if we write Bhojpuri, then our marks will be cut. And if that
happens, no matter what the result, we will all fail.)

The legitimisation of a language seems complete when the practitioners of other languages themselves believe that the right way
to use a language is the one which the school prescribes. Here,
both the students as well as the teachers can be seen using different
varieties in different domains, but in the formal school space, they
intuitively shift to the 'standard' variety of Hindi. The language gets
normalised when it seems normal to use a certain variety of language over others. In the aforementioned statements, it is obvious
to the students that one is normally supposed to write the answer
in the same language in which the question is framed. The obvious-
ness and discomfort that ensues when he is questioned, indicates
a similar assumption of normality. And the student also realises
the possible consequences of not adhering to the school norms of
language, that is, of failing in the examination. What remains un-
obvious is the fact that in the process of normalisation, the process
of marginalisation is completely overlooked. Here, it is the 'local'
influence which has to be discarded. There are punitive sanctions
attached to not using the correct language.

Banarasi/Bhojpuri Sub-culture in the School

So far, the school space is seen as mainly associated with Hindi
and not other locally used varieties. Hindi, in the aforementioned
examples, gets defined by differentiating it from the local varieties.
When I ask Ramsaran about Banarasi, he advises me to go to the

ghats, the famous riverfront of the city and the tea stalls because these are the places where it thrives. Banarasi, referring to both the natives of the city and the language, is associated with *mauj* or a carefree attitude, whereas the school is an institution which disciplines and trains. So, it was 'natural' that Banarasi cannot and should not exist in schools. It is the regionally and nationally recognised official language Hindi which is considered appropriate for schools.

At this point we may recall the useful distinction between what Woolard (1985) describes as the realm of 'status', gained by standard languages and the realm of 'solidarity', which is more associated with social traits of cultural proximity, likeability and trust. Both the realms of language-use are considered important in social interactions depending on the context and domain of language-use. Annamalai (2001) has also referred to separate domain of language-use for formal and informal ways of speaking. This different way of speaking in different occasions and locations is frequently employed by senior school teachers to justify their own contradictory positions with respect to the popular variety of languages. Many senior teachers in school settings accept that they practice Bhojpuri language at home and how its use is important in certain contexts. However, their role in school demands that they are seen as practicing and enforcing use of standard language alone.

> It is important to respond to people in their own languages. We have taught our children that they should speak to their grandparents in Bhojpuri. I myself speak to the school staff in their language, that is, Banarasi. It makes everyone feel nice…
> —Shankarlal, 59, Hindi teacher and School in-charge (till 2006)

Here, Shankarlal is reiterating the home–school divide that separates his practice of Bhojpuri and Hindi. There is a tacit suggestion that it is the school staff of non-teachers, cleaners, peons, etc., who use the more local varieties, and who sometimes need to be communicated in the same way. The dominant culture of the school remains attached to standard Hindi, as seen in the classroom practices. However, the conceptions of separate domains are not wholly useful in explaining the practice of non-standard varieties in school, if domain is understood only in terms of spatial separation. Quite often the same school space is shared by both the varieties of languages.

In spite of the initial denials by the teachers, it is quite common to see the acceptance of the co-existence of popular varieties of Hindi at some school platforms, mostly in informal and at times in formal platforms. Students use these languages in informal contexts to express feelings of closeness with their friends and show a special kind of bond which cannot be expressed in Hindi. Among students, such moments usually occur when there is an absence of supervision by the teachers such as during fights or when among close friends. These are moments when norms of standard language are relaxed.

For example, during a couple of the free classes which I attended, they have storytelling and joke-sharing sessions. Very soon, when everyone is at ease, the students start sharing jokes in creative ways by elaborating small episodes and adding animated expressions, and by changing the voice and tone of their speech. One common strategy employed by students to evoke laughter, is by mixing their speech with some expressions from Bhojpuri. Such performances are always appreciated by the entire class and rewarded with a heavier applause.

The use of non-standard varieties was also observed in the informal spheres, particularly in the absence of supervision by the teachers. However, on some occasions, even teachers figure centrally in the talks about use of Bhojpuri and Banarasi in school.

Me: *School me Bhojpuri kab bolte ho aur kiske sath?*
(When do you speak Bhojpuri and with whom?)

Shivam: *Jyadatar ladai me* (chuckles)
(Mostly during fights)

Me: *Ladai ho jati hai to Bhojpuri me bolte ho?*
(Do you speak it when you fight?)

Shivam: *Han.*(Yes)

Me: *Aur tum?*(And you?)

Rajesh: *Jyadatar friends ke sath ... Ma'am kabhi kabhi ...*
(Mostly with friends ... actually sometimes ...)

Me: *Aur teachers dantate nahi hai Bhojpuri bolne se?*
(Don't your teachers scold you for that?)

Rajesh: *Ma'am ye bhi ek bhasha hi hai.*
(It is also a language)

Prakriti: *Ma'am wo kya dantenge? Wo apas me khud hi baat karte hai Bhojpuri me...*
(Ma'am, how can they scold us? They themselves use Bhojpuri among themselves...) (laughs with others).

Me: *Tumne suna hai?*
(Have you heard them?)

Prakriti: *Yes.*

Here, the students are admitting to their use of Banarasi/Bhojpuri among friends and during fights among friends. They are also aware of the use of the same by their teachers. In the previous section, we have seen similar awareness on part of students about the norm of Hindi to be followed in the formal school discourse of teaching/leaning and evaluation. Here, they seem to be aware of another discourse of practicing local variants in the school. They also appear relaxed about the possible threat of being caught, because they know it is not going to cause any serious trouble if it is kept outside the formal sphere of school functioning. These languages are definitely very popular and are used for completely different reasons than the standards. In contrast to standard Hindi which is used, as per students' accounts, for attaining high scores in subjects; these are used as expression of intimacy, trust, fun and solidarity.

One particular episode in school is quite pertinent to bring the element of solidarity to its most embodied form in school platform, in full public display. During special occasions it is quite common and normal for students to prepare for some sort of folk performance, in the form of folk songs or devotional songs. In fact school culture is such that these two themes are most preferred by the teachers apart from patriotic songs. For devotional and folk songs, verses composed in the *bhakti* tradition of poetry[3] and written in popular folk languages such as Brajbhasha, Rajasthani and Bhojpuri are most popular and extensively used in formal school platforms.

During Children's Day celebrations on 14 November,[4] a number of programmes are being organised by the teachers with the help of students in a hall which is also used as a classroom for Class 9. The hall is too small to accommodate all the students, so the seating arrangements are made by carpeting the floor on which all the students were made to sit. The teachers are offered chairs and they sat near the other end of the hall, facing the children. The space between the teachers and students is used as the stage for performances by the students.

The programme starts with the delivery of a lecture by Shankarlal sir on Jawaharlal Nehru and his love for children. The students are not so involved in the speech and give a customary clapping at the end of speech. This is followed by a *bhajan* (a devotional group song) sung by the students and accompanied by their music teacher on the harmonium. Thereafter, a student from Class 8 recites a poem on Nehru.

Ek din sapne me mere chacha Nehru Aye
Maine poochha chacha se tumhe kyun Gulaab hi bhaaye.
(One night uncle Nehru visited me in dreams
I asked him why he likes only roses)

The poem is recited with a lot of emotion and is quite well received by the students through claps. However, the most interesting and exciting programme of the day comes towards the end, in the form of a folk song performance by the students themselves.

Bada neek laage nainan tore babua ...
(Child! Your eyes look so beautiful ...)

The song is melodious and its sweet lyrics immediately held the students' and teachers' attention in a visible manner. The audience got so animated and engrossed in the performance, that they start participating in it by matching the rhythm of the song with their claps. Soon, even some people from the audience started singing along and the teachers also join in by swaying their bodies and clapping together. With this performance, the programme comes to a happy end and all the teachers congratulate the team members for their performance.

This was one of the few occasions at a formal platform in which both the students and teachers break the strong norms of hierarchical order, which is usually followed in the classroom situation. A rare occasion, when for a while, the students and teachers both participate at equal level by singing together spontaneously and not as part of a necessary order. The song definitely triggered a level of intimacy and a sense of solidarity among all the participants. In this sharing, apart from music, the lyrics of the song and use of terms such as *neek* (beautiful) and *babua* (child) must have played a very important role. Through this episode we can decipher a positive meaning attached to the practice of Bhojpuri in the school space, in which both teachers and students see these varieties as the languages of intimacy and fun, suggesting a close bonding and solidarity which is usually not seen in the formal domains of the school.

The notion of solidarity has been employed by Woolard (1985) who argued that alternative language markets develop not because it provides a space free from 'norms'. Rather these develop and flourish because of the presence of a different kind of 'community pressure', perhaps of peers in informal contexts. She refers to this aspect of language response, as solidarity, in which the traits of likeability, attractiveness, sense of humour, openness, trustworthiness and generosity are valued more. Thereby, she makes a distinction between affective market of solidarity and status market of a language.

These experiences suggest that the other varieties like Banarasi and/or Bhojpuri do exist in the school and tend to appear in moments and spaces away from the requirements of the formal discourse of the school. Sometimes, these appeared even in formal situations like official celebration of Children's Day where performance occurred in a controlled situation, nevertheless, transcended the embodied notions of formality.

Both the students and teachers[5] can be seen as participants of the presence and development of a counterculture to the dominance of standard Hindi in the school. It is clear from their examples, that the use of Banarasi represents moments of fun and close bonding among teachers and students alike. Banarasi is also seen as a popular and more intimate way of connecting with friends. Its presence, in the unsupervised quarters of the school, suggests an attempt to escape the formality and discipline of the dominant discourse of the school.

Urdu in a Modern School

We have examined how HKHSS negotiates official and market ideologies of modernity in its offering of Urdu in the main syllabus, and how Urdu is now a language of cultural distinction among the sparse Muslim elite and Islamic religious leaders. A modern school like HKHSS can offer Urdu only as an optional subject (refer Chapter 4). The school principal finds merit in offering Urdu to students with the conviction that it is a living literary tradition which needs promotion, despite neglect by the state. However, his modern outlook fails to imagine a creative way of introducing it in the school, rather than as just another optional subject which attracts limited students.

Urdu is offered as an optional subject in the school along with Drama. This arrangement arbitrarily divided the students. It was, in principle, open for all the students. However, it failed to attract students from the Hindu community. Abdul, the Urdu teacher, expresses his despair on the decline of Urdu in general, and also specifically in the case of the school. He believes that Urdu calls for a lot of effort and time in learning, which is not permitted by the tight school schedule. The school has allocated only 3 periods every week to the subject, which in his view is grossly insufficient for learning Urdu. Moreover, the school, due to its space constraints, does not have any designated classrooms for optional subjects like Urdu. So, Urdu classes are held wherever the teacher could find adequate space, sometimes in one of the office rooms and sometimes in the music room.

He also stressed that the students, though belonging to Muslim families, do not have the environment of Urdu at home, which makes it even more difficult for them to learn Urdu. He also believes that learning of Urdu in its valued form is increasingly becoming difficult in modern schools. He contrasts the logic and pedagogy of learning in modern schools with that of the community life. Learning within a community in close proximity of one's close kin-groups, nurtures a tradition of learning which is accessible to people like him and Mr Bakhtiyar. It is termed as *Taleem* which follows a different tradition from that of modern institutions. The Urdu teacher of the school, who writes Urdu prose and poems (in the Devanagari script) for magazines, stressed the point that the legacy of Urdu is sustained by institutions other than the school.

> No, in my opinion schools teach only subjects. Tehzib, and the way we speak, our culture and such things, we learn from our families. We have a complicated web of relationships in Banaras... The joint family, relatives and neighbourhood (Jaitpura) have contributed in maintaining our tehzib (culture). In our family, media and other influences have not affected our language.
>
> —Abdul, Urdu teacher

The same link of family and kin-groups is also mentioned by the school principal, when he recalled the tradition of Urdu in his family. Ironically, he seeks to keep that tradition alive with the logic of the modern school, by including it in the curriculum, against all odds.

We may recall here the contrast in the family environments of people like Abdul and Mr Bakhtiyar, who grew up in families where Urdu was still in practice, and those of the students who are from lower-middle-class Muslims families with very little exposure to learning in a formal setting. Such students never use Urdu at home; they use a variety which is a hybrid of Urdu, Hindi and their version of Banarasi.

He also claims that a student who completes his/her education in Urdu till Class 8 should be able to read an Urdu newspaper, if they get the right environment both in school and at home. Both of these conditions, unfortunately, remain unfulfilled for the students of HKHSS. In such a scenario, only those students, by his estimate 20 per cent of all, can do relatively better in the Urdu course. These are students with previous exposure to Urdu-learning in a madrasa or from a *maulvi* at home. These students are interested in Urdu because of their religious orientation, which provides them a grounding for learning the language, rather than for Urdu literature.

The students of Urdu, on the other hand, are not very sure if they know enough Urdu. For many of them, it comes as part of their religious identity of being Muslims who are expected to learn it.

Shaukat, in Class 8, claimed that in this school, no one except Abdul Sir knew *asli* or real Urdu. Real Urdu is very difficult to learn and very few in Banaras know it.

Ahmad (2002) argues that Urdu has become the preserve of madrasa-trained religious leaders rather than the upper-class, educated elite among Muslims. Such madrasa-educated religious leaders are the main practitioners of Urdu. Their training in the language emanates from a different system of learning meant for a different kind of field.

The mufti of the Gyanwapi Mosque in Banaras, is one such practitioner of Urdu. He switches between Hindi–Urdu, his mohalla speech *Alaipuria* and chaste Urdu, depending on who he is talking to. He claimed that the speech of Muslims varies by the locality in Banaras, and that it should not be confused with pure Urdu, which one can only learn by its proper taleem. When he delivered the guest speech on the occasion of Independence Day in HKHSS, his speech was laden with Persianised Urdu words and had nothing in common with the languages used by the students of the school and most of the teachers, his audience. But, his audience, including the school staff, remained unperturbed by their lack of comprehension of his speech.

It is important to mention here that distinction of language is maintained best when it is made exclusive. The language of the maulvi (preacher) is very difficult to understand for the majority of his listeners, and in spite of that, or maybe precisely because of it, the majority revere him. It creates a peculiar situation for Urdu in this school, whose authority is reduced to a domain which has not much resonance with school life in modern India. The alternative space of Urdu seems too distant from school activities that it cannot sustain itself in the larger scheme of affairs.

English and the School: The Hope of Progress

In Banaras, everyone uses *Theth Bhojpuri* at home, but (they) will send their children to English-medium schools anyway ... *Angrez banana chahte hain* ... (they want to make them English)
—Shankarlal, 59, Hindi teacher and School in-charge (till 2006)

Angrez banana chahte hain here refers to the supposedly widespread desire among parents in Banaras to make Englishmen out of their children. The statement captures the post-colonial dilemma of a tense relationship with a language which once belonged to the colonisers. However, there has been a change in the representation of English in the Indian society, because of the emergence of English as the language of both the national as well as international market. It has also been argued that English has now become a part of Indian identity (Advani 2009; LaDousa 2014).

In Banaras, which has been a stronghold of both the Hindi movement in the pre-independence era and the 'Banish English' movement in the post-independence period (refer Chapter 3), it is significant that English is increasingly being seen as the language of progress. This trend has extended to not just the upwardly mobile upper middle-class but also among the lower middle-classes, and among the first generation of school-goers, even though their articulations may retain a complexity.

In HKHSS the mandate is very clear for all, that in the near future, it will be converted to an English-medium school. The preparation for the same is already underway, as is evident from the Chairman's address on Annual Day (refer Chapter 4). Some of the subjects such as Mathematics, Science and basic Computer Science are already being taught in a bilingual mode in primary section. Many of the students cite English as their favourite subject and that they would like to learn it more than any other language, although none of them identify it as one of the languages used at home.

There are two English teachers in the school. One among them speaks with me in English, while narrating his experiences of teaching English in the school and in general. He belongs to a village near Mughalsarai, some 20 kms away from the city of Banaras. He received his school and college education there, and then started staying at a rented house in the city of Banaras. Like many others, he works beyond school hours and gives classes in English as a private tutor as well as in a coaching institute.

> I have seen some changes in their (students') attitude towards English. There are some students in Classes 6, 7 and 8 who try to speak English… The teachers in my time were very different from the present times. They didn't use English. But now, people have become more conscious about using English. They have started using English words more frequently. Now, parents are keener to make their children learn English. They would ask the tutors to teach English so that they learn to speak it.
>
> —Amar, 30, English teacher, HKHSS

However, the other English teacher, an elderly person in his late 50s, has contrary views. He has worked for the district court for quite some time as a clerk and started working in the school after his retirement. He is critical of the growing obsession with English and English-medium schools in Banaras. He believes that students from such schools face problems in learning various subjects in a foreign language. He contrasts the current schooling system with Indian mode of learning. He points out that in older times, a student of medicine, that is, the son of a *vaidya* would start learning his subject quite early, whereas modern students learn English and other subjects till Class 12, and only then start studying Medicine. Pointing to another dilemma of education in the English language, he says that it is of no use for practical purposes in Banaras.

> *Untalees kise kehte hain nahi pata to Banaras jaisi jagah me kya karenge? Rikshe wale se kaise baat karenge? Aajkal hum Angrezi ko itna mahatva dete hai ki Hindi ya Urdu me chahe jitni bhi achhi baat kahi jaye uska koi mahatva nahi hai. Jo English me kahega use khas shikshit kaha jayega...*

'When one does not know what the word for thirty-nine is, what would we do in a place like Banaras? How would one talk to the rickshaw puller? But now, we have started valuing English so much that it does not matter how good the content is if you are speaking in Hindi or Urdu. Nowadays, one who says it in English is seen as especially educated ...'

—Sharma, 55, English teacher, HKHSS

This is one of the few critical remarks on English-language education in the school. Dhiren, who is sitting along, joins in the discussion and agrees with Sharma, but asserts that everyone wishes to learn English in modern times.

> *Sab log chahte hain English bolna... Jo virodh karte hain wo bhi bolte hain...*

'Everyone wants to speak English... Those who oppose it also speak it...'

He then gives the example of the descendants of Bhartendu Harishchandra in present-day Banaras, who prefer to use English rather than Hindi. For him, Bhartendu Harishchandra is a central figure who carved out a separate space for Hindi in the literary world. Adoption of English by his descendants, is presented as a testimony to the larger trend of wider and greater acceptance of English in most unexpected quarters.

His statement about the desire for learning English does hold true for most of the students and parents who send their children to HKHSS. We have examined similar aspirations for a better future for their children through schooling in English in our previous chapter. Though the desire is present across class and community affiliations, it is more strongly voiced in families which rely only on salaried employment and high-ranked jobs, for the fulfilment of such hopes.

Consider the example of the mother of Alok, a student of Class 7 in HKHSS. She believes that the medium of a child's schooling does make a difference to his/her future career in present times, and that one has to struggle a lot in life otherwise. To her, Hindi and English (asserting that the latter was a must) had become very important. Contrasting with her parents' generation, she said that it was possible only in those older times for people to make progress in life even if they studied in the Hindi medium. She wants to send her children to an English-medium school, but she could not do so because she fears that they might not be able to cope with a sudden change. She strongly feels that in HKHSS, the teachers should talk to the students in English, and that there must be enough practice of English. The school, on its part, assured her that they are soon going to change their medium of education to English. To what extent her expectations have been met in the school of her (constrained) choice is another matter.

It is quite interesting to see the different set of expectations on part of parents who seek English education for their children, but are constrained in their social and economic resources. Their desire that their current school, a Hindi-medium school, should make necessary arrangements for learning English within its own limits, is remarkable.

English in Classroom Practice

The classroom practices during language classes, as we have also examined in the case of Hindi, mainly focus on maintaining order and completing the course on time rather than developing the kind of communicative competence that some of the parents aspire for. The reason for this mismatch in hopes and reality of English learning in most schools is that basic resources needed for learning English are not available in the school. Such resources include good number of teachers specifically trained to impart English skills in a cultural milieu of which English is not a part. It also includes the availability of a lot of books and other reading materials and resources in and outside the school, which can foster an environment where creative learning can flourish. A child-centred pedagogy which is sensitive to the local context of the child is another necessity which is found wanting in most schools, even if they claim to be English medium.

As per official policy statement on curriculum of English language, the classroom pedagogy for learning English needs to be specially designed to develop real communicational competency (Advani 2009; NCERT 2005a). Similarly, in HKHSS, the classroom practice of English, which in the case of many students is the sole source of exposure to English, is not suitable for learning any language, let alone English.

Every class begins with the teacher first trying to control the classroom order and then most often proceed to the reading exercise. Reading of the prescribed textbooks is done either by the teacher himself/herself (to save time) or by the students. Explanation of the text usually is reduced to translating the text into Hindi. The lessons of the textbooks are usually completed by engaging in few exercises which are creative in nature. The most commonly completed exercise in class is to find the meaning of difficult words and to answer the questions given at the end of the chapter. There is usually no reference made to the use of supplementary readings, storybook sessions and use of library or creative writing exercise.

In such a poorly equipped learning environment, engaging with the children and with the subject at hand is always in conflict with the norm of classroom order. In one of the rare classes, when the teacher does make an effort to engage the children, the classroom order gets disrupted which in turn disappoints the teacher. Consider the following scenario when I attended Sharma's English class:

I sit in one of the front rows arranged sideways with Sankar, Pritam and Rahul Joshi. The students do not seem much affected by the presence of the teacher. Pritam is looking at a visiting card and takes out the textbook only when the teacher announces that he will punish those students who have not brought their books.

The teacher starts the class with a reading exercise from the textbook. He reads in a high pitch so that he can be audible to all the students in the class. He asks them to underline the difficult words. When a student asks whether they should underline the words that are difficult to understand or those which are difficult to read, the teacher asks them to underline both. The students raise their hands anticipating that the teacher will ask them to start reading. But he asks them to be quiet, to listen to him, and to follow the lines that he is reading by putting their fingers on the sentences in the textbook. He starts reading aloud and explains the meanings of the words such as galloping, turn about, clatter, etc. He gives examples and draws the images of running horses, trains, etc. This leaves the children thrilled and they get animated, and some of them start making the sounds of running horses' hooves. When there is much noise in the class, the teacher asks them to be quiet in the class or else he will stop telling them interesting things. Rajesh, Rakesh, Sankar and Munir keep standing and answering the casual questions by the teacher. As soon as the bell rings, they start packing their bags and closing their books.

This was one of the few occasions when I find the classroom environment to be so animated. However, inside the class, the teacher fails to maintain order which has bearings for his impression in school as a teacher who cannot control his class. In an ironical development, during my later visits to the school, I come to know that Sharma was removed from service because of his inability to discipline the students. The contradictory pressures of learning a language, which is foreign to the students, and the need to maintain discipline in classrooms, become apparent. Learning English in a setting like HKHSS is only possible through greater involvement and participation of students in the classroom and by encouraging their voices, not by silencing them for the sake of discipline.

In all the language classes, the emphasis is on explaining the content of the textbook rather than on mastery of the language. The language component of the subject is dealt with only by identifying the difficult words and giving their meanings. Again, the alternative uses of the words are not discussed. Sometimes, students are required to read out aloud the passages from the text. The teachers only check if some words are mispronounced. These, along with some odd questions about the text, are among the few ways in which teachers engage with the text and the students in the school.

In a different context, Dr Chaturvedi, an elderly journalist and a noted literary figure, remarks that there had not been much of a change in the practice of English language in the city, even when one sees a mushrooming growth of English-medium schools. He claims that this can be verified by examining the trends of circulation of English newspapers or the sale of English books in the city, which he is sure has not seen any upscale movement because of entry of English-medium schools.

However, English is desired by the middle and lower middle-classes for getting an edge over other candidates in the local job market, as we have seen with the families associated with HKHSS. These families could not provide an environment which is rich enough for the learning of English which they so much desire. None of the students in HKHSS has access to English at home other than programmes aired on TV through private cable networks. Some of the families try to make up for this lack by appointing a private English tutor. Those who can afford, send their children to costlier English-medium schools. The principal sends his children to attend one such school and so does an exporter of Banarasi sarees, Salim.

The principal of a reputed and high-fee-charging English-medium school in Banaras explained how it is important to acquire certain skills in English to get a job in the schools of Banaras. He even asserts that a command over spoken English is more important than having academic qualifications for getting a job in an English-medium school which gives a marginally higher scale of salaries. He even shows me a file containing the applications of candidates for the post of teacher in which a qualified candidate was rejected with the remark that the candidate is not using 'correct' and 'fluent' English. Here, the expectation of competence in English is extended to the realm of communication skills. The principal himself is on the verge of retirement and likes to use Bhojpuri and Hindi at home, but is bound to enforce the use of English in an English-medium school. There are mechanisms of punishment for defaulters like levying a fine on those students who do not speak in English. He justified this by saying that parents are willing to pay the high fees of the school because they want their children to be fluent in English.

What is interesting in all these observations is the fact that there is a great desire to learn English among families from varying class positions. Particularly, there is an excessive concern with mastering communicational skills in English. This concern is articulated in terms of the promise of economic opportunities that English is supposed to bring. However, the schools for the middle-classes do not have the adequate resources for teaching/learning the same. Similarly, studies on discourses of mobility have pointed out the gap between the promise and the reality of English education in India.

Conclusion

Schools are the major sites of learning the cultural resources which are important to function in larger communities. The languages learnt in the school are examples of such resources and the nation-state is an example of such a community, both of which have higher social prestige than other kinds of languages and communities.

But, this formulation also conceals the violence implicit in the process where only certain forms of identities are legitimised at the expense of others. Both teachers and students contribute to the process of legitimisation. Teachers engage in classificatory process on the basis of class and status categories which affect their identification of students in terms of their use and their learner identities at school. On the other hand, some students also internalise ideas about good and proper language to be used in school and act accordingly, also, at times, ridiculing the others for failing to do so.

The process of the construction of standard languages such as Hindi, Urdu and English seems to be common, that is, through the marginalisation of the varieties which are used at the local level. But, their respective fields are different. The standard and 'pure' Hindi now gets defined against what is termed as the local influences of family occupation, class and caste, among other markers of identities. In this respect, denial and shame, associated with these other varieties such as Bhojpuri and Banarasi are also examined. Here, Hindi is seen as representing the 'modern school culture' and is hence respectable. Banarasi/Bhojpuri varieties seem to exist more in the informal sphere of schools, where it assumes a different meaning by being associated with close bonding, intimacy and fun. Its use falls in the realm of achieving solidarity through language-use. The learning of Urdu in the school continues only in a token form by continuing to enrol students from a particular community while failing to provide the adequate support-base for learning it.

English, in contrast, represents the promise of an affluent future and participation in a wider community across classes and communities. Though it is not yet a language which is practiced by the students of HKHSS, yet they hope to learn it for a better future. The classroom learning of this school is, however, not designed to fulfil all their expectations. The English-medium schools of Banaras cater to a high-income group. A school like HKHSS also aspires towards a similar status in the school-market of Banaras, and is continuously striving in the same direction.

Notes

1. Used as interjection in the speech. Here believed to be used by those engaged in the saree business, especially the weavers.
2. Mohammad, a teacher in the nearby college and Chairperson of Noorjehan Girls' School also claimed that there was a specific variety used by the Ansaris, and that it

developed because of the contact between the local and immigrant populations. Julehti is believed to contain words from Brajbhasha, Awadhi, Bhojpuri and even some Bengali.

3. Bhakti means devotion and this tradition of poetry in Hindi literature dates back to the fourteenth century India.

4. The birth anniversary of Jawaharlal Nehru is celebrated in most schools in India as Children's Day because of Nehru's famous love for children.

5. Sometimes, the female teachers did not approve of and even complained about the male teachers often using the crude language of Banaras within the school premises.

7
Conclusion

School se zubaan tootati hai ... Jo log padh lete hai unhe Hindi aa jati hai ...

School breaks (open) the speech ... Those who are able to read, acquire Hindi ...

—Sazia, 32, Nargis' Mother

azia, a resident of Kachi bagh in Banaras, speaks of a Hindi which is linked with schooling. She is alluding to the power of a school which can cause *zuban* (tongue or speech) to lose a particular way of speaking and acquire a new form of speech. The metaphorical use of *tootna* (to break), is significant when used with reference to the experience of schooling, because it indicates the loss of language identities which are associated with one's home. However, breaking away from such identities can also be interpreted as getting ready to embrace the new ones. In educational contexts, it means embracing the identities associated with schooling in contemporary times, being able to use standard languages in formal contexts. In both these senses, breaking conveys a loss of culture as well as the possibility of gaining a foothold into a new one. In the aforementioned epigraph, Sazia refers to the loss of the rigidity of a tongue which is unaccustomed to using a standard language like Hindi. To describe her acquired ability of such communication, she narrates her experience of travelling for Haj, when she had to use Hindi with a fellow woman passenger from Kashmir. Her own cultural world of an Ansari family settled in the weavers' lane in Banaras is densely woven in networks of kinship and neighbourhood ties, and it resonates with speech forms which range from Hindi–Urdu, Banarasi and *Julehti*. In her domestic world, use of 'pure Hindi or Urdu' is a complete misfit and would invite scorn and ridicule from family members. That world is in complete contrast with the airport where she chanced to meet a woman from a completely different cultural world. The airport represents a modern impersonal space, a transient abode of people always in move and pausing to communicate, if at all, in a highly standardised and impersonal way of speaking (Gupta 2000). It is in such alien circumstances that her childhood learning of language in a school context comes to her rescue. It is also pertinent to note that Sazia received her primary education of elementary Hindi and Urdu in a government madrasa. Even with the minimum language training gained from schooling, she finds herself (and her tongue) to be prepared for encounter with strangers in the impersonal setting of an airport. Her story encapsulates the power of standard languages in the lives of ordinary people in non-metropolitan centres, the power which can be both enabling and alienating at the same time.

Learning a standard language like Hindi proves to be an enabling experience for many, because of its function as a medium of connecting with people in formal spaces. This is especially true of people whose everyday speech is different from the standard varieties taught in schools. It is argued that standardisation of language in modern societies creates communicative fields, which enables one to connect beyond a small group. Acquisition of these language skills is also seen as providing a sense of cultural proximity to a modern community of the nation-state. Schools and languages associated with schools are often construed as bridges that bring in this notion of proximity to the cultural and economic ideals of modernity. In this pursuit, the choice of a school with the right pedagogy of such language becomes crucial for people not using standard language in other walks of life. But these very institutions and techniques of modernity, schools and their processes of language-learning, function in ways that often widen the existing gaps between people stratified by class and status markers.

Standard languages in the realm of education also assign social status on certain speakers and inflict silence on others. In other words, such languages can be seen to possess a dual character, functioning both as efficient ways of communication for participation in a larger society and also as representing the legitimacy of the official identities in a nation-state. This double-faced nature of standard languages, at once enabling and disabling, calls for a critical reading of language in the institutional context of school.

Historical literature has provided ample proof that the standard language, rather than being a common language, is usually the language of the dominant group in society (Anderson 1983; Brass 1974; Hobsbawm 1996). The myth of commonality of culture implicit in the idea of a nation-state is a result of the projection of cultural homogeneity by concealing the cultural fault lines. Critical studies of modern governance techniques in erstwhile colonies present a different vantage point to understand some of these fault lines. Cohn (1985) has illustrated the effect of colonial knowledge-building exercise on the status and inter-relations of languages in the Indian context. It is further argued that colonial governance techniques, in their attempts to map and make sense of the cultural realities of a colonised society, create 'enumerated' and discrete communities out of groups whose boundaries have been fuzzy and overlapping (Chakrabarty 2002; Kaviraj 1997). In such societies, with traditions of multilinguality independent of literacy traditions, the issue of standard languages in educational context gains special relevance. The colonisation process which place languages in hierarchic relation with each other, results in people identifying with prestige varieties of languages even when they are not using it in practice. This process has been reported and brought to notice in Indian context by political commentators as well as the sociolinguists (Brass 1974; Khubchandani 1977; Dasgupta 2001).

These insights are crucial in explaining how schools tend to reproduce the existing relations of the dominance of social and symbolic order. In this work, the role of the school as a modern institution has been examined in legitimising language varieties recognised by the state over others. In the process, it also explores how the identities of class, status and gender are shaped by the schooling process.

Class, Status and Mobility
Aspirations through Schooling

Schooling and its relation with mobility can only be understood with reference to the nature of economy and the associated symbolic and cultural fields (Bourdieu 1985). In Banaras, the divide between the salaried classes and those in traditional occupations like the saree industry, along with the parents' exposure to education, are significant in defining their relation with schools. These linkages between economic and cultural fields, particularly with reference to the complexity of the middle-class category in India, are not given due attention in the literature documenting the mobility strategies of parents through children's schooling. Keeping in view the large presence of unorganised sector in India in terms of actual employment, the notion of middle-class identity has to be carefully examined using a multi-layered approach. An understanding of the economic field of Banaras and its linkages with the educational field reveals differential relation with schooling, within a lower-middle-class category of the school-going population. Reliance on school education and standard language cultures for entry into the job market is found to be high among a certain section of the middle classes. Those families, who have made the transition from traditional forms of employment, rely more on standard schools for better future prospects of their children. On the other hand, because of the specific nature of the Banarasi Saree Cluster, families associated with it are not so dependent on schooling. Continuing in the same sector, calls for different kinds of skills and values to be learnt in sites other than the school. Conversely, a move towards greater economic integration in sectors which till recently were relatively independent from national markets, increases the overall reliance on schooling for social mobility. The crisis in the Banarasi saree industry has weakened families' reliance on the traditional occupation. Now, many of them aspire to learn the skills valued in markets beyond their traditional occupation. The choice of modern schooling in a school like HKHSS gives them that hope. In this context, the school's offering of English, Hindi and minimal training in Urdu for Muslims gains significance.

Schools are not just seen as instruments of social mobility in economic terms but also as bestowing social prestige in their association with high-culture markers. However, access to different kinds of schools and educational capital is highly differentiated by class and status. In other words, not all kinds of schools are accessible to everyone and parents do not make a free choice in the educational market. Their choice is almost always constrained by considerations of cost and affordability and also depends on their estimation of the overall standing of a school in the local school-market. For some families, choice of a Hindi-medium standard school over a madrasa is a movement towards participation in a wider community of school goers. This movement, relatively under-reported in existing literature on school choice in India, is significant as it reflects negotiations with community-specific norms of schooling which are deeply gendered in nature. In that sense, modern schools which provide secular education with facility for coeducation of boys and girls, even if confined in their localised context, remain a stepping stone for families in their search for prestige associated with better schooling. Here, the gendered educational strategy of sending the son of the family to study 'Computer Science' in Bangalore is not meant for economic betterment alone, but also to add to the family prestige that their cultural world has expanded from the limits of Banaras to a metropolitan level. From the standpoints of the upper echelons of middle-class category, the same school appears to be limited in its potential because of its status as a Hindi-medium school, while for many others, it works fine as a school that prepares their children's grounding in the standard language culture. The fraction of the middle-class associated with this school is not the upper middle-class that LaDousa (2005) has identified, whose actual reference group is placed in a metropolitan centre and whose expectations no school in Banaras can fulfil. However, families with different degrees of reliance on and associations with schooling, share at a certain level, some common expectations from a school. These expectations are expressed both in economic and symbolic terms. The learning of valued, marketable resources such as skills in useful 'prestige' languages such as Hindi and English is one of them.

Classificatory Techniques, Cultural Boundaries and Prestige Languages

The modern classificatory techniques of governance, such as census operations, have always been a contested site where crystallisation of communal identity takes place (Anderson 1991; Chakrabarty 2002). The scholarship on Hindi nationalism has rightly pointed how religion is used as a boundary, demarcating a particular form of Hindi as representative of the nation (Brass 1974; Kumar 2005d). This mobilisation around a form of Hindi based on Hindu religious identity contributed to further polarisation between Hindu and Muslim elites of north India as speakers of two distinct languages, and was reflected in varying trends of identification with these languages in census and survey reports (Brass 1974; King 1989). The very rationality of these techniques defined their limits in their inability to report about multilingual contexts, where linguistic boundaries are not sharply defined.

These issues also have methodological implications for critical social science research concerning language identities. The way languages are conceived and classified or categorised by linguists and government officials is influenced by colonial traditions, and are often different from those of the actual practitioners of the language, and the former often superimpose their own categories upon the latter (Annamalai 2001, 36). The standard-language ideologies or the belief in particular forms of language-use seem to be affecting not just the ordinary people living in 'standard-language cultures', but also the specialists such as linguists and academia in their work, and the latter seem to be reinforcing the ideology through their work (Milroy 2001). It calls for a more sensitive approach to fieldwork and cultivating an ability to listen to multiple ways of talking about one's home language.

The case of a Hindi-medium school, catering to Hindu as well as Muslim students, having links with differing sectors of economy shows that class, community and status identities interact in complex ways in speakers' identification of language varieties. It is reflected in students' talk about their languages used at home and in school. In this context, only certain languages from a broad repertoire of speech are initially reported. The other varieties emerge in discussions much more gradually and are described in more borderless terms, unlike standard Hindi and Urdu. It can be argued that prestige varieties of languages tend to be more strongly demarcated from each other and from the popular varieties within same speech community. For example, among Muslims, often seen as a community of Urdu speakers, the internal boundaries between and popular language-use appears to be strong.

In the account of parents and teachers, it emerges that the division between high Urdu and high Hindi is maintained on the basis of their association with Muslim and Hindu elites respectively. In other words, standard Hindi and pure Urdu continue to be valued because of high-status group positions of Hindu and Muslim elite. Even though Hindi is used by everyone, the use of Hindi at homes, in this context, is still seen as an attribute of the educated middle-class, who are either working as professionals or in regular salaried jobs. The scholarship on social process of boundary making and maintenance consider such folk classificatory practices as definitive of group relations (Barth 1969; Lamont and Molnar 2002). These practices signify that thickening and dissolving of cultural boundaries have to do more with the relationship between groups and the significant 'others' defined by these relationships. It is in this process that Urdu becomes the language of the Muslims, and Hindi, that of the Hindus, at first glance. However, if examined closely, Urdu remains the language of the cultural elite among the Muslims, while Hindi becomes the language of the educated middle-class Hindus (and Muslims). Still people tend to identify with a 'prestige' variety of language, whether they actually use the language or not.

Linguists and anthropologists have often made use of a concept of differential functions of different languages or varieties in different domains whereby prestige variety of language is used in formal domains while other varieties are used in informal domains (Annamalai 2001; Woolard 1985). However, subjective evaluations of languages keep changing as per changes in political and economic contexts as we have examined with reference to the development of standard Hindi ideology. It is important to understand how these processes play out at school level and to what effect.

Legitimisation of Languages in School and its Limits

The ethnographic study of the school context reveals its limited success in perpetuating the legitimacy of norms of standard language associated with middle-class or the high-status group. It is limited because such legitimisation has to face resistance of several types. In this process, the teacher's role emerges significantly. The cultural divide between the high-prestige forms and low-prestige forms of language is shared by teachers and effectively used for constructing the norms of language-use for school. They often engage in identifying students with their parents' occupation and construe a notion of 'culture of education' which is accessible to only a few students. Here, the teachers also engage in classificatory processes based on notions of social identity of students. The conflation of social identity onto the learner identity of students has obvious implications for teaching–learning process, whereby students with the 'right background' gain positive learner identity in teachers' evaluation. The evaluation of students on the basis of right kind of language-use is accepted by teachers and students alike, suggesting the kind of normalisation that Bourdieu theorised in his work (1991). In this process, 'home culture' of the majority of students is devalued and juxtaposed to the formal 'school culture'. It is in this context that privileging of norms of Sanskritised Hindi in formal school space through teaching–learning and evaluation regimes lead to devaluation of popular languages.

Still, legitimisation of language only *appears* to be complete as there are ample instances of cultural resistance towards norms of standard Hindi, whereby these norms are restricted to the formal space of the school. The non-formal space is constructed by students and teachers where norms are not followed. The space is created for sharing a sense of solidarity, intimacy, trust and fun. All these instances of resisting the dominant norms within school space, however, are not strong enough to change the official school culture. In this process of legitimisation, the officially mandated language curricula and its teaching is supported by the dynamics of language at local level. The legitimation appears complete because amidst several conflicts there is coherence between localised language hierarchies and the official language curriculum.

A more serious challenge to the legitimacy claims of standard Hindi is posed by a growing demand for quality teaching of English from many parents, a demand which is taken much more seriously by school administration and efforts are made to achieve a semblance to a semi-English-medium school, if not a full-fledged one.

Educational Planning for Pedagogic Goals

The pedagogic issues of learning of languages have rarely been given the due attention in public discourses around languages. These discourses do not focus on a child and her needs; rather, they look at the language from instrumentalist view as one enabling the creation of a national market. One such discourse constructs education in English language as a guarantee of class-based mobility. The other discourse, which has often been propped up against the former, is one which emphasises education through one's mother tongue. This construct of mother tongue has been a politically contested term. In the competitive political scenario of India, the claim of mother tongue education has been effectively utilised to garner government support for either use of regional languages or for minority languages within a region. In both the discourses, as far as their emphasis on use of a standard form is concerned, they remain similar in their approach, and disagreement lies only in the language adopted. There is also a trend, relatively marginal at policy level and almost absent from popular discourse, which critiques the exclusive reliance on a standard language model of education. This approach is adopted in the framing of NCF 2005 and its position paper on teaching of Indian language. The approach lays stress (theoretically) on the need for a method of learning that is sensitive to the local context of a child and encourages multilingual approaches to language-learning. While this policy proposal appears radical in its formulation, its implementation in curriculum framework in India remains extremely difficult for its limits in being able to define only the textbooks in the absence of any structural transformation in the schooling system.

The school context in Banaras, particularly the lower end private school-market, presents the limits of the official schemes for language-learning in schools. These limits are found to be at structural levels, which place schools and particularly the low-paid teachers in a disadvantageous position to carry out educational reforms based on child-centred pedagogy. In this particular school, where the school principal expresses an interest in bringing such reforms and directs teachers to update themselves on pedagogic issues, the actual classroom practice only promotes a mechanical route of learning. In the classrooms, language-learning is reduced to a mere following of the teacher's directions and the completion of a given task. Any creative engagement with the language is rarely seen, neither on the part of the teachers nor that of the students. Even in the local school-market, a school is assessed more in terms of its students' ability to clear state conducted examinations, than anything else.

In a private school with low investments and inadequate support for teaching as a profession, a language curriculum fails to engage with students at all. Low social and economic status of teachers in an insecure work profile emerges in a stark contrast with the prestige languages that they are required to teach. In such a scenario, language classroom becomes restricted to a mere exercise of lesson completion. The teachers also fail to make sense of the 'reforms' in textbooks prepared at metropolitan centres and directed at them by school administrators. When these structural

factors of teachers' position in educational hierarchy and a centralised process of developing a curriculum and implementing
reforms combine with a pedagogy of language that emphasises
only a correct use and punishes any deviation, it adds to the reproduction of dominant language ideology in school. That is when the
popular languages in the city such as Banarasi and Bhojpuri and
other variants thrive in the alternative spheres of life and also find
their voices in the informal domains of school life. However, their
contrasting position vis-à-vis standard languages are reinforced
by the status and class-based classificatory processes in which
teachers engage within school. For the lower-middle-class families that it is associated with, the school promises to be a vehicle
of social mobility. But it is not always successful in imparting the
language skills because of its structural limitations. The school's
success in establishing the standard language ideologies and
failure in its pedagogy of language presents before us one major
challenge of democratising the process of language-learning in a
post-colonial society.

Annexure

A Note on the Methodology and Fieldwork

In the city of Banaras, I sought to explore the issue of legitimacy of certain languages in schools. I wanted to examine how the dominant languages are constructed, transacted in modern educational institutions by focusing on the official/standard languages in the school context. Through this exercise, I also hoped to understand the consequences of the standardisation of languages in societies where variability and diversity have been the norm. In Banaras, Hindi is the dominant language in terms of its numeric strength in census results, as well as in its political recognition. Other major languages recognised by the state and offered in schools are English, Urdu and Sanskrit. Apart from these standard languages, there are popular languages like Bhojpuri and Banarasi which are practiced commonly on everyday basis but not recognised at official level. These popular languages resonate the city life in every nook and corner, and yet remain unaccounted in the official domains. I was curious to know how people construct their and other's identities vis-à-vis the second category of language varieties in their everyday lives in and outside school. Any such work has to essentially deal with two key issues simultaneously. These are issues of voice and authenticity. First issue is related to the question of who can claim to speak for whom. The second one is the question of validity claims of construction or representation of a particular cultural world. Both call for a sensitivity to power relations in the social science research, and demand a writer's awareness of relative positions of power in any ethnographic work which claims to speak for its subjects. These issues need to be carefully and sensitively addressed in a sociological investigation of languages in the educational domain.

The issues of authenticity and voice have been a major concern of anthropological research, and quite often focused on the question of relationship of the fieldworker with her field in terms of insider-outsider debate. While one tradition of anthropology upholds that objectivity of social research demands a certain distancing of the researcher from the field, a more recent tradition believes that when one speaks for the familiar or one's own 'culture', the voice becomes more authentic (Danahay 1997). In both traditions, familiarity with a culture and space bestows a distinct sense of authenticity to the voice of the researcher. From these perspectives, the urban space of Banaras is a culturally familiar space for me, because I grew up and was schooled in the same city. This familiarity with school life in one's city of upbringing brings in a different kind of engagement with the field. One is constantly reminded of one's own school experiences and begins to make sense of those lived aspects from new perspectives. The continuous dialogue with the self about the past and present experiences has bearings on reflections about cultures in the present. This critical awareness about the self in relation to one's field site is not an entirely new concept in anthropological studies. In the past few decades, a certain tradition in these lines has been identified as autoethnographic approach to research. It is a way of producing an account of social world which (re)reads into the narrator's past experiences in order to make sense of cultural practices in the present. While traditional approaches to fieldwork have been suspicious of any hint of subjectivity, in more recent times, the reflexivity which is bound with such projects is believed to be crucial for a sensitive and fair approach to fieldwork.

Deborah Reed Danahay in her work (1997) locates autoethnography within a reflexive turn in anthropology. In this approach, the insistence on distancing of "self and society" is questioned and the focus is on their interplay in social theory. In Danahay's view, this approach stands at the intersection of three genres of writing—native anthropology where subjects of ethnography become the authors of study of their own group; ethnic autobiography by members of ethnic minority; and autobiographical ethnography where author brings her own subjective experiences in her ethnographic account (p. 2; 1997). Such ethnographers also live in what is termed as "border zone" or "contact zone" of two cultures, simultaneously living the lives of native as well as of a non-native (Warren 1997).

This assertion about need for reflexivity, and transcending the dichotomy of objectivity and subjectivity is particularly true with regard to studying schools. The study of education is inevitably a study of cultural and geographic displacement. Danahay (1997) mentioned in the context of schooling in France, that any study of educational narrative is simultaneously a story of leaving "home". Her study is based on an examination of narrative accounts of two peasant-origin teachers in France, who wrote about their own schooling experience with a sense of cultural loss. Their engagement with education and with their "native-cultures" differ significantly from each other, and yet retain a common theme of cultural distance brought in through formal education in standard languages. From this perspective, any study of language in education, therefore, necessarily becomes a reflexive exercise to understand power struggle over issues of culture and knowledge.

These reflections underline the political–ethical commitment that research has to be sensitive to all narratives of "leaving home" while describing school experiences. In Indian context, Thapan (2014) has argued that while studying schools, every researcher has to engage with one's past experiences, in order to make better sense of the present as experience by others and to make sense of their understanding. The understanding of past is necessarily enmeshed with our present endeavour as social scientists (Thapan 2014).

In the present work, a similar attempt has been made to bring in a reflexive understanding of self and society in two ways. One, it consciously strives for an awareness of the politics of representation and power relations in writing about people's use of language. Two, this awareness shapes and is in turn shaped by reflections on my childhood experiences of an Assamese upbringing, while being schooled at a Hindi medium school of Banaras and finally adopting both the languages as part of one's identity. These two points are significant for the researcher as one engages with the field at a deeper level, unafraid of embracing the subjectivities associated with living a culturally conflicted life.

Growing up Bilingual in a Monolingual Hindi World

When I was exploring the possible sites for fieldwork, familiarity with a language and its local variations was a must. The choice of Banaras was easy for me, as I grew up in this city and received most of my education (mostly in Hindi) there. I acquired not just an easy fluency in Hindi but also a hold of a form of Hindi which is known for being *klisht* or difficult. Additionally, it provided an ideal site of engagement at professional level where my affective and academic interests coincided. I was a native to the schooling in Banaras, and also retained a sense of being an outsider. I claim the dual identity, as I see myself, a "product" of Hindi medium schooling in Banaras without having the native claims over Hindi as my mother tongue. My primary language was Assamese as both my parents were Assamese speaking, and our family stayed in Banaras because of my father's job.

On hindsight, my association with the city is also mired in a sense of cultural dislocation, the sense of being "away from home" as described by Danahay (1997). This was the city where I almost failed to keep track of the shifts in my primary identity, from an Assamese to that of a hyphenated identity of a Hindi-speaking-Assamese. In the family context, our language was Assamese, even as we lived amidst Hindi speaking people and did not have any family relatives in the city. Very soon, the world of formal Hindi encompassed my Assamese world. Soon I started inhabiting both the worlds within my own family, when I would speak with my mother in Assamese and switch to Hindi with my sibling. I was completely immersed in this hybrid world. It was much later, in the course of my research that my early childhood memories of the language shifts, of yearly travels, and of the switching between the two languages—Assamese and Hindi, revisited me with a new perspective.

My confidence in the formal domains grew along with my high scores in every subject in school, including Hindi, which was supposedly non-native for me. This easy switch and mastery of formal Hindi amidst native-Hindi speakers, has always been a cause of mystery among my colleagues from both Hindi and non-Hindi world. Now, I realise that my childhood experiences were dominated by influences of Hindi learnt at school and my neighbourhood in a residential colony away from the heart of the city, both of which worked towards facilitating my entry into the Hindi world and I developed a certain ease in it, which I (regrettably) could not develop in what I believed to be my native language. Now I also know that the ease was limited in nature, mainly because it restricted me to the formal aspects of life in schools and offices, the world of formal communication, the world of impersonal and non-intimate relations. More importantly, my initiation into the school Hindi was actually facilitated by my service-class background which was not rooted in Hindi in a native way. An entry into Hindi world from a non-native background was made possible only through a culture of reliance on formal lessons, textbooks and other literary and popular literature in Hindi. Ironically, the absence of a more grounded experience of Hindi at home worked to my advantage at school. In those days, I completely ignored people with a different or a more "authentic" use of language, partly because of the invisibilisation or mutedness of their world to an average middle-class family. My completely urbanised world operated smoothly with a smattering of *shudh* Hindi and a bit of English. Complete unfamiliarity with the use of local variants of Hindi led to my strange assimilation into only one side of the city world. I was completely out of bounds with the "rustic" or more "authentic" world of Banarasi within Banaras.

It was not until long in my student life that I could reflect back on my association with the city through the prism of language politics. After the completion of my doctoral dissertation, when I shifted base as a sociologist to a non-Hindi region, I had better opportunity to reflect over my association with Hindi and rework my ideas about language and its interplay in the field of education. These reflections about how one achieves ease of expression in certain realms of life and voiceless-ness in others, was crucial during this research. However, it would be wrong to suggest that all realms of life command equal recognition and power in the real world, particularly for social mobility within professional arenas. My classroom peers with a lack of access to the formal codes were the ones who were left behind in the long career of a researcher's life that I embarked upon, and eventually ended up being able to write about these experiences from a relatively safe and powerful position.

Studying Schools and Linguistic Identities

In this work, sensitivity to the methods of fieldwork and the tools of research was imperative. Every critical researcher is faced with the dilemma of engaging in Science, and also, trying to question its methodology so that it may be made less oppressive. These concerns and questions guided me in taking a participatory and reflexive approach to the field through an ethnographic study of a school community, with the hope of building relationships of trust and respect, rather than of hierarchy. I am mainly following the interpretive approach to understand cultural experiences in an institutional setting. In this approach, the researcher engages with the subject in an exercise of understanding the meaning of the things of culture. The approach has been famously described by Geertz:

> '... I take culture to be those webs, and the analysis of it to be, therefore, not an experimental science in search of law but an interpretive one in search of meaning.' (Geertz 1973, p. 5)

The interpretive approach has limited generalisability, but this is compensated by the richness of information which is explored. Here, verifiability may sometimes be difficult, but the trade-off has the benefit of allowing us to make sense of "the normalcy and particularity of others". The cultural interpretations often come in the form of "thick descriptions", and with an awareness that these are "interpretations of the second and third orders" (Geertz 1973).

Apart from a keenness to the meanings of the things of culture, the researcher also has to be conscious of the power dimension of knowledge-construction exercised through modern institutions and technologies. From this perspective, an exercise to make sense of different meaning systems or cultures is fraught with the dangers of furthering the same power relations which one seeks to uncover and question.

In this work, I deal with the cultural identities of groups and their experiences, conflicts and dilemmas of modernity through an exploration of their association with standard languages. Languages are also part of culture, but they signify power relationships, too. Particularly, the language of the classroom in a school is a cultural code which has to be mastered by the students, and is not simply a transparent medium through which the academic curriculum is transmitted (Mehan 1987, p. 125). Here, I am making use of sociological conceptual tools to decipher the meaning of these codes, and their effect on social relations in a particular setting. Therefore, the objective is not a study of languages per se, or even of languages in the school. It is a study of social processes and relations in an institutional context, where language is only one of the markers used by the actors and groups to relate to each other. In this exercise, I take the cultural identities of groups to be dynamic and fluid, and their cultural boundaries to be fuzzy and permeable. Although issues of identity politics often arouse deep-rooted passions, it is also a widely shared idea that every culture is plural, interactive and never wholly *sui generis*, and that its identity is plural, fluid and open. The idea that culture is a plural construct and is always dynamic, when applied to a polity, can bring about a completely new way of organising a society which respects diversity (Parekh 1999).

Since one of the objectives was to examine the standard languages as historically constructed products, I thought of employing terms like language varieties rather than the conventional and hierarchic categories of languages and dialects. Language varieties emphasise the dynamic nature of languages, and examine variations as part of a continuum rather than placing them in dichotomous and hierarchic categories of dialects vs. standard languages. An effort was made to avoid looking at languages as essentialised products and emphasise the processual aspect of constructing them. The languages taught in the school are, therefore, examined with a view to understanding the processes through which the norms of standard languages are constructed in the school. An emphasis on language varieties necessitated that the norms of standard languages are examined vis-á-vis other popular languages.

In this study, the classificatory processes at school are significant in drawing language boundaries at the intersection of identities of class, caste and gender. These classificatory processes are an important feature of modern scientific enterprise which continues to affect much of social science research. I take my cues from Cohn's work on knowledge and power in colonial societies, where he has argued that techniques of mapping, surveying, or any form of classifying a cultural reality often lead to a control over the same and set hierarchical relations in place (1996). Therefore, a conscious attempt is made to avoid using classifications which lead to a reification of identity.

Throughout this work, I have assumed cultural identities to be fluid and not rigid in nature. This pursuit has its own challenges when applied to examine languages. The major question regarding conceptualising and using multilingualism, and using it as a methodological approach comes from the realisation that dominant discourse on language has made it difficult to talk about people's conceptions about languages. The emphasis on diversity of Indian languages in academia has not necessarily taken due cognisance of the fact that this diversity is not necessarily consisting of discrete language groups alone. Language boundaries are fluid and permeable. And we have already discussed how scientific enterprise of knowledge accumulation intrinsic to colonial rule has led to building up of the conception of language in discrete and insular terms. Such an awareness of power relations puts the researcher in a dilemma to avoid reification of language varieties in the process of writing about people's conceptions of language.

Orsini (2012) in her recent work on north-Indian languages has suggested a methodology of doing a multilingual literary history. She argues that the effort has to be towards writing a different, more comprehensive and thicker history than a textbook-ish one which alludes to power relations. Drawing from her work, an attempt is made in this work to take multilinguality seriously. This requires a reflexive approach in methods of inquiry and a carefully cultivated practice of listening. It meant listening to assertions of identities as well as to be attentive to the contexts in which these assertions appear and vanish. For this, I interacted with students alone and also in group situations, not just in classrooms but also outside. I accompanied students to their homes, met and interacted with parents and siblings at home. I started my visits to the field in March 2006 and continued my fieldwork for one academic year at school. Each visit would last for 2–3 weeks at a stretch. I made visits to the field in October 2007 and again in January–February 2008. Apart from schools, I also visited some of the educationists and key literary figures of Hindi, Bhojpuri and Sanskrit in Banaras. Through this exercise and by engaging with the above methodological issues about how to study culture, languages, educational processes in a site which is familiar yet strange, I tried to make sense of the normalcy and particularity of the world of schools in my city.

The School as a Field

The school is a relatively easy field to gain entry, but difficult to stay in without affecting the set of relationships in its everyday routine. Every researcher faces this dilemma of assuming a role that enables one to enter in an empathetic relationship with others and still being able to write about it. A more honest attempt can only be made with an awareness of the relative position of the researcher in the field. During this research, my identity as a University educated middle-class and upper-caste woman, putting me at varying positions of advantages and disadvantages had to be negotiated with. My background made everyone communicate with me in their Khariboli version of Hindi which was easy for me. Although I could understand Bhojpuri and Banarasi varieties which were also used by them, I could not use it in the same way as others did. In the process, I also came to recognise and understand the minute differences of tone- and suffix-use that would mark one variety of Banarasi from another.

Though initially my entry into the schools of Banaras was relatively easy, the idea of a longer and sustained research in a particular school was not a welcome thought for most school administrators, and took quite some time convincing them to allow me to stay and work. In many cases, I had permission to talk to the school management alone and some selected teachers in most of the schools I visited. And since I was interested in exploring schools of various kinds, this initial exercise helped in giving me an overview of different kinds of school. The school I finally settled for a more detailed examination, was Hind Kishor Higher Secondary School.

In this school, I was easily accepted by the school administration, teachers and students. The school principal was particularly interested in the project once we found a shared interest in children's educational literature. He was also interested in the language question, which also had to do with his own predicaments of being a middle-class Shia Muslim running a commercial school. He often expressed a sense of loss of power that emanated from decline in social status of nobility, acquired hereditarily, and maintained through cultural resources like fine Urdu.

These shared interests on issues of education and language politics, enabled me an easy entry into the various dimensions of school life. My easy access to the principal initially made some teachers a little hesitant, but over a period of time, when they saw me completely immersed in school life, their inhibitions melted away and they did not find my presence threatening. During my stay, I actively sought to retain the role of a researcher during fieldwork. Some teachers were familiar with that role, having enrolled in PhD programmes elsewhere, but they did not understand why I continued to hang around in the school for so long. They treated me with respect and love, and also invited me for their outings like picnics, excursions, etc.

In school, I interacted with the students and teachers during their free time. When a certain level of comfort set in, I would also sit through some of the classes. My eagerness to get into a classroom where I could interact with students was initially viewed with some suspicion. Gradually, some of them allowed me to sit in their classes. But, this acceptance within the school also thrust upon me the position of a pseudo-teacher, which I consistently kept resisting. On few occasions, the teachers would request me to go to their classes on my own; this also allowed them a rare free period from their busy schedules.

Still, the conflict of roles would occasionally spring up and cause some embarrassment. Once, I was sitting and jotting down some notes on one of the small benches in the small verandah near Kamla, a school attendant. I was sitting there because of the fresher air and better light. At that moment, one of the office assistants, Reema, asked me to sit inside the staff-room:

'Madam, you should sit inside, in the staff-room. It doesn't look nice that you are sitting outside.'

The outside bench was meant for either helping staff of the school or for the outsiders, while schoolteachers were supposed to sit in chairs inside the staffroom.

Students, on the other hand, were more open from the beginning and seemed to enjoy the attention and enquiry of an adult who looked like their teachers. Sometimes, they would ask me *why I asked questions and made notes.* I would simply tell them that I wished to write a book about them, which seemed to make them very happy. Many of them invited me to their homes to meet their parents and other family members. My relations with the children also went through alternating phases of confusion and ease. Initially, they took time to come to terms with the fact that I would be in their school and in their classrooms without being a teacher. However, the transition to the name *Didi* (elder sister) from the more distant *Ma'am* didn't take much time. It took another couple of months before the students were comfortable enough with me to take me to meet their families. By this time, they had become warm and friendly with me, inviting me to their homes and sharing their games, jokes and food. Although I interacted with everyone in the school, yet, most of my observations were based on my contact with students of the upper-primary- and junior-high-school levels, i.e., from Classes 6 to 9. I decided on the age group of 10 and above, because by this age, students are more articulate and are better able to identify the languages of their homes and talk about it.

Even as I visited many households from a variety of occupational background, none of them came from very underprivileged economic background, or from the ranks of wage-labourers; as such students were few in numbers in a private school. For family members, a woman who comes from school is often seen as a teacher. They would try to place me within the familiar set of roles associated with the school. In household setting, I was usually led to talk to the women first, and only later, to the men of the household. In some families, the men and women of different generations all ended up having long chats with me and inviting me to come over again. All of them treated me with great respect and reverence, and invariably sent me back well-fed and humbled. With the students' families, all the interactions were informal. Despite my denials, they would think of me as a sympathetic school staff, and would sometimes share their concerns about the school with the hope that I could do something for them.

Social science research is an exercise that evokes humility when a researcher armed with "knowledge" on the subject matter fails to provide any answer to the simple queries of a person about his/her troubles of daily life. As social scientists, we are initially trained to think more in terms of issues, and not with personal troubles. It was during the course of my fieldwork that I realised, this was precisely the cause of my helplessness in offering any solution to the everyday troubles of human life in the social context. My baggage only provided me with the tools and techniques to make sense of their world, but not always to act and bring about a change; if at all, clarity about the desired change is there. However, the self-reflexivity gained in the process also allows one to appreciate that the ability to transcend the common notions of self and society is linked with the ability to write and do ethnography. This power to write has a limited reach, and sometimes has the danger of reproducing existing social hierarchy. Then one is left with the question, "is it not a power worth exercising?" As long as the hope prevails that a better understanding of the dynamics of "self and society", and of the complexity of the field of education and of its cultural politics can find its way to contribute to the building up of a critical knowledge that has transformatory potential, the answer remains affirmative.

Bibliography

Acharya, P. 1998. 'Bengali Bhadralok and Educational Development in Nineteenth Century Bengal'. In *Educational Development and Underdevelopment*, edited by S. S. Kaul, 25–38. New Delhi: SAGE Publications.

Advani, S. 2009. *Schooling the National Imagination: Education, English, and the Indian Modern*. New Delhi: Oxford.

Agnihotri, R. K. 2007. 'Identity and Multilinguality: The Case of India'. In *Language Policy, Culture, and Identity in Asian Contexts*, edited by A. Tsui and J. Tollefson, 85–204. Mahwah, NJ: Lawrence Erlbaum Associates.

———. 2015. 'Constituent Assembly Debates on Language'. *Economic & Political Weekly* 50 (8): 47.

Ahmad, I. 1966. 'The Ashraf–Ajlaf Dichotomy in Muslim Social Structure in India'. *Indian Economic and Social History Review* 3 (3): 268. New Delhi: Manohar.

———. 1978. *Caste and Social Stratification Among Muslims in India*. South Asia Books.

———. 2002, June 15. 'Urdu and Madrasa Education'. *Economic and Political Weekly* 37 (24): 2285–87.

Althusser, L. 1971. 'Ideology and Ideological State Apparatuses (Notes Towards an Investigation)'. In *Lenin and Philosophy*, edited by L. Althusser, 85–125. New York, NY: *Monthly Review Press*.

Anderson, B. 1991. *Imagined Communities: Reflections on the Origin and Spread of Nationalism*. London: Verso.

Annamalai, E. 2001. *Managing Multilingualism in India: Political and Linguistic Manifestations*. New Delhi: SAGE Publications.

Appiah, A. 2005. *The Ethics of Identity*. Princeton, NJ: Princeton University Press.

———. 2002. 'Does Education Have Independent Power? Bernstein and the Question of Relative Autonomy'. *British Journal of Sociology of Education* 23 (4): 607–16.

———. 2004. *Ideology and Curriculum*. New York, NY: Routledge.

Arum, R. 2000. 'Schools and Communities: Ecological and Institutional Dimensions'. *Annual Review of Sociology* 26: 395–418.

Ashcroft, B., G. Griffiths, and H. Tiffin. 1995. *The Post-colonial Reader*. London and New York, NY: Routledge.

Austin, G., 2009. 'Language and the Constitution: The Half-hearted Compromise'. In *Language and Politics in India*, edited by Asha Sarangi, 41–92. New Delhi: Oxford University Press.

Ball, S. J. 2003. *Class Strategies and the Education Market*. London: Routledge.

Barth, F. 1969. 'Introduction'. In *Ethnic Groups and Boundaries: The Social Organisation of Culture Difference* (Essays presented at a Symposium held at Bergen, Norway, 23–26 February 1967), edited by Fredrik Barth. Little, Brown and Company.

Baruah, S. 1999. *India Against Itself*. New Delhi: Oxford.

Batra, P. 2010. *Social Science Learning in Schools*. New Delhi: SAGE Publications.

Bayly, C. 1983. *Rulers, Townsmen and Bazaars: North Indian Society in the Age of British Expansion, 1770–1870*. Cambridge: Cambridge University Press.

Benei, V. 2009. *Schooling India: Hindus, Muslims, and the Forging of Citizens*. New Delhi: Permanent Black.

Bernstein, B. 1971. *Class, Codes and Control*, vol. 1. London: Paladin.

———. 2003. 'Social Class and Pedagogic Practice'. In *Class, Codes and Control: The Structuring of Pedagogic Discourse*, edited by Basil Bernstien 63–93. London: Routledge.

Beteille. 2003. 'The Social Character of the Indian Middle Class'. *Middle Class Values in India and Western Europe*, edited by Imtiaz Ahmad and Helmut Reifeld, 73–85. New Delhi: Social Science Press.

Bhargava, R. 2010. 'Secular States and Religious Education: The Indian Debate'. In *The Promise of India's Secular Democracy*, edited by Rajeev Bhargava 301–34. New Delhi: Oxford.

Bhattacharya, N. 2003. 'February. Rewriting History'. Seminar (522). www.india-seminar.com

Bhattacharya, U. 2013. '"Globalization" and the English Imperative: A Study of Language Ideologies and Literacy Practices at an Orphanage and Village School in Suburban New Delhi'. Unpublished Thesis. Berkeley: University of Berkeley.

Bhog, D., and Ghose, M. 2014. 'Writing Gender in: Reflections on Writing Middle-school Political Science Textbooks in India', *Gender & Development*, 22 (1): 49–62.

Bhokta, N. P. 1998. 'Marginalization of Popular Language and Growth of Sectarian Education in Colonial India'. In *Education, Development and Underdevelopment*, edited by R. Kaul, S. Shukla, and R. Kaul, 65–78. New Delhi: SAGE Publications.

Bismillah, Abdul. 2008. *Jhini Jhini Bini Chadariya*. Delhi: Rajkamal Prakashan.

Borpujari, H. K. 1998. *NorthEast India*. Guwahati: Spectrum.

Bourdieu, P. 1976a. *Language and Symbolic Power*. Cambridge: Harvard University Press.

Bourdieu, P. 1976b. 1991. 'The Production and Reproduction of Legitimate Language'. In *Language and Symbolic Power*, edited by J. Thompson, 23–58. Cambridge: Harvard University Press.

———. 1984. *Distinction: A Social Critique of the Judgement of Taste*. New York: Harvard University Press.

———. 1985. 'The Social Space and the Genesis of Groups'. *Theory and Society* 14 (6): 723–44.

———. 1986. 'The Forms of Capital'. In *Handbook of Theory and Research for the Sociology of Education*, edited by J. G. Richardson, 241–58. CT: Greenwood Press.

Bourdieu, P., and L. Wacquant. 1992. *An Invitation to Reflexive Sociology* edited by John G. Richardson. Chicago, IL: University of Chicago.

Bowles, S., and H. Gintis. 1976. *Schooling in Capitalist America: Educational Reform and the Contradictions of Economic Life*. New York: Routledge.

Brass, P. 1974. *Language, Religion and Politics in North India*. Cambridge: Cambridge University Press.

———. 2004. 'Elite Interests, Popular Passions, and Social Power in the Language Politics of India'. *Ethnic and Racial Studies* 27 (3): 353–75.

Braithwaite, E. K. 1984. 'History of the Voice: The Development of National Language'. In *Anglophone Carribean Poetry*. London: Beacon.

Brown, M., and S. Ganguly. 2003. *Fighting Words: Language Policy and Ethnic Relations in Asia*. London: MIT Press.

Bucholtz, M., and Hall, Kira. 2010. 'Locating Identity in Language'. In *Language and Identities* edited by Carmen Llamas, and Dominic Watt, 18–28. Edinburgh: Edinburgh University Press.

Byrne, B. 2006. 'In Search of a "Good Mix"'. *Sociology* 40 (2): 1001–17.

Casolari, M. 2002, April 13. 'Role of Benares in Constructing Political Hindu Identity'. *Economic and Political Weekly* 37 (15): 1413–20.

Chakrabarty, D. 2002. 'Governmental Roots of Modern Ethnicity'. In *Habitations of Modernity: Essays in the Wake of Subaltern Studies*, edited by Dipesh Chakraborty, 80–97. New Delhi: Permanent Black.

Chanana, K. 2001. 'Hinduism and Female Sexuality: Social Control and Education of Girls in India'. *Sociological Bulletin* 50 (1): 37–63.

Chand, V. 2011. 'Elite Positionings Towards Hindi'. *Journal of Sociolinguistics* 15 (1): 6–35.

Chatterjee, P. 1989. 'Colonialism, Nationalism, and Colonised Women: The Contest in India'. *American Ethnologist* 16 (4): 622–33.

———. 1998, February 7. 'Community in the East'. *Economic and Political Weekly* 33 (6): 277–82.

Cohn, B. 1985. 'The Command of Language and the Language of Command'. *Subaltern Studies* 4: 276–329.

———. 1996. *Colonialism and its Forms of Knowledge: The British in India*. Princeton, NJ: Princeton University Press.

Collins, J. 1988, December. 'Language and Class in Minority Education'. *Anthropology and Education Quarterly* 19 (4): 299–326.

Collins, J. 2009. 'Social Reproduction in Classrooms and Schools'. *Annual Review of Anthropology* 38: 33–48.

Dalmia, V. 1997. *The Nationalization of Hindu Traditions: Bhāratendu Hari Chandra and Nineteenth-century Banaras*. Delhi: Oxford University Press.

———. 2003. 'The Locations of Hindi'. *Economic and Political Weekly* 38 (14): 1377–84.

Danahay, D. E. R. 1997a. 'Leaving Home: Schooling Stories and an Ethnography of Autoethnography in Rural France'. In *Autoethnography*, edited by D. E. R. Danahay, 123–44. New York, NY: Berg.

———. 1997b. *Autoethnography*. New York, NY: Berg.

Dasgupta, J. 1970. *Language Conflict and National Development*. Berkeley, CA: University of California Press.

———. 2003. *Language Policy and National Development in India*, 21–50. London: MIT Press.

Dasgupta, J., and J. Gumperz. 1971. 'Language, Communication and Control in North India'. In *Language in Social Groups*, edited by John Joseph Gumperz 129–50. California: Stanford University Press.

Dasgupta, P. 2001. 'Introduction'. In *Managing Multilingualism in India: Political and Linguistic Manifestations*, edited by E. Annamalai, 9–29. New Delhi: SAGE Publications.

Deshpande, S. 2003. 'The Centrality of the Middle Class'. In *Contemporary India*, edited by S. Deshpande, 125–50. Delhi: Penguin.

De, A., Khera, R., Samson, M., and Kumar, A.K.S. 2011. 'PROBE Revisited: A Report on Elementary Education in India'. *OUP Catalogue*.

Dirks, N. B. 1996. 'Foreword'. In *Colonialism and its Forms of Knowledge*, edited by B. Cohn, iv–xii. Princeton, NJ: Princeton University Press.

Dodson, M. S. 2002. 'Re-Presented for the Pandits: James Ballantyne, "Useful Knowledge," and Sanskrit Scholarship in Benares College During the Mid-nineteenth Century'. *Modern Asian Studies* 36 (2): 257–98.

Donner, H. 2005. 'Children Are Capital, Grandchildren Are Interest'. In *Globalizing India*, edited by J. A. Fuller, 119–39. London: Anthem Press.

Drury, D. 1993. *The Iron School Master: Education, Employment and the Family*. New Delhi: Hindustan Publications.

Dube, L. 1997. *Women and Kinship*. Tokyo: United Nations University.

Duranti, A. 2004. *A Companion to Linguistic Anthropology*. Malden, USA: Wiley and Blackwell.

Errington. 2001. 'Colonial Linguistics'. *Annual Review of Anthropology* edited by Joseph Errington, 30: 19–39.

Evans, S. 2002. 'Macaulay's Minute Revisited: Colonial Language Policy in Nineteenth-century India'. *Journal of Multilingual and Multicultural Development* 23 (4): 260–81.

Fernandes, L., and P. J. Heller. 2006. 'Hegemonic Aspirations'. *Critical Asian Studies* 38 (4): 495–522.

Fine, M., and L. Weis. 2003. *Silenced Voices and Extraordinary Conversations*. New York, NY: Teachers College Press.

Fishman, J. 1966. *Language Loyalty in the United States*. The Hague: Mouton and ERIC.

Foley, E. Douglas. 1991. 'Rethinking School Ethnographies of Colonial Settings'. *Comparative Education Review* 35 (3): 532–51.

Fraser, N. 2000. 'Rethinking Recognition'. *New Left Review* 3: 107–20.

Freitag, S. B. 1989. *Culture and Power in Banaras*. Berkeley, CA: University of California Press.

Friere, P. 1970. *Pedagogy of the Oppressed*. New York, NY: Continuum.

Gal, S. 1988. 'The Political Economy of Code Choice. In *Code Switching: Anthropological and Sociolinguistic Perspectives*, edited by M. Heller, 243–63. Berlin: Mouton De Gruyter.

Geertz, C. ed. 1973. 'Thick Description: Toward an Interpretive Theory of Culture'. In *The Interpretation of Cultures* 3–29. New York, NY: Basic Books.

Gellner, E. 1983. *Nation and Nationalism*. Oxford: Basil Blackwell Publisher.

———. ed. 1987. 'Nationalism and the Two Forms of Cohesion in Complex Societies'. In *Culture, Identity, and Politics*, 6–28. New York: Cambridge University Press.

Ghose, D. B. 2014. 'Writing Gender'. In *Gender and Development* 22 (1): 49–62.

Giroux. 1983. 'Theories of Reproduction and Resistance'. In *The New Sociology of Education: A Critical Analysis, Harvard Education Review* 53 (3): 257–293.

Goswami, N. 2011. 'Multiple Identities and Educational Choices: Reflections on Ansari Students in a School of Banaras'. In *Frontiers of Embedded Muslim Communities in India*, edited by V. K. Jairath, 174–95. New Delhi: Routledge.

———. 2015. 'Costs, Security and Discipline: Gendering the Debate on School Choice in India'. *Indian Journal of Gender Studies* 22 (2): 243–64.

Government of India. 1991. *Census 1991*. New Delhi: GoI.

———. 2001. *Census 2001*. New Delhi: GoI.

Gramsci, A. 1971. *Selections from the Prison Notebooks*, edited and translated by Quintin Hoare and Geoffrey Nowell Smith. New York, NY: International.

Grierson, G. 1967. *Linguistic Survey of India*. Varanasi: Motilal Banarasidas.

Gupta, D. 2000. *Culture Space and Nation-state*. New Delhi: SAGE Publications.

Habermas, J. 1989. *The Structural Transformation of the Public Sphere*. Cambridge, MA: MIT Press.

Haeri, N. 1997. 'The Reproduction of Symbolic Capital'. *Current Anthropology* 38 (5): 795–816.

Hall, K., and N. Chad. 2015. 'Code-switching, Globalisation and Identity'. In *The Handbook of Discourse Analysis*, edited by Deborah Tannen, Heidi E. Hamilton, and Deborah Schiffrin, 597–671. Sussex: John Wiley and Sons.

Harris, J. 2011. 'Middle-class Activism and the Politics of the Informal Working Class'. *Critical Asian Studies* 38 (4): 445–65.

Heath, S. B. 1983. *Ways with Words*. New York, NY: Cambridge University.

Heller, M. 1999. *Linguistic Minorities and Modernity*. London: Longman.

Hobsbawm, E. J. 1983. *The Invention of Tradition*. Cambridge: Cambridge University Press.

———. 1996. 'Language, Culture, and National Identity'. *Social Research* 63 (4): 1065–80.

Jain, M., and S. Saxena. 2010. 'Politics of Low Cost Schooling and Low Teacher Salary'. *Economic and Political Weekly* 45 (18): 79–80.

Jaiswal, A. 2012. 'The Changing Occupational Structure and Economic Profile of Textile Industry of Banaras'. *Journal of Social Science* 30 (1): 89–98.

JNNURM. 2006. *City Development Plan for Varanasi*. Varanasi: Feedback Ventures.

Joshee, R. 2003. 'A Framework for Understanding Diversity in Indian Education'. *Race Ethnicity and Education* 6 (3): 283–97.

Kachru, B. 1986. *The Alchemy of English: The Spread, Functions, and Models of Non-native Englishes*. Oxford: University of Illinois Press.

Kachru, Y., and T. Bhatia. 1978. 'The Emerging Dialect Conflict in Hindi: A Case of Glottopolitics'. *International Journal of the Sociology of Language* 1978 (16): 47–58.

Kamat, A. R. 1985. *Education and Social Change in India*. Bombay: Somaiya Publications Private Limited.

Kaviraj, S. 1997. 'On the Construction of Colonial Power'. In *Language Politics in India*, edited by A. Sarangi, 141–58. Delhi: Oxford.

Khora, S. 2008. 'Teacher Motivation: Role of Values and Social Support'. *The Indian Journal of Social Work* 69 (1): 33–44.

Khubchandani, L. 1977. 'Language Ideology and Language Development'. *Linguistics* 15 (193): 33–52.

King, C. 1989. 'Forging a New Linguistic Identity: The Hindi Movement in Banaras, 1868–1914'. In *Culture and Power in Banaras: Community, Performance, and Environment, 1800–1980*, edited by S. B. Freitag, 179–202. Berkeley, CA: University of California Press.

———. 1994. *One Language, Two Scripts*. Bombay: Oxford University Press.

Kumar, K. 1985. 'Educational Experience of Scheduled Castes and Tribes'. In *Sociological Perspective in Education*, edited by S. C. Shukla and K. Kumar, 328–347. Delhi: Chanakya.

———. 1988. 'Origins of India's "Textbook Culture"'. *Comparative Education Review* 32 (4): 452–64.

———. 2001. *School ki Hindi (School Hindi)*. Delhi: Rajkamal.

———. 2005a. 'Colonial Citizen as an Educational Ideal'. In *Political Agenda of Education*, edited by K. Kumar, 25–48. New Delhi: SAGE Publications.

———. 2005b. 'Appropriate Knowledge: Conflict of Curriculum and Culture'. In *Political Agenda of Education*, edited by K. Kumar, 49–72. New Delhi: SAGE Publications.

———. 2005c. 'Meek Dictator: The Paradox of Teacher's Personality'. In *Political Agenda of Education*, edited by K. Kumar, 73–96. New Delhi: SAGE Publications.

Kumar, K. 2005d. 'Quest for Self-identity'. In *Political Agenda of Education*, edited by K. Kumar, 123–55. New Delhi: SAGE Publications.

———. 2008. 'Partners in Education?' *Economic and Political Weekly* 43 (3): 8.

Kumar, N. 1988. *The Artisans of Banaras: Popular Culture and Identity, 1880–1986*. Princeton, NJ: Princeton University Press.

———. 1998. 'Lessons from Contemporary Schools'. *Sociological Bulletin* 47 (1): 33–49.

———. 2000. *Lessons from Schools: The History of Education in Banaras*. New Delhi: SAGE Publications.

———. 2008. *The Politics of Gender, Community, and Modernity: Essays on Education in India*. New Delhi: Oxford University Press.

Kymlicka, W., and B. He. 2005. *Multiculturalism in Asia*. Oxford: Oxford University Press.

LaDousa, C. 2005. 'Disparate Markets: Language, Nation, and Education in North India'. *American Ethnologist* 32 (3): 460–78.

———. 2007. 'Of Nation and State: Language, School, and the Reproduction of Disparity in a North Indian City'. *Anthropological Quarterly* 80 (4): 925–59.

———. 2014. *Hindi is Our Ground, English is Our Sky: Education, Language, and Social Class in Contemporary India*. New York, NY: Berghahn Books.

Lamont, M., and V. Molnar. 2002. 'The Study of Boundaries in the Social Sciences'. *Annual Review of Sociology* 28: 167–95.

Lareau, A. 1985. 'Social Class Differences in Family–School Relationships'. *Sociology of Education* 60 (2): 73–85.

———. 2002. 'Invisible Inequality'. *American Sociological Review* 67 (5): 747–76.

———. 2004. *Unequal Childhoods: Class, Race and Family Life*. Berkeley, CA: University of California Press.

Madan, A. 2012. 'Making Schools Work'. *Journal of Educational Planning and Administration* 26 (4): 591–602.

Manjrekar, N. 2003. 'Contemporary Challenges to Women's Education: Towards an Elusive Goal?' *Economic and Political Weekly*, 38 (43): 4577–82.

Mahajan, G. 1999, December. 'Rethinking Multiculturalism'. New Delhi: Seminar (484): 56–61.

———. 2002. *The Multicultural Path: Issues of Diversity and Discrimination in Democracy*. New Delhi: SAGE Publications.

Mahanta, A. 2008. *Journey of Assamese Women, 1836–1937*. Guwahati: Publication Board Assam.

Majumdar, M. 2011. 'Politicians, Civil Servants or Professionals?' *Contemporary Education Dialogue: Teachers' Voices on Their Work and Worth* 8 (1): 33–65.

Majumdar, S., and N. Kumar. 2003. 'A Postcolonial School in a Modern World: Vidyashram: The Southpoint'. *Economic and Political Weekly* 38 (29): 3049–55.

Mehan, H. 1987. 'Language and Schooling'. In *Interpretive Ethnography of Education: At Home and Abroad*, edited by G. Spindler and L. Spindler, 109–136. Mahwah, NJ: Lawrence Erlbaum Associates.

MHRD. 1968. *National Education Policy*. New Delhi: MHRD, GoI.

———. 1986. *National Education Policy*. New Delhi: MHRD, GoI.

Milroy, J. 2001. 'Language Ideologies and the Consequences of Standardization'. *Journal of Sociolinguistics* 5 (4): 530–55.

Mir, F. 2006. 'Imperial Policy, Provincial Practices'. *Indian Economic and Social History Review* 43 (4): 395–427.

Nambissan, G. B. 1994. 'Language and Schooling of Tribal Children: Issues Related to Medium of Instruction'. *Economic and Political Weekly* 29 (42): 2747–54.

———. 2010. 'The Indian Middle Classes and Educational Advantage'. In *The Routledge International Handbook of the Sociology of Education*, edited by M. Apple, S. Ball, and L. Gandin, 285–95. New York: Taylor and Francis.

National Knowledge Commission. 2008. *National Knowledge Commission Report*. New Delhi: NKC, GoI.

NCERT. 2005a. *National Curriculum Framework*. New Delhi: NCERT, GoI.

———. 2005b. *The Position Paper on Teaching of Indian Languages*. New Delhi: NCERT, GoI.

———. 2006. 'Teaching of Indian Languages', Survey Report. New Delhi: NCERT, GoI.

Oesterheld, J. 2007. 'National Education as a Community Issue: The Muslim Response to the Wardha Scheme'. In *Education and Social Change in South Asia*, edited by K. Kumar and J. Oesterheld, 156–95. New Delhi: Orient Longman.

Ogbu, J. J. 1981. 'School Ethnography: A Multilevel Approach'. *Anthropology and Education Quarterly* 12 (1): 3–29.

Orsini, F. 2012. 'How to Do Multilingual Social History?' *Indian Economic and Social History Review* 49 (2): 225–46.

Ortner, S. B. 1998. 'Identities: The Hidden Life of Class'. *Journal of Anthropological Research* 54 (1): 1–17.

Pai, S. 2002. 'Politics of Language: Decline of Urdu in Uttar Pradesh'. *Economic and Political Weekly* 37 (27): 2705–08.

Panda, G. 2015. 'Maternal Involvement in Everyday Schooling'. *Indian Journal of Gender and Society* 22 (2): 219–42.

Pandey, G. 1989. 'The Bigoted Julaha'. In *The Construction of Communalism in Colonial North India*, edited by Gyanendra Pandey 66–108. New York, NY: Oxford University Press.

———. 1990. *The Colonial Construction of Communalism in North India*. Delhi: Oxford University Press.

Parekh, B. 1999, December. 'What is Multiculturalism?' Seminar (484). http://www. india-seminar. com/1999/484/484% 20parekh. htm

Parsons, T. 1959. 'The School Class as a Social System: Some of its Functions in American Society'. *Harvard Educational Review* 29 (4): 297–318.

Pathak, A. 1998. 'Education and Moral Quest'. New Delhi: Aakar Books.

Pitroda, S. 2006. *Language Letter*. New Delhi: National Knowledge Commission, Government of India.

Proctor, L. M. 2010. *Discourses on Language, Class, Gender, and Education Mobility*. Iowa City, IA: University of Iowa.

Rai, A. 2002. *Hindi Nationalism*. Hyderabad: Orient Blackswan.

Ramachandran, V. 2005. 'Why Teachers Are Demotivated?' *Economic and Political Weekly* 40 (21): 2141–44.

Ramanathan, V. 2005. *The English–Vernacular Divide: Postcolonial Language Politics and Practice*. Clevedon: Multilingual Matters.

Ramaswamy, S. 1997. *Passions of the Tongue: Language Devotion in Tamil India, 1891–1970*. Berkeley, CA: University of California Press.

Rao, S. S. 2008, September 6. 'India's Language Debates and Education of Linguistic Minorities'. *Economic and Political Weekly* 43 (36): 63–70.

Reay, D. 1996. 'Contextualising Choice: Social Power and Parental Involvement'. *British Educational Research Journal* 22 (5): 581–96.

———. 1998. 'Engendering Social Reproduction'. *British Journal of Sociology of Education* 19 (2): 195–209.

———. 1999.'Linguistic Capital and Home: School Relationships'. *Acta Sociologica* 42 (2): 159–68.

———. 2010.'Identity Making in Schools and Classrooms'. In *The Sage Handbook of Identities*, edited by Wetherell, Margaret and Chandra Talpade Mohanty 277–95. London: SAGE Publications.

Rege, S. 2010. 'Education as "Trutiya Ratna": Towards Phule–Ambedkarite Feminist Pedagogical Practice'. *Economic and Political Weekly* 45 (44/45): 88–98.

Ruud, Arild Engelsen. 2003. *Poetics of Village Politics: The Making of West Bengal's Rural Communism*. New Delhi: Oxford University Press.

Said, E. 1978. *Orientalism*. London: Routledge and Kegan Paul.

Sarangapani, Padma M. 2003. 'Indigenising Curriculum: Questions posed by Baiga vidya'. *Comparative Education* 39 (2): 199–209.

Sarangapani, P. 2009. 'Quality, Feasibility and Desirability of Low-cost Private Schooling'. *Economic and Political Weekly* 44 (43): 43–67.

Schiffman, H. 1996. *Linguistic Culture and Language Policy*. London: Routledge.

SenGupta, A. 2007. *Report on Conditions of Work and Promotion of Livelihoods in the Unorganised Sectors*. New Delhi: National Commission for Enterproses in the Unorganised Sectors.

Showeb, M. 1994. *Silk Handloom Industry of Varanasi*. Varanasi: Ganga Kaveri Publication.

Silverstein, M. 1979. 'Language Structure and Linguistic Ideology'. In *The Elements: A Parasession on Linguistic Units and Levels*, edited by R. Clyne, W. Hanks, C. Hauffbaur, 193–247. Chicago: Chicago Linguistic Society.

Simon, B. 1998. 'Language Choice, Religion, and Identity in the Banarsi Community'. In *Living Banaras: Hindu Religion in Cultural Context*, edited by B. Hertel and C. Humes, 255–68. New Delhi: Manohar.

222 Legitimising the Standard Languages

Singh, S. B. 1996. 'Settling Process and Spatial Pattern of Linguo Cultural Groups in Varanasi City'. *National Geographical Journal of India* 42 (1&2): 116–32.

Sinha, S., and B. Saraswati. 1978. *Ascetics of Kashi*. Varanasi: NK Bose Memorial Foundation.

Taylor, C. 1994. *The Politics of Recognition* (A. Gutmann, Ed.). Princeton, NJ: Princeton University Press.

Thapan, M. 1986. 'Aspects of Ritual in a School in South India'. *Contributions to Indian Sociology* 20 (2): 199–219.

———. (Ed.). 2014. *Ethnography of Schooling*. Delhi. SAGE Publications.

Thirumalai, M. 2005, September 4. 'Language Policy in the Motilal Nehru Committee Report, 1928, the Seeds of the Indian Constitution'. Retrieved from: http://www.languageinindia.com/may2005/motilalnehrureport1.html

Tsui, A., and J. Tollefson. 2007. *Language Policy, Culture, and Identity in Asian Contexts*. Mahwah, NJ: Lawrence Erlbaum Associates.

Varman, R., and M. Chakrabarti. 2007. 'Case Studies on Industrial Clusters: A Study of Kanpur Leather & Footwear, Varanasi Silk Saree and Moradabad Brassware Clusters'. Report submitted to DSIR New Delhi: IIT Kanpur.

Viswanathan, G. 1989. *Masks of Conquest*. New York, NY: Columbia University Press.

Waldrop, A. 2004. 'The Meaning of the Old School-tie'. In *Education and Democracy in India*, edited by A. Vaugier-Chatterjee, 203–28. New Delhi: Manohar.

Warren, K. B. 1997. 'Narrating Cultural Resurgence'. In *Autoethnography*, edited by D. E. R. Danahay, 21–46. Oxford: Berg.

Willis, P. 1977. *Learning to Labour: How Working Class Kids Get Working Class Jobs*. Farnborough: Saxon House.

Wong, T. H., and M. W. Apple. 2002. 'Rethinking the Education/State Formation Connection'. *Comparative Education Review* 46 (2): 182–210.

Woolard, K. A. 1985. 'Language Variation and Cultural Hegemony: Toward an Integration of Sociolinguistic and Social Theory'. *American Ethnologist* 12 (4): 738–48.

———. 2005. 'Language and Identity Choice in Catalonia: The Interplay of Contrasting Ideologies of Linguistic Authority'. UCSD Linguistic Anthropology Working Papers Series.

Woolard, K. A., and B. B. Schieffelin. 1994. 'Language Ideology'. *Annual Review of Anthropology* 23: 55–82.

Wortham, S. 2011. 'Linguistic Anthropology of Education'. In *A Companion to Anthropology of Education*, edited by B. A. Levinson and M. Pollock, 137–53. Malden: Wiley and Blackwell.

Wright, E. O. 1985. *Classes*. London: Verso.

Index

About the Author and Series Editor

Author

Nirmali Goswami is Assistant Professor of sociology in Tezpur University. Born to Assamese parents and brought up in North India, she switches between Hindi, English and Assamese languages. She studied in Banaras Hindu University and the Indian Institute of Technology Kanpur. *Legitimising the Standard Languages* is her first book. She has published on issues of gendered nature of school choice in India. Her current research interests include feminist reading of identity politics in Assam.

Series Editor

Meenakshi Thapan is Professor of Sociology at the Delhi School of Economics and Co-ordinator of the D.S. Kothari Centre for Science, Ethics and Education at the University of Delhi. She was Co-ordinator of the European Study Centre Programme, University of Delhi (January 2010–March 2012) and country partner (India) for the EU FP7 Project on EuroBroadMap. She has also published *Life at School* (1991, 2006), *Living the Body* (SAGE 2009) and edited *Ethnographies of Schooling in Contemporary India* (1997) with SAGE.